8758

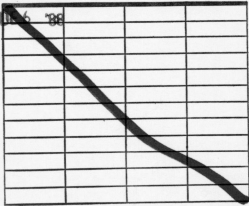

The British Parliament

The
British Parliament

by

ROLAND YOUNG

NORTHWESTERN UNIVERSITY PRESS

Evanston

Contents

Introduction

One should perhaps offer some convincing reason for writing a book on Parliament when so many excellent books on this topic have already been written. Like others, I have found Parliament to be a subject of compelling political interest, and if no other reason presented itself, it seemed personally rewarding to work out an interpretation of how Parliament works, or appears to work. Parliament may be compared to a rich diamond lode, still worth mining, and many facets of Parliament are relatively unstudied and unrecorded.

More than that, Parliament has a significant role to play in modern times. In some respects Parliament is unique, and it is, foremost, an essential part of the complex network of government which the British have developed over the centuries. Yet, in a broader sense Parliament carries the flag for all of us. It often serves as a model for the parliamentary bodies of other countries, and its Members are well aware that the actions taken at Westminster, or the manner in which Westminster does things, have an influence extending beyond the shores of the British Isles. Parliament is sedulously observed, its procedures studied and emulated, and training courses are conducted within the Palace of Westminster for the benefit of parliamentarians and parliamentary officers of other countries.

Parliament lies at the vortex of political controversy, where there is conflict between the parties and between the Members and frequently between Parliament and the Government of the day, and in carrying out its functions the proper role of Parliament may at times appear to be ambiguous. One may raise the question, for instance, of the relationship between ministerial responsibility and parliamentary freedom. If the Government (a term used here to describe collectively the Ministers of the Crown, drawn from Parliament) proposes legislation, if it determines

Introduction

whether or not to conduct an inquiry, if it controls the purse strings, determining how much to spend and how much to tax, what is left for Parliament to do? What degree of independence does Parliament have or require? Or again, if political parties are compelled to maintain a solid front, what chances exist for individual dissent or the expression of ideas disavowed by the party leaders? And how are the leaders developed within Parliament? Are there political bosses outside Parliament who are able to dictate the policy Parliament will be compelled to follow? How do the various interest groups make their opinion known, and are such groups able to influence the content of legislation or the careers of the Members of Parliament? And lastly, how influential is the House of Lords with its truncated powers, and how can one explain its sustained and perhaps increasing popularity? I have attempted to discuss some of these questions in the following chapters.

The purpose of this book is not to extol or to criticize Parliament, or to measure its impact in other lands, or to compare its procedures with those of other legislatures. It is primarily concerned with coming to an understanding of Parliament, and it has been written from the point of view of a detached outside observer who has no revelations to make and no axe to grind. I have observed Parliament for some years, as opportunity has afforded to one whose home is not in Britain, and through a set of fortuitous circumstances I have been able to attend a number of sessions in the past few years. These personal observations have been supplemented by interviews, conversations, and readings, as well as by the observation of and comparison with other parliamentary bodies. In providing a framework for the material, I have deduced a generalized pattern of politics, one which, it seems to me, Parliament has intrinsically shaped for itself, and I have illustrated this pattern with case examples drawn largely from recent events. It is hoped that by combining the theoretical and the concrete in this fashion, the work of Parliament as a whole can be comprehended and that the supporting illustrations will transmit something of the flavour of parliamentary life.

In preparing a book of this nature one assumes many personal obligations, and I extend my warm thanks to all of those nice people in Parliament and those associated with Parliament who have so kindly assisted me. I wish also to thank the United States Educational Commission and the John Simon Guggenheim Memorial Foundation for making it possible for me to carry on this study. Although in my comments I have attempted to be objective and fair, I should indicate my bias at the outset by stating that I found Parliament endlessly fascinating, even the more barren stretches between the dramatic clashes of partisan foes. The enthusiastic comment of a new Life Peer on his impression of the House of Lords may with equal pertinency be applied to all of Parliament: 'It's a great place!'

ROLAND YOUNG

Evanston, Illinois,
May 1961.

CHAPTER I

The High Stakes of Parliament

What goes on in Parliament? How do Members gain their own ends or secure a point against their opponents? What is fair and what is foul in parliamentary warfare? What, indeed, are the high stakes of Parliament for which the partisans contend?

In a restricted sense, the events that take place in Parliament are the concern of the immediate participants—the Government and the Opposition, indeed all Members and Peers who attempt to make their influence felt. They are also the concern of those directly affected by what Parliament does: the government departments, controlled by the laws of Parliament and answerable in some fashion to Parliament for their actions; the British public, who pay the taxes levied by Parliament; and even foreign governments. Indirectly, also, the actions of Parliament are the concern of those a step or two removed from the arena of political conflict: they include the people of the free world who support the peaceful resolution of domestic conflict; those who live in the newer nations now experimenting gingerly and self-consciously with parliamentary institutions; and those in the lands of the dictators who may find in the parliamentary model a method of achieving personal freedom and political stability.

THE CLAIMANTS

The right to raise issues for Parliament to consider is a political prize of some consequence, and the various claimants jostle with each other for a favourable position in the parliamentary queue. It is now agreed that Parliament must take certain action every year, such as appropriating money, and that the Ministers of the Government have special

13

claims on the time of Parliament; but the opportunity for Members not in the Government to bring other items before Parliament is competitive and controversial.

In times past there have been many claimants for the time and attention of Parliament. Indeed, the history of Parliament could be developed in terms of the relative influence of these claimants at historic periods, of those who have had access to its various proceedings and attempted to make their influence felt. We will not attempt here to reweave the threads of this interesting story but rather limit ourselves to describing the relative status of these claimants at the present time. The claimants include the Queen, in whose name official action is taken; H.M. Government, in modern times commanding a position of great political strength; the Opposition, mobilized to challenge and even replace the Government, if the opportunity occurs; Private Members and Private Peers, who have certain parliamentary rights even in a period of strong parties; municipal corporations, who can petition for the enactment of private legislation; individual citizens, with their right to petition; organized groups, who attempt to influence the actions of Parliament; the Church of England Assembly, some of whose measures must be approved by Parliament; and those individual litigants who are permitted to lodge an appeal to the Appellate Committee of the House of Lords. Some of the relationships between Parliament and the claimants are not as important in the political struggle as they once were, and they may be considered to be the continuation into modern times of the political pattern of an earlier period when the Government was less clearly defined and when the functions of Parliament were both more extensive and less specific.

In developing the business of Parliament, the following three questions are pertinent: What proposal is to be considered? Who can make the proposal? When will it be considered? The traditional topics of parliamentary interest, as they have developed over a period of time, are the enactment of legislation; the appropriation of money and the levying of taxes; debates on policy; and the evaluation and criticism of Ministers. As we will see later, these areas of concentration have evolved to Parliament in its historical development from an older, judicial-type body. Parliament clings tenaciously to its historical links and in many ways, even now, it is not completely 'modern'. One may identify Parliament with the Legislative function in the classical trilogy of Legislative, Executive, and Judicial, but this classification is not altogether accurate or complete. Important phases of parliamentary life would be left out if one restricted its functions within such narrow limits, for one is still reminded from time to time of the fusion of governmental functions which prevailed in the Middle Ages. There is, for instance, a subtle and complex relationship between the Crown, the Privy Council, the Government, the Courts, and Parliament that defies simple classification. At this point one can say simply that Parliament is now, as it has been historically, one of the institutions of government which, on some matters, must be consulted. Consultation is the key, and Parliament is sovereign in the sense that if its consent is required and there is a conflict of wills, the will of Parliament prevails. Parliament has the final word.

However contentious it may have been at one time, there is no longer any dispute over the proposition that Parliament has a legitimate interest in the management of government affairs, and the grand role of Parliament in the broader process of government is unchallenged. However, there is occasional disquiet over the performance of Parliament, and it is sometimes claimed that Parliament has less influence over policy than it once had, that it has failed to develop adequate techniques of control, that too much is done *for* Parliament and not enough *by* Parliament—in short, that Parliament is not always the centre of political controversy.

THE QUEEN

The role played by the Crown in a constitutional monarchy is not always clear. The ceremonial display where the pomp and circumstances of office are given full play are reminders of the reality of monarchy, and in the pageantry of the State Openings of Parliament one has another example of the symbolism of authority that pervades British political practices. It is more difficult, however, to describe or assess the role played by the Queen in the more prosaic and confidential aspects of political life. Even though the actions of the Government are taken in the name of the Queen, the relations between Parliament and the Monarch are more than symbolic; the Queen plays a special part in convening and dissolving Parliament and in selecting a Government; messages from Parliament are sent to and received from the Queen; Parliament is housed in a royal palace, and it debates and approves the financial supply given to the Queen.

It could be argued, I believe, that the special deference owed to the Queen provides a subtle type of restraint on partisan conflict. On issues which require the sanction of the Queen, approval is expected and routinely given, but the procedure nevertheless assumes that there is a superior political authority, neutral between the parties and governed by chivalrous standards of public conduct, who must give consent. The effective decision on convening and dissolving Parliament, for instance, is made by the Prime Minister, but the additional obligation of securing the Queen's consent may provide some check on possible impulsive action and it creates an assumption of fair play. Again, the selection of certain types of personnel offers another example where the rigors of partisan competition are held in restraint by the intervention of the Monarch. The method of selecting the Prime Minister, for instance (described more fully in Chapter III), places a premium on choosing a leader whose ability is already acknowledged, and the requirement that the Queen must make the final selection may serve to blunt the sharp edge of personal rivalries. It may also be noted that the major permanent officers of Parliament are appointed in the Queen's name, and even the doorkeepers wear the royal medallion. While it is possible for a system of political patronage to operate in such circumstances, this is not the case at present, and the high offices of Parliament are placed beyond the realm of partisan politics and given an ennobled claim to office. The obligations of service extend beyond party and even beyond Parliament. The Queen may also have some influence in creating new titles and in adding names on the Honours List, but in this speculative area there are few reliable facts on which to make a judgment.

In carrying out the business of Parliament many messages, mostly of a formal nature, are sent to and from the Queen, and even such piquantly titled procedures as 'prayers to the Queen' are no more than attempts to influence the Government to disallow a rule. Moreover, the Queen is kept informed of events that occur in Parliament, and one of the Government Whips prepares a daily letter for the Queen's eyes only.

The short ceremony in which the Queen's consent to Acts of Parliament is announced adds a touch of pageantry to the proceedings and is yet another visible link connecting the present with the past. C. P. Ilbert, a former Clerk of the House of Commons, has described the event as it takes place in the House of Lords (with the Commons standing behind the bar): 'Nothing can be more picturesque,' he has written, 'than the ceremonies which attend the signification of the Royal assent to legislative measures passed by the two Houses. The three silent figures, scarlet robed and cocked-hatted, who sit in a row like some Hindu triad, in front of the vacant throne; the Reading Clerk who declaims in sonorous tones the prolix tautologies of the Commission; the Clerk of the Crown and the Clerk of Parliaments, who, standing white-wigged and sable-gowned on either side of the table, chant their antiphony, punctuated by profound reverences, the one rehearsing the title of each Act which is to take its place on the statute book, the other signifying, in the accustomed form and manner, the King's assent. "Little Pedlington Electricity Supply Act". "Le Roy le veult". Between the two voices six centuries lie. The Parliament at Westminster is not only a busy workshop; it is a museum of antiquities.'[1]

The institution of monarchy is not a controversial political topic, and the issues of basic political loyalty, or of republicanism, do not arise. The monarchy would appear to be as popular now as at any period in the past. As for financial support, the requirements of Her Majesty are met by special legislation (the Civil List), under which £475,000 is provided annually. This amount was recommended by a Select Committee and accepted by Parliament in 1952. Annual payments to five other members of the Royal Family amount in all to £157,000.

THE GOVERNMENT

In the ideology of Parliament it is assumed, foremost, that there *must* be a Government, comprising a known and specific set of Ministers who are recruited from the membership of Parliament itself and subject to its direction and influence. The image develops of the Government acting as the head of the great bureaucracy, giving instructions on policy and making certain that the instructions are in fact carried out. In the language of Parliament, the Government collectively, and the Ministers individually, are responsible for administering public affairs. As this theory has developed, a specific relationship between the Government and Parliament has become manifest: the Government administers and leads; Parliament supports the Government and holds it responsible. The assumption that there must be a Government is rudimentary to the whole system, and it now seems so obvious and is so widely understood and accepted that it need not be emphasized. However, the assumption

---

[1] C. P. Ilbert, quoted in Redlich, *The Procedure of the House of Commons* (1908), Vol. 1, pp. v–vi. See also Sir Ivor Jennings, *Parliament* (1957), on this and other topics: *viz.* 'The Importance of Being Ancient', pp. 13–22. Other works on Parliament include the following: P. A. Bromhead, *The House of Lords and Contemporary Politics* (London, 1958); Lord Campion, *An Introduction to the Procedure of the House of Commons,* 3rd ed., (London, 1958); Strathearn Gordon, *Our Parliament,* 4th ed. (London, 1952); Sir Courtenay Ilbert, *Parliament: Its History, Constitution, and Practice,* 3rd ed., (Cambridge, 1950); K. R. Mackenzie, *The English Parliament* (Penguin, 1959); Herbert Morrison, *Government and Parliament: A Survey from the Inside* (London, 1954); Peter G. Richards, *Honourable Members, A Study of the British Backbencher* (London, 1959); Eric Taylor, *The House of Commons at Work* (Pellican, 1951).

does not have universal validity for other relationships between Parliaments and Governments may exist, and the present arrangement is a development from earlier practices. Granted, then, that there must be a Government, formed from Parliament itself, it follows that within Parliament the most important of all the stakes, the goal that overshadows all other goals, is the ability to organize the Government.

The Government now has such a preferred position in parliamentary affairs that it exercises a commanding influence over the business of Parliament and the allocation of time. In the consideration of public bills, the position of the Government is unchallenged, and it is strong enough to control the flow of legislation and the form in which it is approved. Remnants of time may be left over for the competitive use of Private Members—that is, all Members not in the Government—but these snippets of time available for their use does not weaken the Government's strong position. In an earlier period, when Parliament was less dominated by Government and the Government was more exclusively concerned with administration, it was not unusual for Private Members to introduce and sponsor important bills and for committees to investigate the need for legislative remedies, but nowadays these lines of action are not significant. The Government sponsors all important public legislation and it decides whether to hold inquiries.

The set of relationships between Parliament and Government forms the mainstream of parliamentary interest. A pattern has developed wherein the Government is the chief proponent of policy; it indicates what actions it wishes Parliament to take and it is expected to explain and defend its policy. Parliament does not necessarily make the important decisions itself, but it can attempt to influence the Government, calling attention to specific complaints and areas of dissatisfaction. Parliament is also constantly sizing up the calibre of those who are, or who might be, Ministers in H.M. Government. The relationship provides a key to the manner in which Parliament is organized, a subject which will be further discussed in Chapter III, and it also provides a key to the kind of action Parliament believes to be politically significant. The interaction may be infinitely subtle as in private conversations, and disputes may be debated within the confines of the party. The conflict may also be open, blunt, and purposely provocative, as is the case with some of the sharp, acrid, and bitter exchanges between the partisans. It follows from the remarks above that some of the important events in Parliament take place confidentially, behind closed doors and unknown to the public. Agreement on some issues may in effect have been reached at some other place, at some other time, and the proceedings in Parliament are an affirmation of this prior agreement.

The obligations owed by Government to Parliament are considerable, and the Government follows the principle that Parliament should be the first informed of all changes in policy. Parliament is given special deferential status and becomes the central forum for discussing public policy. The Government must secure the consent of Parliament for all new legislation, for some types of subsidiary legislation, for annual appropriations, and for taxes. The Ministers must be prepared to defend their policy in public debate, and the House of Commons may expect the Prime Minister himself to make important statements of policy. This point of view was once put somewhat tartly by Mr. William Ross (Lab.), who was dissatisfied because the position of the Government was given by a Parliamentary Secretary, who would ordinarily be expected to make the less important statements of policy. 'We want the Prime Minister,' he said, 'not the office boy.'[1]

It is somewhat ironic that the application of the principle that Parliament must be informed first may on some occasions exclude Parliament and the public from the process in which policy is actually made. The policy may be developed by the departments in camera and kept confidential so as not to prejudice the rights of Parliament to discuss the topic. However, by the time Parliament is officially informed, the effective decisions may have been made, and Parliament may not be aware of the forces which shaped the legislation, or of the arguments of the proponents, or of the position taken by the various interested groups.

The Government constantly permits its actions to be evaluated, criticized, and even condemned, and it is accountable in the sense that Parliament is consulted and has the opportunity to debate, to criticize, to ask questions, and even to reject. The Government is endlessly informing Parliament, explaining its programme and defending its policies, and Mr. R. A. Butler (Cons.) once surmised that 'There is probably no Executive in the world . . . which is more constantly in touch with the legislature than the British Government is with the British House of Commons.'[2] The Government is normally frank and open, but it can determine the extent to which Parliament should share its confidences and on some occasions it will tell no more than it is reluctantly compelled to tell after being goaded and scolded. The Government some-

---

[1] House of Commons Debates (henceforth H. C. Deb.), (London, H.M.S.O.), 5th November 1958, col. 973.
[2] *Ibid.*, 31st July 1958, col. 1,629.

times plays its hand close to its chest and Parliament may have singular difficulty in prying out the desired information.

The relationship between Parliament and Government sometimes exhibits a circuitous political process, characteristic also of other phases of British politics, wherein anticipated action is controlled at a somewhat earlier stage in the total process. This prearranged backstopping can go on endlessly as one anticipated decision is earlier anticipated; and in some cases the final decision becomes ceremonial, the necessary arrangements and compromises and canvassing of opinions having been made previously and perhaps confidentially. In the case at hand one may begin with the simple assumption that Parliament has the legal right to make the final, binding decision—that it is 'sovereign', in the words of the legalists. The Government may anticipate the wishes of Parliament, however, by making a preliminary decision which is subsequently approved by Parliament and firmly supported by a party majority. We may add further embellishments to the process. Some discerning Members of Parliament may attempt to influence the Government to make the preliminary decisions which Parliament will subsequently be asked to confirm. Although the process may appear to be cut-and-dried once the Government has spoken, there may be considerable pulling and hauling before the Government makes its proposals in a White Paper or a Bill and before it marches its majorities through the lobby in Parliament to win final approval.

In modern times, the Government prepares the important measures placed before Parliament, explaining and defending them and in some cases convincing its own supporters. In general, then, the Government assumes full responsibility for developing the legislative programme, extending from the initial preparation and the co-ordination, through the debates and the consideration of amendments until the measures are finally approved in the division, when the Members are physically separated by going into the lobbies to vote.

The legislative proposals brought before Parliament will have been considered previously by the departments: inquiries will have been held, documents prepared, and issues formulated. The preliminary work is frequently carried on by special groups appointed for this purpose, such as departmental committees, advisory committees, and Royal Commissions. In preparing the legislation, these groups may carry on their own deliberations, make recommendations, and attempt to resolve in a preliminary fashion the issue which Parliament will eventually be asked to approve. Representatives of interested groups may appear before these special groups, and the Government anticipates and attempts to resolve the political conflicts before the proposals are sent to Parliament. Accordingly, many of the proposals brought before Parliament have been fully rationalized with arguments set forth in the supporting documents.

The information received by Parliament is supplied primarily by the Government, supplemented by the pleas of pressure groups and the information which Members can supply on their own account. The Government feeds into the maw of Parliament a steady stream of facts in the form of White Papers, departmental reports, reports of royal commissions, courts of inquiry, working groups, study groups, committees of the Privy Council, and the like. There are few areas where Parliament itself attempts to mobilize information, and these areas are mostly concerned with the Select Committees having control functions. The underlying assumption is that the Government has the primary responsibility for supplying Parliament with the information required for enacting legislation and debating policy; it supplies the facts and makes the necessary rationale. Parliament may itself create a committee to investigate and report, although the more usual method is to persuade the Government to undertake an inquiry. The creation of a commission or tribunal may reduce political tempers, and Parliament may refrain from debating the matter while the commission is sitting.

The failure of Parliament (on the whole) to mobilize information for itself is explained partly by the belief that Government is responsible for taking the lead and partly by the internal structure of Parliament. Facts are supplied in such abundance by governmental departments that considerable resolution would be required if Parliament were to accumulate facts on its own. More than this: finding facts may be tiresome and tedious and Members may be loath to add more burdens to their eixsting commitments. Parliament is not organized so that it can take independent action. What group would mobilize the facts? Where would they get the information? How would the information be fed into the parliamentary organization? The present theory of parliamentary control makes slight provision for Parliament's having access to independent resources of information.

However, what cannot be done within the formal structure may be done outside the formal structure. Members may become independently well informed, and the party committee may secure information through informal inquiry, and interparty delegations are sent on missions to various parts of the Commonwealth. In addition, the Library of the

The High Stakes of Parliament

House of Commons supplies answers to inquiries and itself carries on research on a small scale.

If further information is demanded, the Government must be persuaded by its critics to create some sort of committee to carry on the inquiry, and there are a variety of forms which may be used. Only rarely does Parliament create its own committees for this purpose, although the committees or commissions created by the Government may contain Private Members as well as Peers. Although the Government does not always give in to pressure and create a commission of inquiry, or a Royal Commission (or whatever the particular form may be), Parliament is frequently able to persuade the Government to look further into a controversial subject. One may note, for instance, the success of Parliament in recent years in persuading the Government to investigate such controversial topics as wire tapping, the bank-rate leak, the use of Government labels on envelopes, the sale of scrap wire by the London Electricity Board, and the allegation of the alleged assault on a citizen by two policemen.

The role of Parliament is conditioned by the influential position taken by the Government in its proceedings. Parliament plays a small part in developing policy, as we have noted; it has a more restricted function of discussing, perhaps changing, and eventually approving the proposals made by the Government. It can raise questions; it can discuss the probable effect of the proposed policy; and it can attempt to persuade the Government to change its mind.

The assumption that Government must be able to carry Parliament along with it means, in practice, the visible support of a numerical majority, but in a broader sense the support of all Parliament is required on many issues. It is not only necessary to satisfy a majority on specific controversial issues but it is also necessary to satisfy all Members of Parliament, most of the time, giving them the assurance and the confidence that they are being informed and that correct procedures are being followed. Sometimes the membership is divided, but on most issues it is Parliament as a whole, or one chamber or the other, which implicitly gives its approval. The reaction of Parliament, extending to its most cantankerous and obdurate Members, must always be considered by Government; and even without the assistance of any formal vote or divining process, it is not difficult to tell when the stern, righteous, and often moralistic opinion of either House has been flouted.

Under the prevailing political system where two strong parties contest for electoral supremacy, the Government normally commands the allegiance of the majority party in the House of Commons, and party solidarity is so regularly maintained that Governments do not normally collapse because they lose the support of their followers. However, the Government must make sedulous efforts to maintain this support, and it must constantly listen to the complaints and criticisms and suggestions of its own supporters. Many of the communications between the Government and its supporters take place in private, perhaps in the secrecy of a party committee where signs of disharmony can be kept from public view. Such signs of disagreement as abstentions or voting with the opposition party indicate a rift which the party must somehow attempt to heal. However, the supporters of the Government are not muzzled, and Members on the back benches may exercise considerable freedom in asking the Government sharp questions or in criticizing policy without withdrawing their general support or voting against the Government. The Opposition will be less reticent in its criticism; although the Government supporters may choose to make their criticism in private, the Opposition will most certainly make theirs in public. Because the Government is so dependent on a majority, and normally expects to have a majority, party defection may seem to be extraordinarily important. The obdurate attitude of a few Members may be able to threaten the Government's position, challenging the entire edifice of political support on which the Government makes its claim for power.

Enough has been said about the power of the Government to suggest that the relationship between the Government and Parliament is infinitely subtle, flexible, sensitive, and critical, and it is at this nexus that some parliamentary governments have failed. On some issues, the Government may have commanding influence, limiting the role of Parliament to formal approval, or it may be able to gloss over actions about which Parliament would like to be informed. Conversely, parliamentary pressures may force the Government to take action; committees may propose amendments not to the Government's liking; questions may lead to debate and debate to an inquiry; and political dissension may result in the removal of a Minister or even the resignation of the Government. Parliament, in effect, must carry water on both shoulders in performing the somewhat contradictory functions of criticizing while supporting, and there is no single formula, no useful label, which describes how Parliament can support the Government and at the same time retain enough independence to exercise effective control. As the narrative here develops, we will see more clearly the various nuances in this relationship and the techniques of control used by Parliament. In the procedural sense, it can be said that one of the stakes of Parliament is the retention by Parliament of sufficient independence of action that it can in fact control the Government.

It may appear from this that Parliament is the prisoner of its own creation; that it has abundant authority in the abstract but little authority in the concrete. Parliament is in an anomalous situation where it is showered with respect and adulation, but it is not permitted to do very much on its own, independent of the Government. Things are done for Parliament which are thought to be beneath its dignity to perform or which might bore the Members or for which its internal organization is not especially adapted or which the Government would rather do. Parliament is 'relieved of its burdens', to use the patronizing cliché. However, one should not conclude that Parliament is without influence; rather, that its influence is not always observable or on the surface. If the Government seems to have considerable influence over Parliament, it is also true that the Government is alert to the need for having the support of Parliament. One reason the Government is seldom defeated may be due to the fact that difficult issues are resolved before the final vote is taken, or even before the legislation is introduced. The force of Parliament is found not only in what it does or in what, conceivably, it might do if it suddenly and improbably asserted its independence; it is also found in the constant pressures and criticisms and comments, expressed both on and off the floor. There is no indication that either the Government or the Opposition or any important leader of political opinion wishes Parliament to be more assertive. There may be some support for giving Private Members more time to introduce legislation for bringing about minor reforms; however, there seems to be general agreement that the development of major policy, and the mobilization of facts by which the policy can be evaluated and criticized, are the responsibility of the Government.

In summary, we can say that the Government has achieved a position of great power with its authority extending over the various departments of the bureaucracy and over the organization and proceedings of Parliament. The Government is expected to take a stand on all major policy issues, and within Parliament the Government is constantly proposing, defending, and explaining. Its broad obligations are to inform Parliament first, to justify its action, to secure Parliament's consent when necessary, and to carry Parliament along with it on all major issues. The actions of Government determine in a large measure the interests of Parliament. Parliament can deliberate, raise questions, and attempt to persuade the Government to change its mind, but the responsibility for initiating policy rests with Government. Criticism may be expressed in many ways, some obvious, some more indirect. Formal motions of censure may be tabled or votes taken on the issue of confidence, but the Government may also be influenced by pressures from within its own party or by dissatisfactions expressed at question time or by informal conversations between Ministers and Members or by the nuances in debate or by the response of Members to speeches by Ministers, all of which may be interpreted as clues to the reaction of Parliament. Criticism and independent action are necessary, but support is necessary also, and at times the various political disputes become consolidated into the single issue: Do you support the Government? By restricting the question in this fashion, Parliament may permit minor issues to go by default, only to be resolved elsewhere.

POLITICAL PARTIES

The political parties also have a stake in the actions of Parliament, for it is primarily through the parties that the business of Parliament is carried on. Parties are interested foremost in survival, in protecting their organization and their ideas and the various interests and groups that support them, and although the ultimate decision on survival, and inferentially on achieving power, is made by the electorate, the actions within Parliament may also affect the result. Granted survival, the parties are concerned with influencing the proceedings of Parliament—in selecting the agenda, in carrying on deliberations, in making the final decision—and the ability to carry out these functions requires organization and discipline and sometimes a display of forensic skills. The parties are highly competitive, and the proceedings of Parliament are organized on the assumption of constant, perpetual, unresolved party conflict. The final prize is command, when a party has achieved the strength and the ability to organize the Government and make the effective decisions concerning public policy. The parties are organized internally in such a fashion that they can pursue these various goals: the majority party forms the Government and attempts to keep its own supporters sweet and the Opposition confused; the Opposition attempts sedulously and persistently to gain a point, to influence policy and procedures, and hopefully to embarrass the Government or even shame it into resigning.

The Opposition now plays an influential role in parliamentary activities, but the term, His Majesty's Opposition, was not used until 1826 and the recognition of an Opposition with specific functions to perform, is a more recent development. Even now, the Opposition is not recognized in the Standing Orders, where the two principal claimants for time are the Government and Private Members. The Government plays the major role in developing the agenda, although it will be expected to consult with the Opposition on the order of business. The Opposition does not normally offer an alternative programme which it may hope to persuade Parliament to accept, but it can select topics for debate and compel the Government to justify its policy. It has complete control over the twenty-six days allotted annually for debating Supply, and during this period it can discuss anything it wishes. The Opposition may also offer amendments, introduce motions, and arrange with the Government the timetable to be followed.

The agenda may develop from the events of the day on matters of urgent public importance, and it is reasonably easy for the Opposition to arrange for such a debate. The competition for time is such, however, that some matters may not get debated at all, or that there will be a time lag between the event and the debate. The report of the Royal Commission on East Africa (1955), for instance, was debated some two years after it had been submitted to Parliament. As an intellectual proposition, the report should have been a constituent part of the colonial debates which took place in the interim, but as a procedural proposition, the report was not taken up until a Private Member interested in the subject was lucky enough in the Ballot (which allots time for Private Members' business) to be able to suggest that it be debated.

The proposals of the Opposition may have developed after discussion within the Parliamentary Labour Party. An instance where the various conflicting viewpoints were accommodated, or papered over, is found in a motion on disengagement in Germany considered in February 1959. Mr. Sydney Silverman of the left wing of the party tabled a motion recommending 'disengagement' in Europe, the exclusion of Germany from military alliances, and the *de facto* recognition of the (East) German Democratic Republic. Mr. Silverman had put his party on the spot, for the policy he advocated was not that of the leaders. An amendment to the Silverman motion was then tabled by Mr. John Hynd of the right wing of the party and endorsed by several former Ministers. Now the party was split, left and right, and the party then gathered together to work out a solution. A new resolution, introduced by Mr. Silverman, emphasized both compromise and unity by listing alternatively the left wing and the right wing sponsors: Mr. Silverman's name was first, followed by Mr. Hynd of the Right; then Mr. Zilliacus of the Left and Mr. Arthur Henderson of the Right; Mr. Mikardo of the Left and Mr. Kenneth Younger of the Right; and by more than sixty other Members.

The parties also have a stake in the deliberations of Parliament: the proponents in advancing, defending, and explaining policy; the opponents in bringing out the components of the issue. It is sometimes said that the duty of the Opposition is to oppose, but its functions are in fact somewhat more varied and extensive than the stubbornness which this bromide suggests. The Opposition has created for itself a special role, acting not only as the conscience of Parliament when the Government might be callous or indifferent but also insisting on accountability and full discussion. It is not an easy role to play and it may lead on to acrimonious debate on both sides of the aisle. The Opposition does not have many concrete powers or independent sources of information; it must nevertheless attempt to persuade the Government to make certain disclosures or to take certain action, and this may lead to vigorous debate. In the constant competition between the parties, various shadings of victory or defeat may be expressed as one party scores off another or a Private Member tells off a Minister. The Opposition is constantly challenging the Government, attempting to break down its confidence in its decisions and forcing it to admit mistakes and bad judgment. Although these small and sometimes petty forays may be personally gratifying to the contestants and thought of as an end in themselves, they may also affect the larger issue of which party will be able to form the Government. The issue is often placed on a narrow fulcrum, as when the debating skill of one Member is pitted against another, and this factor often adds zest and thrust to the debates.

On some issues which seem to have little public appeal or are thought to be nonpartisan, the political parties may express no opinion and take no stand, and the latitude given to Members may produce alignments that have little resemblance to the normal partisan split. Such nonparty alignments may develop in support of Bills introduced by Private Members or of proposed amendments to legislation, and many of the topics chosen for debate (especially in the House of Lords) have no obvious partisan division. It may be inferred, then, that political parties are interested in most debates but not in all of them, and there are aspects of public policy on which the parties take no stand.

The political parties also have a stake in the final decision made by Parliament, where the outcome is considered the supreme test of party strength. The division tests the ability of the Government to command the support of its own party and of the Opposition to maintain a vigorous and united protest. In the division, numbers count, and the party organization sees to it that the requisite number of Members or Peers are in their place at the proper time to vote correctly. Although the Opposition is constantly defeated, the division nevertheless can be used for asserting and reasserting a point of view and, tactically, as a weapon with which to harrow the Government. Partisans are expected to support their party, and although abstention may be forgiven, to vote with the party opposite is normally considered a cardinal political sin in which respectable Members do not indulge. In the effort of parties to shore up their support and mobilize all possible sources of strength, cross-voting in Parliament on major issues has been all but eliminated. The pyramid of power can at this point be too readily toppled by the dissenter, although dissent may be expressed in other ways.

If the Government loses a major division, its position may be considered precarious, but in modern times the various Governments have been strong enough, or prudent enough, to make the necessary adjustments before risking defeat in the lobby. The Government will be less disturbed by defeats on minor issues, which may occur in the House of Lords or in Standing Committees, and it occasionally permits free votes. Although the parliamentary parties may be tolerant of internal opposition and willing enough to overlook the occasional abstention, the constituency organizations may be less so; they may wish to reprimand the dissenting Member and perhaps even to end their association.

The great political parties also have a stake in the elections, and the next election is never far from the consciousness of the party membership. This duality of interest is reflected in the organization of the parliamentary parties; they are primarily concerned with the business of Parliament but they also have close relations with the external party structure, which is especially concerned with fighting an election, and individual Members in addition develop their own personal arrangements with their constituencies. The elections have a multifarious effect on Parliament: they determine the composition of the membership in the House of Commons, they indicate which party will be able to organize the Government, and to an extent they influence the selection of the issues to be considered by Parliament. The elections also affect the relationship between the parties. In the period before elections, there is a noticeable increase in the sensitivity of Members: tempers will rise; it may be more difficult to secure interparty agreements; and there is a

28

temptation to resort more frequently to the use of invective. Following the elections, the tension of the party conflict may carry over for a year or more.

Our consideration of the influences shaping the business of Parliament would be incomplete without inquiring into the part played by external political parties which have their own research organizations and attempt to develop political issues. In fact, the question is sometimes raised whether Parliament has been transformed into an agency which merely follows and ratifies the party line. However influential the external parties are in some areas, Parliament is by no means a supine captive which takes' orders and carries out instructions. Parliament has an independence of its own, a function to perform, which the external parties have not crushed. It is difficult, however, to state with any precision the nature of external party influence, partly because the relationship between the parties and Parliament is often vague and unclarified. The controversy in the Labour Party, following the General Election of 1959, was in part concerned with the location of power within the party: whether the Party Conference can speak authoritatively, formulating policy and strategy and binding everybody with its bloc votes, or whether the party is a pluralistic organization with elements and areas of autonomy and independence.

In general it may be said that the external parties are more influential in some areas of parliamentary activity than in other areas; they stimulate political thought and attempt to formulate issues on some questions, but they do not advance a complete pattern of policy. The agreements reached at party conferences have a commanding influence over the policy of the respective parties, although the Conservative tradition reserves for the leaders some freedom of action. They may ignore, if they wish, the decisions of the conference but the leaders also like to keep the party contented and they may be inclined to go along with the wishes of the conference. Both parties follow the rule that the external parties should not interfere in the day-to-day operation of Government or in the relations between Government and Parliament, and Mr. Attlee in particular made it plain in 1945 that policy decisions would be made by the Government and not by the Labour Party Executive. The external political organizations may influence attitudes and help to conduct elections but they do not tell Parliament what to do, and the internal partisan organization of Parliament is not run by a caucus.

The High Stakes of Parliament

THE MEMBERS

The careers of individual Members, also at stake in the actions of Parliament, are shaped by the demands for leadership found there and by the opportunities available for self-expression. From the total aggregate of the membership of both Houses, the leaders must evolve who will be responsible for the fortunes of the Government and the Opposition. Members are constantly evaluating the talents of their colleagues and forming an opinion whether they can be trusted with high office. The hierarchy of leadership is relatively small, and those who are successful in the competitive struggle receive large rewards in the sense of having influence within Parliament over certain types of policy. The period of testing and trial and waiting may go on for a long period, but under optimum conditions some Members are fortunate enough to become Ministers very quickly indeed. An instance where personality and competence were recognized and rewarded, assisted by the luck of the elections, is found in the career of Mr. Iain Macleod, who was elected to Parliament in 1950 and became Minister of Health two years later, with other ministries to follow. But there is no sure road to the top. An ambitious and able Member of the minority party may undergo years of frustration—perhaps never becoming a Minister—and Members of ministerial calibre may lose favour within their own party.

The membership of the House of Commons may, for convenience, be divided into several groups, although the divisions may sometimes overlap. In the first group are the leaders who hold special office within the party hierarchy—that is, the Government and the Opposition. In the second group are the former leaders, those who have once held high office. Members in this group are normally Privy Councillors and as such have certain parliamentary prerogatives. In the third group are the full-time Private Members, those who are diligent in attendance and in debate. In the fourth group are those who attend less regularly and perhaps have no committee assignments; they may be engaged in full-time jobs outside Parliament.

In exercising influence over the business of Parliament, Private Members are the underprivileged ones, and they are often kept on a very short leash. They may ask questions; with good fortune and some perseverance they may choose the topic for short debates; with even better fortune and greater perseverance they may be able to sponsor legislation successfully; and they may participate in debate, providing they can catch the Speaker's wandering eye. There is also a nether world of parliamentary activity, where Private Members put down motions that are practically never considered and collect supporting signatures that are rarely required for a division. Such motions may nevertheless have some influence. They may be put down for the purpose of revealing to the Government the strength of sentiment behind some proposal, and the sponsor of a popular cause may be able to collect several score and perhaps even hundreds of signatures for his proposal. Again, the tabling of a motion may be part of the in-fighting within a party, and a motion may be used to express the opinion of a dissident group. We have seen how Mr. Silverman used his motion on military disengagement to press his views on the party. Following the Suez military operation in 1956, a number of motions unfavourable to American foreign policy were tabled by Conservative Members, but they were withdrawn after Mr. Macmillan had visited the United States and the tension between the two countries had decreased. Motions may, indeed, persuade the Government to take some kind of action, even though the motion itself is not voted on. In 1959, Members from both parties signed a motion tabled by Sir David Robertson, a Conservative, asking for an investigation of the police behaviour in Thurso, Scotland, where the police had supposedly struck a boy, and although the Government had initially opposed a further investigation, it eventually gave in to the demand and created a Committee of Inquiry.

The right of a Private Member to introduce legislation is acquired (primarily) by Ballot, and at the beginning of each session the Speaker's Sweepstakes, as they are called, are held. The Ballot is popular with some Members, those with hobbies to promote and who enjoy the challenge of shepherding a Bill through Parliament. Members who are not interested in sponsoring legislation may nevertheless be encouraged by the party Whips to put their names down, and the Whips may even suggest legislation that might be introduced. A Member who is fortunate in the Ballot need not be burdened down with an assignment for which he has no heart but can delegate to another Member the opportunity for promoting the legislation. The interest in the Ballot extends to the public, and there are many groups and associations who would like special legislation enacted but who have been unable to persuade the Government to take up their cause. Sir Keith Joseph has commented that Members who are lucky in the Ballot become, for a short period of time, 'the centre of enormous pressures from the panacea mongers and the reformers of this world.'[1] Even though lucky in the Ballot, a Member

[1] H. C. Deb., 28th November 1958, col. 718.

television; that the pig farmers have been lobbying their Members 'to put home pig farmers in a better position to compete with overseas bacon suppliers'; that a reception has been given in the Palace of Westminster, where Members may book rooms; that the Anti-Ugly Action Group has met with Members regarding the development of Piccadilly Circus; and that all-party delegations have put to the Minister the claims of Scotland for locating a Ford plant there.

In a sense, the Government and the Opposition leaders are the custodians of the 'national interest' whereas Private Members on the back benches are permitted to take a more narrow, parochial view of policy. The Private Members may attempt to persuade the leadership to keep in mind the particular interests with which they are concerned, including local and regional interests. The pattern is maintained, then, of the Government proposing solutions, or asking that its own solutions be accepted, and Parliament attempting to influence the decisions of the Government sometime before giving its final consent.

Municipal corporations may sponsor private Bills, which are introduced by petition and follow special procedures, and there is an area in law where private litigants may appeal to the House of Lords. Parliament also has some control over Measures passed by the Church Assembly. Such Measures are first considered by an Ecclesiastical Committee consisting of thirty Members (fifteen from each House) which can comment on the substance and the legal effect of the Measure but which has no power of amendment. Normally, parliamentary approval of the Measures of the Church Assembly is formal and noncontroversial, but Parliament, after a sharp debate, rejected the proposed revision of the Book of Common Prayer in 1927–28. On this issue there was considerable lobbying from several quarters, and the Church of England itself was split on the merits of the revision.

THE PROCEDURES

The effectiveness of the procedures may also be considered to be one of the high stakes at issue in the actions of Parliament. At times the processes are under some strain as attempts are made to have them satisfy competitive and sometimes contradictory demands. In the parliamentary tradition, the procedures must be fair and just, and in the House of Commons the towering figure of the Speaker plays a part. The procedures must be able to regulate debate in such a fashion that some definite action follows; and they must be flexible enough to permit the significant issues to be brought before it and to be resolved. Parliament is an arena of political conflict, where real issues in society are considered under controlled conditions, and it is necessary that the procedures not only permit the conflict to be raised but also to blunt its edge so as to permit resolution. The process itself is often complex, with special procedures followed in making law, appropriating money, debating policy, questioning Ministers, reviewing orders, and completing various technical undertakings such as issuing writs of election. A mastery of procedures may be an essential first step in acquiring influence in Parliament. An endless parade of issues is brought before Parliament for consideration, and it is necessary that the integrity and the utility of the procedures be preserved in resolving these issues.

In settling the business of Parliament, one is in effect allocating scarce commodities between competing claimants, and one of the factors in the equation is the perverse item of time. Demands on the time of Parliament have increased with the rise of popular democracy and the widespread extension of governmental authority. The electorate and the Members are increasingly articulate, and Members are expected to speak up, to advocate or defend some particular cause. Pressures are brought on even the most laconic Member to say something, to influence somebody about something, not just sit there in reflective silence. The demands on Parliament are so extensive that there is not time enough to satisfy all of them, and this shortage of time leads to procedural controls exercised by political hierarchies. It might be possible to create more time by delegating work to committees or to the Government, but this in turn would affect the traditional role of Parliament and would lead to problems of a different nature.

As in other aspects of Parliament, the routine followed in determining its business is highly stylized. The sessional orders, enacted for each session, determine the general order of debate according to the category of the proposal and the nature of the claimant, and there is a well-developed rhythm in the hours, days, weeks, and sessions in the life of a Parliament. One knows what to expect! The rules are somewhat obtuse, reflecting as they do the many attempts made by Parliament to secure a workable compromise between the various conflicting demands. It is not a new problem. Between 1837 and 1960 some nineteen committees studied methods of improving procedures governing the consideration of public business. The tactics followed by the Irish Members in the 1870's and 1880's showed that Parliament could be rendered powerless by a small group of wilful men, to give them the name applied by President Wilson to a cabal of filibustering Senators, and the subsequent revision of the rules increased the authority of the Government and the Speaker of the House of Commons. There is no need to repeat the technical arguments on this subject, and much of the story has been described by Josef Redlich in his meritorious three-volume work, *The Procedure of the House of Commons*, which appeared in 1908. The regulations now in effect are essentially a product of the nineteenth and twentieth centuries. The need for adequate or improved procedures continues to be discussed, and as recently as 1959 a Select Committee considered the imaginative proposal made by Sir Edward Fellowes (the Clerk of the House) for decentralizing the work of the House of Commons.[1]

There is perhaps little public interest in the business of Parliament, as it is developed week by week, but in Parliament itself the topic commands singular attention. There is not time enough for everybody to do what he wants to do. There are more Members who wish to make speeches or to sponsor legislation than can be accommodated, and the Government also has proposals that it would like Parliament to consider. Sir Herbert Butcher once remarked that he was depressed by the thought that whatever arrangements may be made for speeding up things, 'the time saved is almost certain to be appropriated by any Government, whatever colour it may be, for pushing forward with its own legislation.'[2]

LENGTH OF A PARLIAMENT

The nature of the conflict between the parties is also related to and affected by the length of a Parliament, which at the present time may last up to five years (and longer if changed by law). The length of Parliament, and the frequency with which Parliament assembles, was for long periods of history an unsettled and contentious topic, but it has now become harmonized with the political struggle and is an issue of great importance to the political parties. The identification of 'a Parliament' with a given period of time is a reminder of an earlier period when the term 'parliament' was a generic name applied to a body of advisers and councillors whom the King summoned for consultation. In the fourteenth century, Parliaments were convened annually, or even more frequently, and in all more than a hundred Parliaments were held in that

---

[1] See *Report from the Select Committee on Procedure* (1959), H. C. 92-1.
[2] *Ibid.*, pp. 22–23.

century. In the fifteenth century, some fifty-seven Parliaments were convened. The meetings of Parliament became more irregular in the sixteenth and seventeenth centuries, for although Parliament was in some ways essential to the King it might also be troublesome, and many years might elapse between the period when Parliament was dissolved and when it was again convened. There was some dissatisfaction with the irregularity of the meetings, and in 1689 the Bill of Rights attempted to define the acceptable constitutional doctrine: 'That for redress of all grievances,' it stated, 'and for the amending, strengthening, and preserving of the laws, Parliament ought to be held frequently.'

During the eighteenth and nineteenth centuries, annual sessions became customary, and the life of a Parliament was fixed legally at seven years; it could be dissolved at an earlier date. In 1911 the duration of a Parliament was shortened to five years, but under the stress of the First World War Parliament continued for almost eight years without a General Election intervening and, in the period of the Second World War, for nine years and seven months.

The circumstantial fact that no fixed date (other than the five-year proviso) governs the length of a Parliament is now a factor of some importance to the fortunes of the political parties. The element of flexibility in the length of Parliament, leading to uncertainty concerning the date of dissolution and of the elections, casts its spell over the proceedings of Parliament. Certain conventions serve as a guide for dissolving Parliament, but the Prime Minister, who advises the Monarch and in effect makes the decision, may have considerable discretion in the matter. Parliament may be dissolved because the support of the Government is withering away, as in 1902; or the support is tenuous, as in 1951; it may be dissolved to secure further approval of a policy, as in 1910 (on curtailing the powers of the House of Lords) or in 1935 (on applying sanctions in the Italo-Ethiopian War). If the Government maintains a steady majority, however, and there is no particular issue to be resolved, these stock reasons for dissolving Parliament may be inapplicable. The indeterminate life of a Parliament means that an election can be fought at any time, and the parties, those in the country as well as in Parliament, are constantly on the alert. The uncertain date of dissolution may colour the activities within Parliament, and the tense atmosphere will increase as the end of the five-year period approaches.

The Prime Minister has, perhaps, a theoretical advantage in being able to select the date for dissolution. In 1958 and 1959, when all eyes were scanning the skies for interpretative signs and omens, Mr. Macmillan remained happily enigmatic, and as the central figure in these bootless speculations he would tease Opposition Members who became overly curious. On one occasion Mr. Fernyhough, a Labour Member, sought to gain some information about the date of the General Election.

'Can the Prime Minister tell us', he asked, 'whether he expects the Summit talks to take place before or after the General Election?'

'Well, Sir,' the Prime Minister responded, 'that depends upon two not absolutely known factors: first, when the General Election will be; and, secondly, when the Summit talks will be.'[1]

Although the Opposition cannot select the dissolution date, it is not powerless in raising issues on which the Election might be fought, and it might be lucky enough to select one that has broad public support and divides the opposite party.

Other broad units of parliamentary time include the fiscal year and the reign of the sovereign. The fiscal year, beginning 6th April, regulates the time for considering the Estimates and the Finance Bill and, incidentally, may limit the time available for elections. The reign of the sovereign governs the documentary dating system; and until the passage of the Representation of the People Act in 1867, the demise of the sovereign was followed by the dissolution of Parliament.

Annual sessions (consuming approximately 160 days) are normally divided into four periods, with periodic risings of indeterminate length at Christmas, Easter, Whitsun, and Summer. There are weekly sessions, for which specific plans are made, and of course daily sessions, where specific time is provided for considering the various items of business.

We have now identified the leading participants in the parliamentary process and have discussed somewhat cursorily their various goals. Among those who are directly concerned with the high stakes of Parliament are the Government, the Opposition, the parties, the individual Members and Peers, and British society itself. We have also mentioned the significant part played by the procedures of Parliament. So far we have spoken in general terms and have used fairly abstract concepts, the better to present a general view of what is considered to be significant in the parliamentary system. In the subsequent chapters we will examine more closely how Parliament works, or appears to work, in actuality, considering first its membership.

---

[1] H. C. Deb., 25th March 1959, col. 1,334.

CHAPTER II

Membership: All Sorts and Conditions of Men

THE HOUSE OF COMMONS

The membership of Parliament runs to an impressive figure, for there are 630 Members of the House of Commons and some 900 Peers in the House of Lords, and it could be argued that the sheer size of the membership is a factor in shaping the form of British politics. With a large membership and broad representation, the prize of office in the House of Commons is spread widely over many constituencies. One might also argue that this prodigality of numbers affects the internal organization of Parliament in which a political hierarchy with considerable influence has developed. Although the focus of this book is on Parliament, it may be desirable to underscore some of the salient features of the electoral system as they affect the composition and the operation of Parliament itself. There is in the electoral system an emphasis on representation of areas, people, parties, groups, and communities, and the representation in the House of Commons, legally based on population and territory, is supplemented by the varied forms of representation in the House of Lords. Representation in Parliament extends to all parts of the country, and, inferentially, to many social groups. If to this extensive representation one adds accessibility on the part of the public, one can envisage Parliament as the centre of a network of political information through which it is informed of controversies and grievances throughout the Kingdom. The network of political information extends somewhat unevenly to the overseas territories as well, although formal representation is not extended to the colonies. There is some representation of Commonwealth countries, acquired or extended on a personal basis, including a few Peers, members of the Privy Council, and Members of the House of Commons.

Membership: All Sorts and Conditions of Men

Various changes have occurred in the electoral system during the development of Parliament, and one may note how former methods for recruiting Members have been supplanted by popular elections and how the electorate has been broadened; how social conflict becomes a part of political and often of partisan conflict; how political parties have developed for controlling the elections; and how groups and individuals compete in still other places to control the parties.

THE DEVELOPMENT OF REPRESENTATION

The development of the electoral system can perhaps be clarified by taking a backward glance at the practice followed during the Elizabethan period and earlier, for the roots of the present system can be seen in this older type of representation. The earlier forms may also provide some perspective as one observes the attempts made by some of the newer nations to develop their own internal systems of representation. But what, we may ask first, does representation attempt to achieve? and on this question there has been considerable theory construction, rationalization, and historical research. The system of representation followed in the Middle Ages may be broadly described as a process by which those directly concerned with an institution could participate in some fashion in its operation. When the early barons became members of the King's council, representation was given to a land-controlling class which had identifiable common interests and which exercised specific controls over other phases of society. Perhaps the fact that the barons formed a permanent, hereditary class, that they controlled men and land as well as money, made it possible for them to develop an autonomous corporate identity which enabled them to be influential in their own right.

Medieval representation was based on functional groups, such as the barons and the clergy, and on communities, which found representation in the House of Commons. Speaking of the House of Commons, Professor F. W. Maitland has said that 'the representatives who appeared in Parliament were not representatives of inorganic collections of individuals, they represented shires and boroughs.'[1] The concept of representation based on aggregates of the population and of representatives chosen primarily by popular elections was the development of a later day.

[1] F. W. Maitland, *The Constitutional History of England* (Cambridge, 1908; reprinted, 1955), p. 85.

Membership: All Sorts and Conditions of Men

In the Elizabethan Parliament, the House of Commons became more powerful, with an expanded membership and a broader basis of representation, and Professor Sir John Neale informs us that the House of Commons began to rival the House of Lords 'in power and influence, if not in prestige.'[1] The idea of representation now became divorced 'from any local ties with the constituency' and it was possible for 'anyone from anywhere to contest an election.' Without the suspension of the residency rule, Professor Neale asks, 'how else could the House of Commons have greatly surpassed the average ability of the community; how else have provided room for the nation's best available skill and leadership; how else have secured that Parliament should be nationally rather than locally minded?'[2]

During the sixteenth century the membership of the House of Commons expanded from 296 to 462, and one raises the question why the membership expanded in such profusion. The changing representation was less the result of planned reform than of chance reaction to new forces in the social system. Some seats were added by extending the representative system to Wales, Monmouthshire, and Cheshire, and under this system the county received two Members and the town either one or two Members. The addition of other seats, in the words of Professor Neale, 'were the results of an apparently haphazard creation or restoration of parliamentary boroughs, excusable by no argument that would be valid today, and certainly having little connection with population'.[3]

Expansion of parliamentary membership was facilitated by the fact that there was no maximum limit placed on the number of towns which could secure representation and no minimum limit placed on their size. Having no stated quota, parliamentary membership was expanded in accordance with the effectiveness of the pressure brought on the Monarch.

Some of the new parliamentary boroughs of the sixteenth century became the rotten boroughs of the nineteenth century, which were the object of electoral reform. The spectacular growth of parliamentary boroughs is sometimes cited as an example of the abuse of royal prerogative, but there seem to be more solid reasons than patronage to explain the growth. It has been contended that the new boroughs were 'really designed to give more adequate representation to the new trading interests' which could not be so readily represented through existing

---

[1] J. E. Neale, *The Elizabethan House of Commons* (London, 1949), p. 15.
[2] *Ibid.,* p. 16.   [3] *Ibid.,* p. 140.

electoral patterns in town or country.[1] Professor Neale, however, has attributed this growth to the increasing popularity of the House of Commons. 'If we ask why the Elizabethan gentry were so desirous of a seat in Parliament,' he says, 'we might answer, as we should answer for more recent times—ambition, dignity, curiosity, a desire to be at the centre of things, or even business reasons.'[2] The country gentry brought pressure on their patrons for more representation, and the patrons, in consequence, brought pressure on the Queen to create new boroughs.

With the increase in the number of Members, the House of Commons gained the support of the local communities and became increasingly tied to them. With its strength augmented, the House of Commons could also be more independent, and it developed 'the spirit and tenacity . . . to challenge and overthrow the monarchy'.[3] There were other results, also, which affected the character of the House of Commons. The size of the constituency was, and still is, relatively small, making possible a high degree of direct personal contact between Members and constituents. On the other end of the spectrum it is possible for the national government to be highly sensitized to local opinion. Moreover, the extension of the membership to small, thinly populated boroughs created political opportunities for candidates who were not permanent residents of the boroughs or counties they represented. The law required residence, but a situation was created where, in theory, any man otherwise eligible for election could offer himself in any constituency. In the meantime, however, the House of Commons became a large deliberative body, of a size which required a well-defined system of internal control if it was to be effective.

Elections were held in the Elizabethan period, but it would be incorrect to describe them by the modern word 'popular'. The county elections held for every new Parliament were controlled or at least strongly influenced by the great families. Elections to a borough seat depended on a different set of factors, and there was no statutory franchise, such as there was in the counties. Professor Neale has reminded us that 'the less we think in terms of a right to vote, the better we shall understand the complexity of the subject. It was the community, not the individual, that was represented. Even in the counties, with their forty-shilling freeholder franchise, this conception was still alive.' In a substantial number of Elizabethan boroughs, the electorate consisted of

---

[1] J. R. Green, *A Short History of the English People* (London, 1915 ed.), vol. 1, p. 383.
[2] Neale, op. cit., p. 148.   [3] *Ibid.*, p. 147.

the corporation of the borough, such as at King's Lynn, where the Member of Parliament was regularly elected by the Mayor, twelve aldermen, and eighteen common councillors. But the pattern was not uniform. 'Elsewhere, popular agitation broadened the franchise—agitation akin to the demand for a voice in the affairs of the town which led to the creation of a second chamber of "commoners" in the governing body. The modern conception of a right to vote . . . drew strength from the competition for parliamentary seats which developed in the second half of the sixteenth century. Rival candidates began seeking support from different elements in the community, thus provoking disputes about the franchise. Then, in the seventeenth century the House of Commons itself helped to break down the medieval preference of the community to the individual, when its standing committee, which dealt with election controversies, applied what we should describe as liberal principles.'[1]

We can enumerate simply the development since then: the growth and identification of a specific electorate; extension of suffrage, with the right of participation in the suffrage broadly extended; and the increased use of a representative base of geographic units having substantially equal populations. The boundaries of boroughs and counties are ordinarily respected, but the empirical standard for allocating representation is the size of population, not communities as such.

PARTY REPRESENTATION

It is not easy to establish a precise date marking the advent of the party system in Parliament. Factions preceded parties and often behaved much like parties; there have been Yorkists and Lancastrians, Cavaliers and Roundheads, Irish Republicans, and many other factional groups, and factions continue on in the present day within the broader party framework.

The date for the origin of parliamentary parties is frequently placed at the close of the reign of Charles II when Parliament was debating the Exclusion Bill (1679–80), which proposed to prevent the succession to the crown of James, Duke of York, on the grounds that he was a Roman Catholic. The Members who supported exclusion were given the name of Whigs by their opponents, and the latter, in turn, were given the name Tories. (The names of the parties were later changed to Liberal and Conservative.)

---

[1] Neale, op. cit., p. 247.

Membership: All Sorts and Conditions of Men

On advice, William III selected a ministry in 1696 from the party forming a majority in the House of Commons (the Whigs); it was also the party to which the King owed his throne. The office of Prime Minister developed under George I, who was unfamiliar with the English language and was disinclined to preside at meetings of the Ministers; the function, or office, was acquired by Robert Walpole in 1721 and held by him for almost twenty-one years. On 28 January 1742, Walpole was defeated by a majority of one vote; on February 2nd, by sixteen votes, whereupon he resigned. This incident was one of the early attempts to enforce ministerial responsibility by compelling the Minister to resign when he no longer enjoys the support of the majority.

Labour candidates first appeared at the General Election of 1892 (when the Labour leader, J. Keir Hardie, was elected), and the Labour Party was officially organized in 1906.

The major political parties now exercise great influence in selecting the candidates and conducting the elections. They are highly competitive and very active, challenging seats even when the chances of victory are very small, and they now control all but one of the seats in Parliament. In the 1959 General Election, Labour contested 621 seats, winning 258; the Conservatives contested 625 seats, winning 365; and the Liberals contested 216 seats, winning 6. In all, there were 1,536 candidates.

The modern electoral system places a light burden on the candidate himself and does not require him to build up a large personal following on his own resources or to impoverish himself in getting elected. The method of selection is relatively informal and is not excessively taxing. The candidate need not (and indeed cannot) spend large quantities of money on the election; he need not be a resident of the constituency he represents; and he is not burdened by any intraparty conflict through such a device as a primary election. An impecunious candidate, even an amateur in politics, will suffer no handicap as such.

As a first step, a candidate must find a hospitable constituency, one which will adopt him as its own, which will raise money to wage the campaign and pay the costs of a full-time party agent to look after the interests of the party and which will support him with enthusiasm at the election. The fact that there is no residential requirement gives the potential candidate considerable scope in looking for a compatible constituency, and he may have to do some shopping around before he finds one. Constituencies vary in esteem, and such factors as accessibility to London or to one's home residence may be considered, as well as the important question of the voting habits of the constituency. Moreover, there will be competitors, perhaps many of them. Even though adopted, a candidate may decide to seek a more favourable constituency if the opportunity arises and at one time it was not unknown for a candidate to hedge against defeat by offering himself as a candidate in more than one constituency. He would resign the surplus seats if elected more than once.

If the potential candidate succeeds in getting his name on a short list of names to be considered, he will be interviewed briefly by the selection committee of the constituency party, and he may be asked to make a few remarks. The final selection may be made at the end of the meeting, and if the candidate is confirmed by the higher powers, as is normally the case, the candidate will begin to nurse the constituency in his spare time and prepare in a quiet way for the next election, which may indeed be some years in the future.

It is not easy to generalize about the nature of the control over adoptions exercised by the party organization, for it is a topic of great complexity, often varying in practice from one constituency to the next; and in the Labour Party there is the additional complicating factor that some candidates are sponsored by trade unions. All national parties attempt to respect and preserve the autonomy of the local unit in making the selection, although the national headquarters will assist the constituency parties by preparing lists of approved candidates.

In the Conservative Party the candidate designated by the selection committee must be confirmed by members of the constituency party, and although normally the choice is approved, there have been cases where party dissidents have requested a 'postal referendum'—the first step towards a primary election! In the Labour Party, the candidate must be approved by the National Executive, and it is possible to reject a candidate because of his political views.

Relatively few people are involved in the total selection process. A potential candidate has to be alert to his opportunities, and he may have to do a good deal of talking and travelling, but the process of selection is on the whole a quiet and unspectacular affair, with conflict and controversy normally kept behind closed doors. The process of adoption does not require the expenditure of very much money, and the successful candidate need please but a small number of people. The candidate who seeks office but is not adopted may conclude that getting into Parliament is no easy matter, and it is true that he has no recourse if rejected, other than the implausible one of standing as an independent.

For the successful candidate, however, the process is often simple, straightforward, and inexpensive.

The candidate is no longer required to finance his own campaign, but money must come from somewhere, and the local branch is responsible for the raising of funds. In the Labour Party, some of the financial problems of the local branches are solved by a system in which trade unions and co-operatives sponsor candidates. The sponsoring organizations are permitted by the party to pay up to 80 per cent of the total amount of election expenses permissible under the law. They may also contribute to the annual costs of the local party organization, and in some cases they further subsidize Members after election. The groups having the largest number of sponsored elected Members following the 1959 General Election were the Miners (31); Co-operative Party (18); Transport and General Workers' Union (14); Union Shop, Distributive and Allied Workers (9); Amalgamated Engineering Union (8); and National Union of Railwaymen (5). The National Union of Teachers also sponsors candidates, distributed equally among Conservatives, Labour, and Liberals. Five of the twelve sponsored candidates were elected in 1959.

In general, the candidates sponsored by the trade unions and co-operatives are found in the safer seats, and their success at the polls is a good deal better than the national average of the Labour Party. In 1945, some 96 per cent of their sponsored candidates were elected, but the percentage has been falling in subsequent elections. In 1959, the trade unions sponsored 129 candidates, of whom 92 were elected, and their allies in the Co-operative Party sponsored 31 candidates of whom 18 were elected. This is an average of 69 per cent. Of the other 461 Labour candidates in the 1959 General Election who did not have this sponsorship, 148 were elected, for an average of 24 per cent.

Each party has a number of relatively safe seats, although these are not necessarily given to the national party leaders, sheltering them from the winds of political competition as a reward for their services; and an examination of the safer seats, those where one party predominates and customarily wins the election, leads one to the conclusion that a political Santa Claus has dispensed his presents in a surprising fashion. Some candidates are always being plagued by the fickleness of elections, as their fortunes are first up and then down; others may begin their careers in relatively safe seats and hold on to them, so the vagaries of elections cause them very little trouble; still other candidates may be adopted for a safer seat after having held or fought one where the political competition was considerably stronger. In the latter case, one may cite the career of Mr. Macmillan, who was twice defeated at Stockton-on-Tees in County Durham before his election to the relatively safe seat of Bromley, Kent. The national party may on some occasions attempt to influence the selection of a candidate, but even so powerful a figure as Mr. Morgan Phillips, the General Secretary of the Labour Party, was unable to find a constituency for the 1959 General Election and was twice turned down by constituency selection committees.

The Conservatives have a large bloc of relatively safe seats in the Home Counties south of the Thames, and there are twenty-five constituencies in Surrey, East and West Sussex, Hampshire, and Kent which consistently give the Conservatives a majority of 55 per cent or better. On the Labour side, a large bloc of safe seats is controlled by the National Union of Mineworkers. Of the thirty-four seats sponsored by the miners, three are held with a margin of 80 per cent or more of the voters; fourteen are held with a margin of between 70 and 79 per cent; ten between 60 and 69 per cent; and three between 54 and 59 per cent. There is a propensity on the part of the Union to award these seats to their own members after service in the Union, and membership in Parliament from a relatively safe district becomes part of the hierarchy of power within the Mineworkers Union. One of the results of using parliamentary membership as a type of Union reward is that the average age of the miner Members of Parliament is high in comparison with other Members; eighteen of the thirty miner candidates in 1959 were over sixty years old.

Education and Occupation of Members, General Election, 1959

EDUCATION

	Conser- vative	Labour	Liberal	Total
Oxford	107	33	2	142
Cambridge	80	14	3	97
Other Universities	31	64	1	96
Eton	73	3	2	78
Harrow	20	—	—	—
Other Public Schools	155	39	2	196
Service Colleges	37	1	—	38
Grammar, Secondary and Combination School	52	86*	—	138
Elementary	5	54	—	59

(* Includes Ruskin College and Labour and Co-operative Colleges.)

Membership: All Sorts and Conditions of Men

	Conservative	Labour	Liberal	Total
Barristers	56	22	4	82
Solicitors	10	8	1	19
Journalists	10	22	—	32
Broadcasters	2	2	—	4
Directors	70	6	—	76
Manufacturers	3	2	1	6
Landowners and Farmers	30	4	—	34
Accountants	5	1	—	6
Publishers	4	—	—	4
Teachers and Lecturers	2	25	—	27
Engineers	3	9	—	12
Surveyors	3	—	—	3
Medicine and Dentistry	1	5	—	6
Brokers	12	1	—	13
Regular Forces	25	3	—	28
Diplomatic Service	3	—	—	3
Trade Union, etc., officials	—	40	—	40
Miners	—	23	—	23
Railwaymen	—	9	—	9
Secretaries	—	3	—	3

(*The Times*, 19th October 1959, based on information supplied by Members for inclusion in *The Times Guide to the House of Commons*, 1959.)

Although both large parties are national in the sense that they compete in almost every constituency, there are some regional differences in the support given to the parties, as the following table shows:

	Conservative	Labour	Liberal	Independent
England	315	193	3	—
Wales	7	27	2	—
Scotland	31	38	1	1
Northern Ireland	12	—	—	—
	365	258	6	1

Membership: All Sorts and Conditions of Men

There has also been a trend in favour of the Conservatives, following the General Election of 1945:

	1945	1950	1951	1955	1959
Conservatives and Associates	213	298	321	345	365
Labour (and Co-operative Party)	393	315	295	277	258
Liberal	12	9	6	6	6
Others	22	3	3	2	1
	640	625	625	630	630

With the growing activities of government, the local demands on the time of Members have increased, and perhaps the greatest demand is placed on Members who represent new and growing constituencies where the social services have not yet been well developed. Many Members spend frequent weekends in their constituencies, conducting 'surgeries' where various grievances are aired. Local interest may be defended in debate, in legislation, and during question time; for example, if the Member comes from a Scottish division he will very likely make speeches on the vicissitudes of the herring fishermen.

The constituency organization may attempt to exercise some control over the Member, and it may expect him to report occasionally on his political performance, although in fact the relationships between a Member and his constituency vary greatly. Some Members, indeed, consider the constituency organizations to be a petty nuisance. However, these organizations can't be ignored, and if a Member disagrees openly with his party in Parliament he will return to his constituency in noticeable haste in an attempt to retain the goodwill of the local party. The power of the constituency organization to deny readoption is one of the sanctions supporting party regularity, and one is led to the unexpected conclusion that local controls over the selection of candidates may help to support the solidarity of the national parties within Parliament. The local party, anxious to win elections, may be impatient if it finds it has embraced a candidate with embarrassing political aberrations, as if the son of a publican became a temperance leader.

The parliamentary candidate has now been relieved from most (and in some cases all) of the obligations of financing either a campaign or the local party office, and the opportunities for a career in Parliament have accordingly been extended to some who could not have afforded one heretofore. However, what is gained in one area may be lost in

D

another, and a Member may, under some conditions, have less political freedom now than formerly. A Member who falls out with his local party organization may be relatively powerless to protect himself, and in recent years some few constituency organizations have been provocative and assertive, even bullying Members into resigning from Parliament or forcing them out of public life by refusing to readopt them.

SPECIAL REPRESENTATION

In addition to the formal representation in Parliament based on population and geography and controlled by political parties, there exists also a species of group representation which ranges from the casual requests and petitions that Members introduce on behalf of their constituencies to a type of contractual arrangement between the Members and the groups whose interests they agree to represent. Some Members become, in effect, conduits through which influence is exerted on the Government. The terms 'pressures' and 'pressure groups' have an ominous ring and are not widely accepted in the vocabulary of British politics; yet, in the broadest and non-invidious sense, Parliament has traditionally been a vehicle for exerting influence on the Government. So it was historically, and so it is in modern times; and the process of Members attempting to influence H.M. Government, of bringing pressures on the centres of power, goes on constantly.[1]

The role played in group representation may not always be obvious. In considering public legislation, representatives of special groups have no right of access to the parliamentary process, and there are no public hearings in the congressional sense of the word in which the views of the various groups are placed on the record. The political parties maintain such a command over the proceedings that in considering Government business no external assistance is necessary to persuade Members or committees to take action. Matters may be taken up with the Government privately, and one of the uses of Parliament is the occasion it provides for Members and Peers to talk to Ministers confidentially.

In a broader sense, however, the representation of group interests plays a significant role in the parliamentary process. The interests may

[1] An examination of group representation in Parliament has been made by Mr. J. D. Stewart in an instructive book, *British Pressure Groups: Their Role in Relation to the House of Commons* (Oxford, 1958). Mr. Stewart has mobilized considerable information on the specific groups that are represented, the associations with which Members are identified, and the tactics and procedures followed by the groups in putting their case before Parliament. See also S. E. Finer, *Anonymous Empire: a Study of the Lobby in Britain* (London, 1958).

be expressed when legislation is being considered or policy debated, and ginger groups may be formed to stimulate interest in certain types of policy. There is, in fact, an intricate system of group consultation and representation that has been built into the British political system. It is found in the administration of policy. It is found in preparing legislation, at which time the Government will normally consult the interested groups. The following remarks, made by Mr. Michael Stewart, a Labour Member, illuminate the procedure sometimes followed in securing partisan and group agreement before the proposal is sent to Parliament for approval. The Bill 'is the result of discussions, spreading over a good many months . . .', Mr. Stewart said. 'I took part on behalf of the official opposition. . . . My right hon. Friends and I took the opportunity to see that we were properly informed of the views of the religious denominations on the various matters that have to be considered.'[1]

Group consultation is also evident in fiscal affairs, and every year the Chancellor of the Exchequer listens to the doleful complaints of taxpaying organizations before making up his budget. Once proposals are before Parliament, the pressures continue: amendments are proposed, resolutions tabled, questions raised, speeches made, Members lobbied, consulted, and persuaded, Ministers cornered, the public aroused. In debate, the views of certain groups may be expressed by Members, and the Speaker seems to know who these Members are and the groups whose opinions they express. The points of view of various trade associations, trade unions, educational groups, churches, and on and on, are given in this manner.

Influence may be engineered by private groups (some of which are permanent) with regularized methods of approaching Parliament, while others are of a more transient nature, organized to exert pressure in particular cases for immediate ends. These pressure groups may be bold enough to hold their meetings of protest within the Palace of Westminster itself, the one requirement being that the meeting will be sponsored by a Member.

The nature of the relationship between Member and group varies considerably, and although normally it would be on an informal basis, with the Member representing the interest of the group just as he would that of any other constituent, in some cases the relationship is more specific, even extending to a contractual basis. One case of Member-group relationship has already been mentioned, that where trade unions sponsor Members and in some cases supplement the salaries and provide

[1] House of Commons Debates (London, H.M.S.O.), 22nd June 1959, col. 870.

clerical aid. Some Members are also designated as 'Parliamentary agents' of firms, associations, and trade unions. The Church Commissioners and Charity Commissioners are represented in the House of Commons by one of their unpaid members. 'He answers questions in Parliament like a Minister, belongs as a matter of course to the party which is in power, and accordingly ceases to be a representative Commissioner on a change in the party complexion of the Government.'[1]

The group or groups with which a Member may be identified is often a matter of public knowledge, but there is no standard practice for revealing the nature of this association and no firm rule governing the financial relations between Members and private associations. In debate, however, it is customary for a Member to declare his interest in the topic under consideration. The direct representation of interests is confined to Private Members; Ministers must dissociate themselves from such alliances and they receive no salaries from external sources.

Under the prevailing theory, then, the Government must be objective, aloof, dispassionate, and neutral; the Ministers should have no competitive outside interests and they do not act as special pleaders for any interest groups; for in the long run the Government must arbitrate and choose between conflicting demands and must make the final decision. The representation of group interests is a part of the process of providing information on which decisions are based, and suggestions are sometimes made that the representation of group interests be increased and be made more specific. In debates on industrial disputes, for instance, it is occasionally proposed that the major, responsible officials of trade unions and of industry should themselves be Members of Parliament in order that the point of view of these groups could be expressed directly.

The nature of the relationship between Members and special groups is largely the concern of the Members, but the question of political and intellectual independence cannot be excluded, and some cases recently have been brought before Parliament on the question of privilege. It has long been established that it is unethical and a breach of privilege for a Member to receive money to influence specific legislation, but other types of relationship raise special problems. In the case of W. A. Robinson, the union became disenchanted with this Member, whom it had sponsored, and asked him to resign from Parliament. When Robinson refused, the union discontinued its assistance. The Committee of

[1] *May's Treatise on the Law, Privileges, Proceedings and Usage of Parliament*, Fellowes and Cocks, eds., 16th ed., (London, 1957), p. 208.

Privileges attempted to distinguish between payments of money 'for promoting or opposing a particular proceeding or measure', which they found to constitute 'an undoubted breach of privilege', and the payment of money for the general support of the Member. In the latter case it said that 'it has long been recognized that there are Members who receive financial assistance from associations of their constituents or from other bodies. A body which provides such assistance must normally be free and entitled to withdraw it.'[1] No breach of privilege was involved. The rule, then, seems to be that a Member cannot be paid for piecework lobbying but that, under the Robinson doctrine, he can be placed on the payroll of an interest group to look after its general interests. And he can be sacked.

There are some restrictions on the extent to which a Member can profit monetarily from the information he acquires in Parliament on a confidential basis. This is the Allighan case. In 1947, Mr. Garry Allighan, a Labour Member from Gravesend, made the charge in *World's Press News* that some Members gave confidential information to newspapers in return for financial reward or revealed information when under the influence of drink. The information concerned events at private meetings of the Parliamentary Labour Party. The Committee of Privileges held that the disclosure of party proceedings was 'a gross breach of confidence' but not of itself a breach of privilege. However, the receipt of payment by a Member in return for information 'obtained through his status as a Member' was a breach of privilege. Allighan was found guilty of the charges he had made against others and was expelled by the House and a second Member, Mr. Evelyn Walkden, was reprimanded by the Speaker.

From the evidence at hand, one may conclude that the representation of group interests flows through Parliament in an uneven stream. Group representation is casual and irregular and it supplements the representation based on population and territory, where the group interests are not clearly defined. It also supplements partisan representation, and Members representing group interests may attempt to influence the policy of the political parties. In some cases, the groups play both sides of the street, appealing alike for the support of Labour and Conservative Members. Parliament, in short, is constantly bringing influence on the

[1] H. C. 85 of 1943–44, p. 5; see Stewart, op. cit., pp. 188–89. Another interesting case concerns Mr. W. J. Brown, the General Secretary of the Civil Service Clerical Association and a Member for Rugby, who also encountered difficulty with his 'sponsor'. See H. C. 118 of 1946–47, and Stewart, ibid., pp. 189–94.

Government, and the Government, the object of the pressures and the influences, remains somewhat aloof, since it has the responsibility for hearing all sides of a question before making the final decision.

The Amateur Politicians. Parliament is representative, but there is another factor which helps to explain its nature and which gives character to its proceedings. In a word, Parliament is nonprofessional. The concept of amateurism is kept in the foreground, providing for the Members a standard for their actions and prescribing their proper role. One of the standards is that Members should engage in politics from a sense of civic duty and not because of financial rewards or other personal gains. The system does not encourage the development of Members as professional party bosses, of men who independently wield great power because they control patronage or government contracts or because of the personal political support they can command in regions or cities. There are no Senators from Wales! There is another facet of the amateur status of the Members. Not being considered professional politicians, Members are not obliged to spend all their time in Parliament and indeed they are encouraged to cultivate outside interests, including those having no political overtones.

The spirit of political amateurism permeates the two chambers, and one finds an atmosphere of spirited *bonhomie* in Parliament, a product of past tradition continued into modern times, and it is one which, it would seem, Members cherish and wish to retain. It is a youthful spirit, where good talk and good companions are valued, but which would be blighted if all Members were fully absorbed in the political struggle. The vision of Members, powerful and opulent, receiving salaries from the State and dominating spacious suites of offices, would not be appealing; it would be a nightmare to be forgotten, not a dream to be realized. Members are not expected to take so concentrated a view of politics that they overlook other values that lie beyond the realm of political conflict. It is admitted that political debate may be tedious, that it is often vexing to have to appeal publicly for votes; but all of the petty humiliations of politics can be endured because public office is considered to be a public service. It would be distorting one's sense of proportion to consider politics a profession which made demands on one's personality and which brought large material gains.

The cult of amateurism is also evident in the attitude of Parliament towards the professional. It is assumed that the professional expert and the technician may be somewhat boring in their single-minded approach; they know too much about some things and not enough about other things. Moreover, it might be difficult to establish a meeting of minds because from the nature of professionalism the amateur politician cannot readily challenge the judgment of the specialist. This bias against the professional is seen also in the doctrine of ministerial responsibility, for Members would prefer to give power to amateurs like themselves who are subject to known rules of social and political behaviour.

The attitude of nonprofessionalism which pervades Parliament is manifested in a variety of ways, including the salaries of the Members, the outside work they engage in, and the hours of the daily session. Salaries are not high, and membership in Parliament may involve some financial sacrifice.

In the Middle Ages and later, Members of Parliament were entitled to wages, normally paid by the community; according to Professor Neale Members of Parliament in the Elizabethan period received wages of four shillings per day for knights of the shire, and two shillings for burgesses, including travelling time to and from Westminster.[1] The practice of communities paying wages to Members fell into desuetude, however, and it became the accepted custom for Members to finance themselves. During the nineteenth century there was some agitation for paying salaries in order that more working men could be Members of Parliament, but regular salaries were not paid until 1911, when Members were given £400 per year. There have been increases since then, and Members now receive an annual salary of £1,750, and for tax purposes an amount up to £750 may be claimed for expenses. Although the salaries of Members are small compared with those of the higher branches of the Civil Service and of the staff of Parliament, there would be considerable opposition to increasing the salaries of Members to any very large sum.

The opposition to increased salaries is based, primarily, on the theory that parliamentary work is a public service and not to be measured by ordinary standards of income. The combination of the theory of amateurism, plus the need in many cases to earn additional income, results, as we have noted, in a situation where many Members supplement their income by outside work.

The value to Parliament of Members holding outside jobs has been frequently stressed, and the following statement made by Sir C. N. Thornton-Kemsley, a Scottish Member, epitomizes this attitude: 'We should be losing something of value,' he said, 'something characteristically British which contributes to the success of the House, if all Hon.

[1] J. E. Neale, op. cit., p. 321.

Membership: All Sorts and Conditions of Men

Members were wholetime politicians. It would be a bad thing if we made it impossible for Hon. Members to do outside work and retain contacts with the professions, commerce, trade and industry. Because there is a certain proportion of Hon. Members who, by reason perhaps of their location or the fact that their business may be in London instead of in distant constituencies, can pursue occupations outside, it is a more lively House of Commons. It becomes a House more in touch with the realities of day-to-day life and a House which has its feet more on the ground than would be the case if it were composed entirely of full-time politicians.'[1]

However, the need for a supplementary income may make some Members less willing to accept assignments in the Government, and there have been several cases in recent years where younger Members have rejected the chance of a ministerial career because they could not afford it.

The outside interests of the Members also affect the hours when Parliament sits, which are designed to accommodate the Members who may have jobs elsewhere as well as the Ministers, who like to spend most of the day in their departments. The House of Commons convenes at 2.30 p.m., from Monday through Thursday, and continues until 10.30 p.m. or later. Many of the important divisions take place at about 10.00 p.m., when the maximum attendance can be mobilized. The House meets on Friday mornings and then adjourns for a long weekend. Committee meetings begin at 10.00 or 10.30 in the morning, but many Members with outside jobs do not participate.

Sometimes the House does not adjourn until after midnight, and all-night sessions are not unknown. Constant attendance on a normal day, from midmorning until near midnight, is an exhausting experience, but except when there is sustained party competition (such as in the 1950–1 Parliament) Members are not expected to be present at all hours, day and night. The fact that some Members work, or are for other reasons unable to be present during the morning hours, creates a division in the membership, and the burden of committee work in particular, which is sometimes considered to be a dull and unrewarding assignment, falls most heavily on some two hundred Members.

Parliament is part of a well-ordered universe, and proceedings are controlled in such a fashion that Members know in advance when attendance is required. The versatile Whip organizations see to it that Members are present at the right time. In return for their considerable

[1] H. C. Deb., Scottish Standing Committee, 19th March 1957, col. 38.

freedom, Members have assumed certain party obligations, including that of being present for the important debates and the crucial divisions.

THE HOUSE OF LORDS

The membership of the House of Lords does not lend itself to easy generalizations. In size, it is immense, and if every eligible Peer attended, one might well wonder how business could be conducted with the decorum which is so characteristic of its proceedings. But on learning that a quorum consists of three, one reverses one's thinking and begins to wonder with what effort the chamber must be kept alive. The story goes that it is never necessary to call attention to the absence of a quorum. One Lord must be speaking, a second presiding, and any third Lord in the chamber automatically makes up the quorum. These extremes are a caricature of the House of Lords, but it is not easy to correct the distortions and draw an accurate picture. Some may approach the House of Lords with certain assumptions of what it is, or should be; others may be perplexed, having no notion of what, in fact, the House of Lords is now permitted to do.

In modern democratic thought, the hereditary aspect is often puzzling, yet membership is not entirely hereditary, and a recent recruit to the Life Peerage has been Mr. Herbert Morrison, who has been a moving spirit of British socialism for forty years and at times a critic of the House of Lords. An understanding of the various functions performed by the House of Lords may provide some insight into the nature of its membership. We can start negatively by saying that the House of Lords has no control over finance and only limited control over legislation; that it cannot make or break Governments, and that no Peer has been Prime Minister since the Marquess of Salisbury left the office in 1902. What, then, does it in fact do? The difficulty in answering this question is enhanced by the fact that the House of Lords performs many functions, and in modern times, when there is rigorous specialization in so many areas, it may be difficult to grasp the nature of such an assembly.

The House of Lords remains now, as it has been for centuries, a multifunctional assembly whose active element is drawn from a variety of sources. One cannot be too precise in enumerating its functions, for they are traditionally and characteristically diffuse and unclarified. On the one hand, they embrace the symbols of high office, replete with gaudy pomp and pageantry, improbable costumes, medieval stage props, genuflecting gentlemen, and the colour and glitter of heraldic display. On the other hand, they include critical, lucid, and informed discussions of public policy. In still other directions they embrace the judicial consideration of legal cases. Again, as in the House of Commons, there are partisan debates over contentious political questions, and legislation is considered and occasionally revised. The various functions are a mixed blend indeed: symbolic and revisionary, critical and political and judicial. These incongruities are capped with the extraordinary office of the Lord Chancellor, who is in turn an impartial judge, a moderator (in that he is Speaker of the House of Lords), an advocate (of legislation), a political leader (who makes speeches at General Elections), a Member of the Cabinet, and a dispenser of what is known as ecclesiastical patronage wherein he appoints to certain church livings within the gift of the Crown. He must be persuasive, partisan, and neutral, and from the nature of his job, ever and forever discreet.

In addition to its more formal functions, the House of Lords constitutes a pool of talent from which Peers may be drawn for limited and specific public service, for example, as members of official delegations, in Commissions of Inquiry, and in Royal Commissions; Peers may be appointed Governors, Ambassadors, High Commissioners, Special Representatives, or Ministers of the Crown. (Terminological distinction: 'Bishops to whom a writ of summons has been issued are not Peers but are Lords of Parliament.' Standing Order 7.) The associations of the Peers extend to many areas of British life, including but not confined to the political parties, and this representative aspect can be seen in the deliberations. The House of Lords is also, and perhaps primarily, a public forum where its members can keep in touch with current policy; where they can speak or propose topics for discussion; where they can inform others and themselves be informed. It is, in a broad sense, a place where a select group of public-minded individuals can meet and debate, where the college professor can talk with a colonial governor, an explorer with a bishop, a physicist with a labour leader, a general with a pacifist.

There is frequently some disquiet about the nature of the membership in the House of Lords, for the selection process does not use some of the more modern techniques for securing representation and establishing responsibility. The fact that all Lords have membership for life excludes control through periodic elections, and the Lords need not claim direct public support or make explicit the nature of their representativeness. Nevertheless, there is a considerable element of representativeness in the composition of the House of Lords, and one may suggest that historically it was the representative and independent element in this body that enabled Parliament to develop as an autonomous, corporate body able to speak authoritatively for the broader whole.

The membership has a diversified range of specialized knowledge, training, background, and skills. The jibe that the cure for admiring the House of Lords is to look at it is more biting than accurate, for the chamber includes among its members a number of men and women of singular ability and reputation and its debates are frequently interesting and of a high calibre. There is a sense of stability and continuity, of perspective and detachment, in the deliberations.

We have said earlier that it is difficult to describe the House of Lords in terms of broad generalizations alone; what is now required is a more detailed inquiry into the components of its membership in terms of appointment, of parties and alignments, and of what may be called the effective membership, which is considerably smaller than the actual membership.

Although some of the Peers have secured membership by heredity, this of itself does not reveal very much about their competence or their opinions, much less about their contribution to the work of the organization. Hereditary Peers are no longer a distinct and identifiable group, and the variety of opinions and views found in the House of Lords is perhaps more extensive than that in the House of Commons. The justification of hereditary offices is occasionally debated, at least inferentially, for it is a point about which the Peers are introspective and frank. The rationale that service should be given 'as a matter of honour' may be taken at face value, although to some it may sound old-fashioned.

A man may consider himself lucky to be able to sit in the House of Lords, but the privilege carries with it obligations also; there is little enough reward in the job, other than the personal satisfaction of serving the country. (I am excluding from this commentary the social side of the peerage, which is independent of the work of the House of Lords and would no doubt survive any parliamentary reform.) Granted then, that the justification of service can be taken at face value, that the Peers have something to contribute to the public, some Peers are nevertheless troubled by a system that compels people to become Members in the House of Lords who otherwise might not wish to do so. The case of the Hon. Anthony Wedgwood Benn is relevant. Mr. Benn, the heir of Viscount Stansgate and an active Member of the House of Commons, did not want to succeed to his father's title, but remedial legislation

Membership: All Sorts and Conditions of Men

freeing Mr. Benn of this obligation was defeated. Following the death of his father, Mr. Benn (now the second Viscount Stansgate) was not permitted to retain his seat in the House of Commons.

It was mentioned above that some Peers are introspective in considering the privileges and obligations they have acquired by inheritance. There are some Peers (the number is not known precisely) who don't believe in the system and do not attend. The qualms of others may be allayed, however, by the continuing support given to the hereditary principle by the British public; one may assume that there are scores of people 'in another place' who would be pleased to be called up to the House of Lords, and that there are also many in the public at large who would not scorn a peerage.

The statistics on hereditary peerages given below do not indicate the relative influence and activity of the various types of peers, but it is nevertheless instructive to observe the particular historical period in which the existing titles were created:

	Created before 1700	Created 1700–1799	Created 1800–1899	Created 1900–1960	Total
Dukes	9	7	4	2	22
Marquesses	1	7	12	7	27
Earls	20	27	57	28	132
Viscounts	1	6	17	83	107
Barons and Baronesses	27	37	164	338	566
	58	84	254	458	854
					others 47[1]
					901

It will be noted that the titles of more than half of the Peers were created in the twentieth century and more than 80 per cent in the nineteenth and twentieth centuries. Titles are still being created at a full-employment rate, including almost 200 in the fifteen-year period, 1945–

[1] The 47 others include 2 Archbishops; 24 Bishops; 16 Representative Peers for Scotland (elected for every new Parliament); one Representative Peer for Ireland (elected for life); 4 Peers of royal blood. The following are not Peers of Parliament: 23 Scottish Peers and Peeresses; 68 Irish Peers; 14 Peeresses of the United Kingdom (except Baroness Ravensdale, who is a Life Peer).

59. The figures for the most recent years are as follows: 1957, eleven hereditary Peers and one law Life Peer; 1958, four hereditary Peers, one law Life Peer, fourteen Life Peers (including four women); 1959, nine hereditary Peers, one law Life Peer and seven Life Peers.

Life Peers. The judges form a particular category of Life Peers, although this category is not exclusive inasmuch as some judges hold hereditary peerages. The Lords of Appeal in Ordinary are members of the Appellate Committee of the House of Lords, and their salary of £9,000 a year must make them the highest paid members of a legislative committee in the world. In alternate weeks, they also sit on the Judicial Committee of the Privy Council. The following Lords of Appeal in Ordinary were sitting in 1960: Viscount Simonds, appointed Life Peer in 1944, Hereditary Baron in 1952 and Viscount in 1954; Lord Morton of Henryton, Life Peer, 1947; Lord Reid, Life Peer, 1948; Lord Radcliffe, Life Peer, 1949; Lord Tucker, Life Peer, 1950; Lord Cohen, Life Peer, 1951; Lord Keith of Avonholm, Life Peer, 1953; Lord Somervell of Harrow, Life Peer, 1954; Lord Denning, Life Peer, 1957; Lord Jenkins, Life Peer, 1959.

The Lord Chief Justice of England, Lord Parker (salary £10,000 annually) was appointed a Life Peer in 1958; Lord Goddard, the former Lord Chief Justice of England, in 1944; and Lord MacDermott, the Lord Chief Justice of Northern Ireland, in 1947. Other Peers who have held high judicial office include Lord Wright, Lord Normand, Lord Oaksey, and Lord Birkett.

After years of discussion, agitation, and indecision, the composition of the House of Lords was modified in 1958 by the passage of the Life Peerages Act, and there was an expectation that the newly appointed Peers would contribute actively to the work of the House of Lords. At the time of the passage of the Act, there was expressed anxiety about the innovation. Some were opposed to increasing the popularity or influence of the House of Lords under any conditions or by any means; others were opposed to weakening the hereditary principle in this fashion. But now that the deed has been done, those who follow the proceedings closely say that the new plan is working well. The newly appointed Life Peers have much to contribute and they have been welcomed into the club; there is no tension, no aloofness, no disparagement, no holding back. In all, 'It was a jolly good idea.'

In making the transmogrification to nobility, the new Life Peers have been somewhat circumspect and even unimaginative in choosing names to conform to their new life and status, and only rarely has a Life Peer taken the plunge and adopted a lustrous title which, for the time being, hides him from public life and even from his friends by temporarily concealing his identity. This is less true with hereditary Peers, and the former Speaker of the House, Mr. W. S. Morrison, created a hereditary Peer, appeared with the handsome title of Viscount Dunrossil of Vallaquie. The choice of names must be approved by the Garter King of Arms, and some new Peers have said that he is not a pliable man to deal with. Lord Morrison of Lambeth has commented publicly on his struggles with the College of Heralds, and Lionel Robbins, the economist, was unable to reach agreement on a name (his own name!) for many months. Some disquiet has been expressed in the House of Lords that an outsider (not even responsible to a Minister!) should have such power over their names, and proposals have been made that this genial function should be transferred to a committee of the House of Lords. This would be a wrench indeed. 'Arms . . . are granted by Letters Patent from the Kings of Arms under authority delegated to them by the Sovereign, such authority having been expressly conferred on them since at least the fifteenth century.'[1]

Who are the Life Peers? In the first three years of the new plan, thirty-five life peerages were created, representing a diversified range of interests. Eighteen of the thirty-five were former Members of the House of Commons; six were women; and thirteen came from Universities, unions, civil service, business, the Church, and the Commonwealth.

The former Members of the House of Commons were as follows: *Conservatives:* Lord Fraser of Lonsdale, Member of the Council, Royal National Institute for the Blind; National President British Legion, 1947–58; Lord Craigton, Joint Parliamentary Under-Secretary of State, Scottish Office; Lord Bossom; Lord Molsom; Lord Alport; Lady Horsbrugh. *Labour:* Lord Stonham (Victor Collins); Lord Robens; Lord Dalton, former Chancellor of the Exchequer; Lord Williams, former Minister of Agriculture; Lord Lindgren; Lady Summerskill, former Minister of National Insurance; Lord Granville-West, lawyer; Lord Morrison of Lambeth, political leader; Lord Taylor, Medical Director, Harlow Industrial Health Service; Lord Shackleton, explorer,

[1] See *Whitaker's Almanack:* The Garter King of Arms is one of the 13 officers of Arms or Heralds College, all of whom 'specialize in genealogical and heraldic work for their respective clients.' There are 3 Kings of Arms: Garter, Clarenceux, and Norroy and Ulster; 6 Heralds: Richmond (and Registrar), Windsor, Somerset, Lancaster, Chester, and York; and 4 Pursuivants: Rouge Dragon, Rouge Croix, Bluemantle, and Portcullis. The Earl Marshal is the Duke of Norfolk. The only other Peer in the College is Lord Sinclair (York, the Herald), an elected Peer for Scotland.

son of the late Sir Ernest Shackleton. *Cross-benches:* Lord Boothby, former Conservative Minister, television commentator; Lord Shawcross, former Labour Attorney-General, Director, Shell Petroleum Company.

The following Peers came from areas outside Parliament: Lord Geddes of Epsom, President of the Trades Union Congress 1954–5, Member (part-time) London Transport Executive; Lord Ferrier (Noel-Paton), business, Director and Chairman of T. & S. Smith Ltd. Group of Companies, Edinburgh, Member of the Church of Scotland Trust; Lord Twining, Governor of Tanganyika, 1949–58; Lord James of Rusholme, High Master of Manchester Grammar School since 1945; Lord Stopford of Fallowfield, former Vice-Chancellor of the University of Manchester, Emeritus Professor of Experimental Neurology; Lord Plowden, Chairman, Atomic Energy Authority; Lord Robbins, Professor of Economics in the University of London, Trustee of the National Gallery and the Tate Gallery, Director, Royal Opera House; Lord Hughes, Scottish Labour Party and company director; Lord Peddie, chairman of the Co-operative Party; Lord Walston, agriculture; Lord Casey, Minister for External Affairs, Australia; Lord Fisher of Lambeth, former Archbishop of Canterbury; Lord Coutanche, Bailiff of Jersey.

The newly appointed women peers are: Lady Elliot of Harwood, social welfare, Chairman, National Union of Conservative and Unionist Associations 1956–7, widow, Rt. Hon. Walter Elliot, P.C.; Lady Wootton of Abinger, former Professor of Social Studies, University of London; Lady Swanborough (Dowager Marchioness of Reading, also known as Lady Reading), Chairman and Founder of the Women's Voluntary Services; Lady Ravensdale (also Baroness in her own right); Lady Horsbrugh, former Minister of Education; and Lady Summer-skill, former Minister of National Insurance.

EFFECTIVE SIZE

During the recent reform of the House of Lords, an attempt has been made to establish the scope of the effective membership. A Select Committee—the so-called 'Swinton Committee'—reporting in January 1956, said that a Writ of Summons to a Lord imposed a duty of attendance but that the House had the power 'both of compelling and of excusing attendance'. It was recognized that many Peers were unable to attend, 'either because they were fully occupied with other important duties, or because they feel themselves unfitted for parliamentary work, or by reason of age, health, or expense'. Without criticizing those unable to attend, it suggested that arrangements be made whereby Lords unable to attend would be relieved of the obligation imposed on them by the writ of summons. Leaves of absence could be granted. In order to sweeten the bait, the Committee recommended that Peers on leave of absence should be entitled to apply 'for places for their wives at the State Opening of Parliament, and for the usual number of places at such functions as Trooping the Colour'. They would also be 'entitled to use the Library, Dining Room, Guest Room, etc., and to give tickets for the Strangers' Gallery'.[1]

In 1958, letters were sent out by the Lord Chancellor asking all Peers to indicate their intention regarding attendance. Some 173 Peers failed to respond to the two letters and were granted leave of absence for the remainder of the Parliament. Only 63 Peers requested leave of absence, which was granted for the following session. As a result of this culling, the potential effective size of the House of Lords was reduced to approximately 625 Peers. One must now make additional distinctions, for the effective and reliable attendance is considerably smaller.

An analysis of the attendance record gives some glimpse of the nature of the House of Lords and the attitude its Members hold towards it. Members find varying degrees of attraction there. Some attend for a specific purpose—perhaps to make a speech, to listen to a debate, to witness a ceremony, to see a friend, or to vote. The following table, giving the pattern of attendance in 1957–8, shows that 518 Lords attended at least once; this figure is more than a hundred below the total number who were not granted leave of absence. The number in attendance drops perceptibly between one time and five times, and from then on the attendance tapers off more gradually for the remainder of the session (108 meetings). Approximately one hundred Lords attended at least 50 per cent of the time, and some few of these had an almost perfect attendance record.

Attended at least

once	518
three times	418
five times	360
ten times	287
twenty times	197
thirty times	165

[1] Select Committee on Powers of the House in Relation to Attendance of its Members; see letter of Viscount Kilmuir, House of Lords Journal, 24th June 1958, pp. 215–217. See also the volume by P. A. Bromhead, *The House of Lords and Contemporary Politics* (London, 1958).

Membership: All Sorts and Conditions of Men

Attended at least

forty times	134
fifty times	99
sixty times	83
seventy times	61
eighty times	46
ninety times	24

Members of the House of Lords are unpaid, although they are entitled to a daily allowance of three guineas plus travelling expenses. This is not a generous award, even for those most regular in attendance, and a Peer who attended, say, half of the sessions, would receive no more than 150 guineas a session. Relatively few Peers are sufficiently independent financially to lead a leisured life, and with the exception of those who have retired most Peers have additional commitments to outside jobs. Even more than in the House of Commons, membership in the House of Lords is a part-time and largely voluntary assignment.

Party membership in the House of Lords is a difficult concept to analyse. On the face of it, the Conservatives have everything their own way; the strength of Labour is low; the Liberals have more representation than in the House of Commons, but not necessarily more than their proportion of votes cast at the polls. In a recent issue of Vacher's *Parliamentary Companion*, 443 Peers were identified as Conservative (or members of an allied party), 41 as Liberal, and 57 as Labour. The overwhelming Conservative strength is in some ways misleading, for party ties may be casual and attendance irregular. Labour Peers are more regular in attendance than the average set by all Peers who attended at least once. Of the 57 Labour Peers, so identified, 51 attended the 1957–8 session at least once and some 25 Labour Peers attended more than 50 per cent of the time. As a result of the spirited attendance of the Labour Peers, it is possible to carry on the formal type of parliamentary procedure, with Government facing Opposition. If the Opposition is bolstered by Liberals, Independents, and weakly-committed Conservatives, it may occasionally defeat the Government. The position of the Opposition in the House of Lords is not so hopeless or desperate as it may seem to be if looking at gross figures alone.

Although the hereditary facet of the House of Lords is often emphasized, there is in fact a kind of guild representation, where the Lords have close associations with specific organized groups in society. The representation of the Church by the bishops is obvious enough. Other

E

65

groups may also be represented, unofficially, and we may note, for instance, the relationship of the following Peers (the list is suggestive only and not inclusive): *Military:* Lord Harding of Petherton; Viscount Alexander of Tunis; Viscount Mountbatten of Burma; Viscount Montgomery of Alamein; Viscount Alanbrooke; Viscount Portal of Hungerford; Viscount Cunningham of Hyndhope. *Press:* Viscount Kemsley (Berry); Lord Astor of Hever; Lord Beaverbrook (Aitken). *Agriculture:* Lord Netherthorpe (Turner), President, Farmers' Union. *Business and Industry:* Lord Sinclair of Cleeve, Chairman, Imperial Tobacco Co.; Lord Weeks, Vickers, Massey-Ferguson, Shell Transport; Lord McCorquodale of Newton, J. & P. Coats, Ltd.; Lord Heyworth, Chairman, Unilever Ltd.; Lord Strathalmond (Fraser), British Petroleum. *Labour:* Lord Forster, Industrial Court, National Arbitration Tribunal; Lord Citrine, General Secretary 1926–46, T.U.C. *Administration:* Lord Strang, former Permanent Under-Secretary of State, Foreign Office; Lord Bridges, former Permanent Secretary, H.M. Treasury and former Secretary to the Cabinet; Lord Milverton (Richards), former Governor of Jamaica and of Nigeria. *Medicine:* Lord Evans. *Universities:* Lord Adrian, Vice-Chancellor, University of Cambridge, Professor of Physiology; Lord Chorley, former Dean, Faculty of Laws, University of London.

The House of Lords is not a place where history is easily forgotten, and one finds in the membership many interesting links with the past and with contemporary history as well. Lord Hastings, an active Peer, bears a title which was created in 1290. The Earl of Huntingdon includes Plantagenet in his names; he is a Labour Peer, with a title created in 1529. The Marquess of Salisbury (once referred to disrespectfully in a journal as Old Sarum) is a member of the Cecil family and has twice been Leader of the House of Lords. The Marquess of Winchester, no longer active, succeeded to his title in 1899 at the age of thirty-seven. Lord Sinha, of Raipur, India, is a Liberal Peer, with addresses both in London and at Lord Sinha Road, Calcutta. Lord Pethick-Lawrence, an active Labour Peer at the age of eighty-eight, was a former Member of the House of Commons and a leader in the suffragette movement; he recorded in a biographical notation that he was 'sentenced to nine months' imprisonment in 1912 for conspiracy in connection with one of the militant demonstrations of woman suffragists'. Viscount Elibank was parliamentary private secretary to Sir Edward Grey, 1910–14. Earl Winterton, still active in 1960, served in the House of Commons from 1904 to 1951 before being called up to the House of Lords (with a United Kingdom title to supplement his Irish title). Hereditary Peers have their own variety of frustration. Lord Hawke, with a title extending back to 1776, has seven daughters. And for a more modern and egalitarian touch, one may note that Lord Lawson, who was Lord-Lieutenant of County Durham, 1949–58, commenced work in a mine at the age of twelve.

In summary it may be said that the House of Lords carries on a number of different functions, including some (such as that of judicial appeal) which are not normally associated with a legislative and deliberative body. Although the hereditary aspect of its membership is pronounced, new talent is constantly being added, including Life Peers. The effective membership (those who attend more than once a session) is less than five hundred, and within this larger group there is a corps of diligent Peers who are fairly regular in their attendance and who make it possible to carry on business in the traditional parliamentary fashion. Partisanship counts for something, but the party ties are more loosely worn than in the House of Commons, and there is a representative element in the House of Lords which extends to many particular groups in society and which, in some cases, re-emphasizes the continuous link of the present with the past.

CHAPTER III

The Pattern of Power

THE POLITICAL STRUCTURE

M any of the events that unfold on the floor of Parliament with such éclat can be anticipated, perhaps even rehearsed in advance, and these events may be influenced by people off the floor who have some interest in what Parliament does. The partisans and the partisan organizations in the background, operating quietly, often without publicity, and even secretly, may prepare the arguments, devise the strategy, and mobilize the support which later will be seen on the floor in full public view. Parliament is organized in such a way that partisans may be able to anticipate in advance at what point in the process their influence will be effective.

In many ways it is meaningful to consider Parliament as a single institution which, for purposes of deliberation, divides its work between two chambers. The unity of Parliament is especially apparent at ceremonial functions, as when the Commons are summoned to the House of Lords to hear an address from the Throne, or to witness the approval of legislation by a Royal Commission, or to hear that Parliament is to be prorogued, or to receive instructions on selecting a Speaker. The unity of Parliament is also apparent procedurally, such as in the consideration of legislation, which must have the approval of both Houses. Symbolically and procedurally, the Commons and the Lords are part of the greater institution.

Several types of organizations are found within Parliament, foremost of which is the strong party system, with its coterie of leaders and its mass of enthusiastic or indifferent followers. Other types of associations are identified with the party, or with particular groups interested in public policy, or with the internal organization of Parliament. These party divisions work within the broad divisions of the two chambers and the several committees, over which a variety of political controls are exercised.

The parliamentary parties share certain characteristics, as if formed by a common mould, but there are also dissimilarities which reflect a different historical development and a different theoretical framework. The routine demands on Parliament, the constant competition between the parties, and the internal relations between the leaders and the followers have helped to shape the particular kind of party organization that has developed within the parliamentary system. The fact that the Government must be drawn from Parliament and be sustained by a parliamentary majority underscores the need for parties to develop a set of known leaders, and there is only an occasional echo here of the political egalitarianism that is such a dominant feature of the political organization of Congress. If there is need for leaders, there is also need for a group of reliable, well-informed and sometimes critical followers, for a party forum where opinion can be expressed, and for procedures for developing party policy.

The party organizations are more complex than their formal charts might suggest, and if one follows the intricate passageways of power for a little distance, he will soon encounter a maze of informal and personal influence. It is quite apparent that politics does not begin and end in Parliament but that the associations there are part of a wider network of political influence. Within the organizations of party (and of Parliament) there are wheels within wheels; some Members have influence on certain types of policy, forming groups or cliques that meet occasionally and perhaps secretly to discuss policy; this type of influence is not recorded officially and is not a formal part of the party structure. The well-developed political organizations in Parliament can be described and analysed, but in addition significant partisan action may take place outside the normal channels of power.

THE LEADERSHIP PRINCIPLE

The requirements of leadership create the great division in Parliament between the Front Benches of the Government and the Opposition and the Private Members on the back benches, between the recognized party leaders and those who at some distance and with varying degrees of enthusiasm support them. In the politics of Parliament there is a continuing theme of latent conflict between the interests of the leaders and the followers. There are other significant divisions and alignments in the distribution of power, but within the parties of the House of Commons the most spectacular division is that between party leaders and the party mass. This great division is supported by Government, if for no other reason than that there are a limited number of ministerial posts available. It is also supported by the Opposition Front Bench, who would be loath to create new parliamentary instruments beyond their control for harassing the Government. Leaders on both sides of the aisle have a common desire to preserve their position and are somewhat niggardly in sharing power with those in the ranks.

The Private Member may in fact have considerable freedom in some areas; he may be able to carry on outside work, leading a leisurely and unhurried life, and he may have considerable scope for expressing his own ideas. However, he will be expected to support his party at the crucial time and to permit the leaders to formulate the policy, make the significant statements on policy in debate, and control the crucial aspects of the parliamentary process. The Private Members, without possessing very much political influence, may believe with some justification that they are politically underprivileged.

The party leaders dominate the proceedings in the House of Commons, and they command or hope to command the allegiance of their fellow partisans. Both parties must produce a set of leaders, one to control the Government, the other to debate and criticize and suggest alternative choices; indeed leadership is such an integral aspect of the system that the attention of Parliament is constantly directed towards the question, Who is to have power? The selection of a group of leaders raises certain problems that are common to both large parties, although there is some difference in the procedures followed in making the choice, in the powers granted to the leaders, and in the relationship between the leaders and the party followers.

In both parties, control tends to be centralized in the hands of a relatively small number of Members. There are also various types of associations among the party mass, who in turn develop their own leaders for more limited purposes, and there is constant interplay between the leaders and the followers. The word hierarchy comes to mind as a term to describe the party organization, for hierarchy suggests a centralized pyramid of authority, a division of function, and a distinct set of leaders. There are various gradations of influence within the parliamentary parties, and such questions as party rank and party influence, of where one stands in his party, are important criteria in evaluating a Member.

The Pattern of Power

Some Members may have more influence within their party than within Parliament, while others may be able to influence Parliament but do not rate high positions in their party. This distinction may be helpful in understanding the meaning or the purpose of some types of political action in Parliament. A proposal may come before Parliament as a result of party manœuvring, the victory of a Member who is skilled in the politics of intraparty conflict but who may have little influence within Parliament. Again, a speech may be made in Parliament, the purpose of which is to gain stature within the party, not to persuade the Members on the other side of the aisle.

However chosen, the leadership must normally maintain the support of the party followers, both inside and outside Parliament, and on some questions it is desirable that the Government leaders extend their support beyond the party and include all Members of Parliament. The leaders must acquire sufficient control over the proceedings of Parliament to perform their respective functions, and this means, for Government leaders, constant surveillance of procedures and party reaction if they are to carry through their policy. The parties must determine the issue they will support and the strategy they intend to pursue. They must be prepared to present a convincing case on the various political issues that arise and to mobilize their forces to make a decision. The party leaders on the Front Benches have the major burden of determining party policy and of carrying it through the various vicissitudes of a parliamentary conflict. The Opposition can influence the selection of the agenda and, to a considerable extent, choose the grounds on which to make a political issue. In these conditions, the Government proposes the broad legislative programme and assumes general responsibility for administration; the Opposition selects the issues to be debated.

There are two aspects of the partisan contest within Parliament. One is external, where the object is to deflect the malevolent plan of one's opponents; the other is internal, where the object is to influence the decisions of the party and perhaps to gain power. The need for firm leadership on the one hand, and the desire for self-expression by the Private Members on the other hand, may create tensions and raise a dilemma in the internal organization of the parties. The leaders may find it less troublesome to be supported by Members who have no overweening ambition or independent ideas and who nevertheless are able to command political support at the elections. Trends in this direction may secure political stability but they make Parliament a dull place rather than a lively political forum where controversial ideas can be

71

debated. Some Private Members might prefer a situation of greater freedom and greater power, where there are more opportunities for speaking and for influencing legislation and where information is broadly accessible. But trends in this direction might encourage political instability by creating pockets of power within Parliament which could challenge the leadership.

Within the parties, all is not static, like a Hindu caste system, and political competition is permitted. There are well-recognized methods by which those on the 'out' can get 'in', or those on the 'bottom' can move 'up', or those 'on top' can be pushed or tripped or otherwise assisted down the slippery slope of power. Both parties have what may loosely be called staff agencies for developing and carrying out party policy, and in particular the Whip organizations are useful in this area. Ministers (and the Leader of the Opposition) use parliamentary private secretaries to keep informed of the opinion in Parliament and especially the opinion held by the Private Members.

The political controls and the party hierarchy are in general accepted by the membership as an essential part of the system, and although there are quarrels over who is to have power, and sometimes over the amount of freedom permitted, there is little expressed discontent with the major contours of the power structure or with the leadership principle. Certain types of relationships between leaders and followers have been developed and are respected, for leaders are not given power, once and for all, without further checks on their actions, and the Private Members are not a homogeneous and united group which sees alike on all issues. Similarly, a well-developed set of relationships exist between the leaders of the two parties, including a method of communicating with each other 'through the usual channels'. Within the parliamentary structure there is not something laid out for every Member to set his hand to, some task where he can give his best efforts and where his merits can be recognized. Members must, to a degree, make their own opportunities, and leadership emerges through a gradual, abstruse, somewhat recondite process. In the House of Commons, everyone counts—but not everyone counts equally.

THE CONSERVATIVE PARTY

The Leader of the Conservative Party, as he is known, is nominally the head of the party both within and without Parliament, and one does not find in the Conservative Party the bifurcation of leadership that

72

characterizes the Labour Party. The Conservative Leader has a free rein in selecting his colleagues, and although he is subject to pressures from within his party and he must constantly retain the confidence of his supporters, he is not bound to yield to their suggestions and there is no organized device by which he can be told what to do. The Leader of the Labour Party (when in Opposition) is more restricted; he has less influence over the choice of his principal colleagues, who are elected by the party; he is not the leader of his national party; and he is subject to some controls by the party caucus. (A Labour Prime Minister, however, would have more independence and freedom of action.) One may also detect a difference in the attitude which party members hold towards their leader. Lord Pakenham, a Labour Peer, has been quoted as telling the Labour Party Conference that 'the Tories treated their leader as if he were the Almighty; Labour sometimes went to the other extreme and treated theirs as if he were Lucifer'.[1]

The external Conservative Party may attempt to influence policy at the annual conferences, but it does not challenge the autonomy of the party within Parliament, and there is but one Leader for the whole party. In a sense it could be said that the Leader, as Prime Minister, is not only the head of the Conservative Party, with all of its ramifications, but he is also head of British society. His influence permeates widely throughout the British culture, in Government, Parliament, and party, in ecclesiastical and university circles, in the courts, and in selecting those whom the Queen will delight to honour. His powers, diffused over a wide area, are often subtle and ill-defined, yet withal a part of many spheres of action. The British culture, with its emphasis on order and continuity and status and tradition, seems to require a secular leader, and although this broader leadership is not rationalized or made specific it goes beyond the realm of political support alone.

In describing the position and power of the Leader, one cannot use such managerial concepts as span of control, specific responsibility, chain of command, or staff and line, for the Leader is in part a symbol, a fount of authority, whose influence may be greater than his formal powers and whose formal powers must be used with discretion. In addition to his authority within the Government, the Leader has considerable influence within his own party: he selects those who will share the Front Bench with him and he appoints the leading officers of the party; he also appoints the Leader of the House of Commons, the Leader of the House of Lords, and the Government Whips in both Houses. How-

[1] *Daily Telegraph*, 30th November 1959.

73

ever, the Leader is not an autocrat, and he is hedged about with conventions and indirect controls, and there is the expectation that he will consult with his colleagues before acting. The procedures he follows are not prescribed by law but are nevertheless understood.

The process by which the Leader is selected is easier to comprehend than to describe, and any formal enumeration of the various steps of the process might easily be misleading. The significant proceedings are for the most part confidential, and no one with full knowledge of events has recreated the entire story of the process at a later date. The process is an example of decisions made by indirection, where controversy is kept under control and concealed from public view, where attitudes are sifted and evaluated but not assigned numerical weights, and where the specified proceedings are used for ceremonial approval. There are no mass appeals or public elections or demonstrations. Opinions are sounded out by those who, it is agreed, should do the sounding, and eventually, without campaigns or public contests, a Leader emerges who is accepted by his party.

To fulfil the requirements of the party bylaws, the Leader is formally elected by an *ad hoc* body consisting of all Conservative Members of Parliament, all prospective candidates, and the Executive Committee of the National Union,[1] but this body has roughly the status and power of the American Electoral College in selecting a President. The party election confirms the choice made previously by the indirect process. A special case arose in 1957 when Sir Anthony Eden, the Leader of the party, resigned as Prime Minister, and it was necessary to move quickly in choosing a new Leader. The Queen subsequently invited Mr. Harold Macmillan to form a new Government and inferentially to become Leader of the Party. It is known that the Queen consulted Sir Winston Churchill and the Marquess of Salisbury, but the views of other party members appear also to have been canvassed. Some revealing correspondence on this point between two Conservative Members of Parliament appeared in the press at the time. One Member claimed that he had not been consulted in the choice of the Prime Minister. The second Member responded that there were channels of communication through which partisans could express an opinion. Anyone in the party could

---

[1] The Leader is normally a Member of Parliament, although in the Election of 1906 the Conservative Leader (and Prime Minister), A. J. Balfour, was defeated. When the new Parliament met in February 1907, Balfour asked Joseph Chamberlain to lead the Opposition during his absence. Balfour was subsequently elected for the City of London at a by-election and returned to Parliament in March 1907. See Earl Winterton *Orders of the Day* (London, 1953), p. 17.

find out for himself what these channels were and to whom he could make his attitude known. On another occasion when the selection of Mr. Macmillan was also under discussion, a third Member, who was part of the information network mentioned above, said that the opinions of the first Member had actually been canvassed though the Member may have been unaware of it at the time.

THE WHIPS

In the large, organized political parties of Parliament, it is necessary for the leaders of the party to keep in touch with the membership, and this function falls within the competence of the group bearing the colourful name of Whips. The Whips see to it that the party members are kept informed of the current business and events and that they are present for the important debates and divisions. They also act as friendly informants, keeping the party leaders apprised of the attitude of the Members and often speaking up on behalf of the interests of the Private Members. The Whips may also act as a channel of communication between the parties concerning topics for debates and the order of business.

The Whip organization supporting the Government arranges for the orderly consideration of the Government's business. It is necessary to plan ahead and to co-ordinate action, making certain that the process in Parliament runs smoothly and that the policy is acceptable to the party. The Whips have no direct control over policy and no power to discipline Members, although from the nature of their position they may be influential in both areas.

The Whips keep in touch with the Members by means of a weekly notice called 'The Whip', which informs Members of various legislative developments and meetings and indicates by bold underlining the time and the degree of urgency when it is desired that Members be present. The notices in the House of Commons are secret, and it is part of the game for the partisans to conceal from each other the various values they place on attendance and their estimate of the significance of the events. The Member is under some obligation to respond to the Whip's suggestion, but the 'whipping', as it is called, occurs only occasionally during the week, and the requirement of attending important sessions is compensated by the freedom to be absent during most of the parliamentary sittings.

The Whips also assist the leaders in appraising the reaction of Members, being especially sensitive to currents of opinion within their own party and to some extent within the other party also. Party discontent may be variously expressed, including such obvious forms as questions or speeches, signatures on resolutions, proposed Bills, letters to the press, abstention in voting, attitudes at party meetings, and of course direct complaint. There have been secret revolts, such as the meeting held by dissident Conservatives at the Carlton Club in 1922 when it was decided to withdraw Conservative support from the Coalition Government headed by Lloyd George.

Each Whip is allocated an area of constituencies and is responsible for the attendance of the Members in that area and for knowing their minds on policy; it is said that Members are frank in their discussions, and in addition, the Whips often gather further information at party meetings. The Government Whips collect, collate, and assess all of these various strands of political information, and the relevant material will be passed on to the Prime Minister by the Chief Whip.

The Whips also play an unobtrusive part in the deliberations. Throughout the long session, hour after hour, one or two Whips from each party are posted on the Front Benches, where they sit like silent sentinels, observing and listening but seldom speaking or engaging in partisan debate. The Whips may be considered to be the active agents within the parties in making party government effective. Although they attempt to influence the attitude of Members and maintain party unity, it is also true that Members attempt to influence them and through them, their party leaders.

The organization of the Whips reflects their unsettled position in the historical development of Parliament, and their status is not completely rationalized. The Whip organization, grafted on to the more traditional order, has close relations with the Government, with the party, with Parliament, and even with H.M. Household. The close relationship between the Government and the Whips is emphasized by the fact that the Chief Whip is Parliamentary Secretary of the Treasury and five of his assistants are Junior Lords of the Treasury. The Chief Whip also bears the title of Patronage Secretary, although in modern times he has little control over patronage; three Government Whips in the House of Commons and five in the House of Lords, all of whom are political appointees, are nominally attached to the Queen's Household and receive salaries. But not all Whips are so fortunate; three Government Whips and all Opposition Whips have no official titles or formal attachment and are unpaid. There is also an element of social status which falls to those Whips who are, in name, attached to the Queen's Household. In Precedence in England, these three Whips—the Treasurer, the Comptroller, and the Vice-Chamberlain of H.M. Household—hold a rank immediately following the Barons and preceding Privy Councillors, the Chancellor of the Exchequer, the Lord Chief Justice of England, and the Masters in Lunacy.

The staff of the Whip organization also reveals the ambivalence of its relationships. The Private Secretary of the Chief Whip is a permanent Civil Servant, Sir Charles J. Harris. It is now customary for the staff to continue in office whichever party forms the Government, and a Member who served in the Labour Government has commented on the 'extraordinary loyalty shown by his staff to the party in office'. (There is a similar arrangement in the House of Lords, where the late Sir Charles Hendriks, nominally an employee of the Treasury, was 'seconded for other duties' and acted as the permanent secretary to the Leader of the House of Lords.) In addition to the Civil Service staff, the Whips' offices utilize employees whose salaries are paid by the political parties. Accommodations for Whips are provided within the Palace of Westminster and the Chief Whip's office is located at 12 Downing Street—to this extent Parliament officially acknowledges the existence of the Whip organization. The salary differential of the various categories of Whips persists, one would suppose, not because the differential is defended but because of the failure or reticence of the leaders to call attention to these inequities.

There is some small difference in the function and composition of the Whip organization of the two parties. The Labour Party develops the policy and the Whips see to it that the policy is carried out within the party. The Whips act as an enforcement agency, upholding the policy which party members know they are obliged to support. The Conservative Party does not bind its Members, and voting in divisions is an individual decision, although there is an expectation that Members will support the party. The Whips may attempt to explain, to persuade, and perhaps to coax, but they cannot order or compel. The Conservative Whips are themselves a kind of club, and the homogeneity of the group is increased by the fact that the Whips themselves select new members (subject to the approval of the Leader). The unity of the group may help to ease the burden, for their work is often tiring and demanding, and they are constantly under the obligation to remain good humoured and sweetly persuasive when dealing with their party colleagues.

The Pattern of Power

PARLIAMENTARY PRIVATE SECRETARY

The Parliamentary Private Secretary is also part of the political network in the House of Commons. The office is strictly honorary, carrying with it no salary and no official responsibilities. The P.P.S. is appointed personally by the Minister concerned, although names of competent young Members may be proffered by the Whips. Within Parliament, the P.P.S. acts as a conduit in providing his Minister with political information. He will attend the meetings of the party committees, keeping his ears open for comment and criticism and praise, and this information he will relay to his Minister. When the Minister makes a speech, the faithful P.P.S. will be sitting on the bench behind, ready to supply notes or facts or to jog the Minister's memory. Within Parliament, the P.P.S. is a kind of political hybrid, his obligations are less extensive than those of a Minister, but he is less free than other Private Members to criticize the Government. He refrains from speaking on topics relating to his own department but he is not restricted from speaking on other topics. In all there are some forty Parliamentary Private Secretaries in the House of Commons on the Government side. If to these one adds the sixty-odd Ministers and the dozen Whips, the Front Bench element of the party can command a force of about 110 Members; behind them are some 100 Members who hold office in the 1922 Committee or in the party committees, and there are also about 140 Members who hold no office, either Governmental or partisan.

PARTY COMMITTEES

The proper function of committees has never been fully rationalized in the parliamentary system, and both Houses of Parliament tend to be anti-committee in the sense that they do not want committees to become independent policy-forming units which can challenge the leaders. There is always concern lest the committees achieve sufficient power to develop policy on their own. Nevertheless, although Parliament has traditionally looked somewhat suspiciously towards committees, one of the more significant developments in recents years has been the rise in importance of the committees of the political parties.

The establishment of the 1922 Committee in the Conservative Party was an attempt on the part of Private Members to increase their influence in policy, and since then there has been a considerable proliferation of party committees. The 1922 Committee was organized by Private

Members to oppose the further participation by their party in the Lloyd George Coalition Government, and it has continued as a committee whose special function is to protect the interests of Private Members. It has its own organization and its own officers, and although the relations with Government may be close, it maintains its own independence and autonomy. In all, then, it can be said that the Conservatives have developed a system where, in effect, power is divided and separated, and when the Conservatives form the Government, the 1922 Committee serves as a forum for raising and reconciling party differences. One finds here a counterpoise to the power of the Leader, a hairshirt irritant to the Ministers, and it is perhaps no exaggeration to say that one of the most effective controls over Government is found within the committee structure of its own party. Ministers attend the 1922 Committee by invitation and not as a matter of right; and indeed they may be cordially invited to attend when the Private Members have something they wish to discuss. Whips attend regularly, not to speak but to listen to complaints and the general tone of the discussions, and they report to the Government.

The Conservative Party policy committees are organized around subject areas roughly corresponding with those of the Government departments. The influence and activity of these committees fluctuate widely, depending in part on the continuing interest shown by the Members and the timeliness of the subject under discussion. The committees may be active in acquiring information, and to that extent the membership will be better informed, but they may also attempt to influence policy and the attitude of the party leaders. It is possible that the committee structure is changing the nature of the party organization by giving Private Members a weapon of considerable strength, but the influence of the committees is uneven; their status only partly defined; yet at times they can be very powerful indeed. The Food and Agriculture Committee, for instance, seems to have brought considerable pressure on the Government in the Crichel Downs case in 1954, when charges of favouritism and irregularities on the part of permanent civil servants led to the resignation of the responsible Minister, Sir Thomas Dugdale.[1]

Realizing the success of the 1922 Committee, the Conservatives began to develop their policy committee system in 1924, and it has grown to such an extent that, in some areas, the Minister concerned must pay some attention to the opinion of the relevant committee. The party is

[1] See R. Douglas Brown, *The Battle of Crichel Down* (London, 1955), pp. 115–20 and *passim*.

able to adjust its differences over policy in private, and some Conservative Members have remarked that since the development of the committee system there has been a trend towards debating and deciding controversial matters within the confines of the party and off the floor of Parliament.

There are some seventeen policy committees in the Conservative Party, in addition to numerous sub-committees. The committee organization is relatively simple, consisting of a Chairman, one or more Vice-Chairmen, and a Secretary, all of whom are Members of Parliament. The party headquarters at Smith Square provides additional staff assistance. Committee membership is voluntary, and in carrying out their work the committees have no power to compel witnesses to attend or to submit evidence. The committees are not, as one might expect, appendages to the 1922 Committee, although disputes within a committee, or between a committee and a Minister, may be referred to the 1922 Committee for further discussion. The Government in no sense controls the policy committees, but they are kept informed of the attitudes expressed through the services of a Whip.

There may be differences of opinion between the Minister and the party committee, and some of the committee members may perhaps hope to persuade the Minister to change his mind. In a similar fashion the Minister may attempt to mobilize the committee in support of his policy, thus increasing his influence with the civil servants in his department or with his cabinet colleagues or improving his bargaining position, say, in negotiations on foreign policy. The committees may also act as the intermediary agent in a conflict between private groups and Government; indeed, the officers of a party committee may be in a strong position to influence policy, and some of the committee elections are no formal matters but are sharply contested on issues of policy. The policy committees of the parties seem at times, and in some areas of policy, to be replacing the Select Committees as a method of securing information; the latter have fallen into partial disuse in modern times, for the consent necessary for their creation is given by the Government rarely and reluctantly.

Various other associations are also organized under the general aegis of the Conservative Party, such as regional groups of Members (Scottish Unionist, Lancashire, etc.), and Members may join such bipartisan associations as the Commonwealth Parliamentary Association, the Inter-Parliamentary Union, and the Parliamentary and Scientific Committee.

The Pattern of Power

The Parliamentary Labour Party is organized along somewhat different lines from its Conservative counterpart, and it may be considered to be a corporate body to which all Labour Members belong, with a Party Committee (the so-called Shadow Cabinet, when the Party is in opposition) at the top of the hierarchy. The meetings of the P.L.P. are attended by leaders and followers alike. The members are expected to act as part of a dedicated and disciplined party, and they are pledged to vote in accordance with party directives and party policy.

The Parliamentary Labour Party is an autonomous body, not subject to the direction of the National Executive Committee of the Labour Party or of any other outside group; however, it was created as an instrument for putting national party policy into effect and its relations with the external party are naturally close. Questions and disputes over policy and personnel that occur within the national party may also find expression within the Parliamentary Labour Party; and the issue of the leadership of the Parliamentary Labour Party will be of singular interest to the national party as well. A complicated set of interlocking relationships exist between the various party units and the trade unions. The Parliamentary Labour Party does not contain all party leaders, and one may note initially that some of the most influential members of the party-at-large are not themselves Members of Parliament, and that some members of the National Executive who are also Members of Parliament are not in the Shadow Cabinet. Many powerful trade union leaders are not in Parliament, but their unions may exercise influence in the Parliamentary Labour Party through their sponsored Members; in particular the union bloc has a strong voice in determining the membership of the Shadow Cabinet.

Inasmuch as the actions taken by the Shadow Cabinet or by the larger group, the Parliamentary Labour Party, may affect the proceedings of Parliament, it follows that internal party manœuvre may be an important aspect of influencing Parliament itself. The P.L.P. meetings are normally closed to the public, but nevertheless a good deal is known about the methods of procedure, the groups, the cliques, the arguments, the issues, the schisms, the conflicts, and the methods of persuasion and manipulation. There are internal disputes over policy (nationalization, disengagement in Europe, the use of nuclear weapons) and over personnel (Gaitskell, Wilson, Jay, Gordon Walker, Castle, and Callaghan, for instance). The unified mass of loyal supporters which the party

F
81

produces in the division lobbies may conceal the vigorous contest for influence that goes on within the party itself.

The annual election of the Parliamentary Committee tends to promote and encourage rivalry within the party. The stakes of victory are high, but the procedure followed in distributing these important offices tends to accentuate rigorous personal competition. The aspirants to leadership are in effect compelled to go on the block every year and to subject themselves to the numerical evaluation of their colleagues. The composition of the party committee would not bind the hands of a Labour Prime Minister, however, and he would retain his freedom of selection. In opposition the Labour Leader may invite Members who are not in the Shadow Cabinet to sit on the Front Bench for important debates and to act as party spokesman in particular fields. Nevertheless, membership in the Shadow Cabinet is a coveted and competitive honour, the next best thing to being in the Government itself. A Member who is selected in the annual poll can sit on the small of his back on the Front Bench, waiting with pleased anticipation the chance to trip up H.M. Ministers on the opposite benches.

The Parliamentary Labour Party holds its elections annually, at the beginning of each session, at which time it selects a Chairman, Deputy Chairman, Chief Whip, and twelve members of the Committee. Once elected, the Party Leader is generally (but not always) re-elected without opposition, and the major partisan contest concerns the remaining membership. Mr. Gaitskell, the present Party Leader, was selected at a meeting of the Parliamentary Labour Party held on 14th December 1955, following a period of tension in which there was some controversy on the successor to Mr. Attlee. Mr. Gaitskell received 157 votes; Mr. Bevan, 70; and Mr. Morrison, 40.

The composition of the balance of the committee is fairly stable, but the elections are nevertheless spirited and the topic of comment, inasmuch as shifts in position may reflect the prevailing pattern of power within the party. The results in 1959 were as follows:

	1959	1958	1957	Also ran, 1959
*H. Gaitskell, Chairman	No contest			Michael Stewart
*A. Bevan, Vice-Chairman	No contest	1	3	*Richard Crossman
*Harold Wilson	1	1	2	Dr. Edith Summerskill
*James Callaghan	2	5	5	*Wedgwood Benn

Sir Frank Soskice	3	4	4 *Mrs. B. Castle
Alfred Robens	4	7	6 Philip Noel-Baker
Fred Lee	5	13	14 Sir Lynn Ungoed-Thomas
*A. Greenwood	6	8	7 Leslie Hale
Tom Fraser	7	12	8 Malcolm Macmillan
George Brown	8	15	9 W. Blyton
Gordon Walker	9	6	11 C. Mayhew
G. R. Mitchison	10	3	2 F. Peart
F. Willey	11	14	16 H. Marquand
Denis Healey	12	20	23 F. Mulley
H. Bowden,	No		Robert Edwards
Chief Whip	contest		Stephen Swingler
			Harold Davies
			K. Zilliacus
			R. Mellish
			C. Pannell
			G. Craddock
			Victor Yates
			Roy Mason
			George Chetwynd
			Arthur Irvine
			E. Popplewell
			J. B. Hynd
			George Rogers
			Frank Tomney

In addition, three Labour Peers are ex-officio members of the committee. They are: Lord Alexander of Hillsborough, the Leader of the Labour Peers; Lord Lucan, the Opposition Chief Whip in the House of Lords; and Lord Faringdon, the elected representative of the Labour Peers.

In 1960, Mr. Gaitskell was re-elected Chairman, after a contest for leadership waged by Mr. Wilson. Mr. Brown replaced Mr. Bevan as Vice-Chairman. The following were elected to the Labour Parliamentary Committee for the session, 1960–1: Mr. Callaghan (1); Sir F. Soskice (2); Mr. Mitchison (3); Mr. Stewart (4); Mr. Healey

* Indicates that the Member is also a member of the National Executive Committee of the Labour Party. The following Members of Parliament were also members of the N.E.C. in 1959–60: Miss Alice Bacon; A. Bevan (Treasurer); A. Wedgwood Benn; Mrs. E. Braddock; James Callaghan; Mrs. Barbara Castle (Former Chairman); Richard Crossman; Tom Driberg; Hugh Gaitskell (*ex officio*); E. G. Gooch; Anthony Greenwood; R. Gunter; Miss M. Herbison; Miss J. Lee (Mrs. Aneurin Bevan); W. Padley; A. Skeffington; Mrs. E. White; Harold Wilson.

(5); Mr. Fraser (6); Mr. R. Gunter (7); Mr. Gordon Walker (8); Mr. Wilson (9); Mr. D. Houghton (10); Mr. F. Willey (11); Mr. Lee (12).

The composition of the Parliamentary Committee gives another indication of the strong position of organized Labour within the party. Five members of the Shadow Cabinet in 1959–60 were also members of the National Executive of the Labour Party (Gaitskell, Bevan, Wilson, Callaghan, and Greenwood). An additional four members of the Shadow Cabinet were sponsored by trade unions and were members of the Trade Union *bloc* within the parliamentary party: they included Mr. Robens (U.S.D.A.W., Union Shop, Distributive, and Allied Workers); Mr. Lee (A.E.U., Amalgamated Engineering Union); Mr. Fraser (N.U.M., National Union of Mineworkers); and Mr. Brown (T. & G.W.U., Transport and General Workers' Union). Sir Frank Soskice and Mr. Mitchison are barristers. Mr. Willey is also a barrister and a member of the London Trades Council. Mr. Healey, an Oxford man and one of the party's intellectuals, is primarily interested in European affairs. He was somewhat lucky in being selected for the Shadow Cabinet in 1959, increasing his rating from twentieth to twelfth, and his success was said to be in part to the support given him by Mr. Gaitskell, who was anxious to add talent to the Opposition Front Bench in the field of foreign affairs. Mr. Gordon Walker, a former Oxford don, is also classed as a member of the intellectual group in the Labour Party. In 1958 he rose from eleventh place to sixth, following his vigorous attack on Government policy in the controversy over the use of cars in elections.

Some Members are more successful in gaining seats on the National Executive Committee than on the Parliamentary Committee. Mr. Richard Crossman, another member of the intellectual group, would no doubt deserve a place on the Shadow Cabinet on the basis of ability, but his recent published comments on the calibre of trade unionists in Parliament may have lost him some support. Mrs. Castle has had considerable success in gaining high office in the national party, and in 1959 was Chairman of the Executive Committee. In the same year, she ranked seventeenth in the parliamentary poll and failed to gain a seat in the Shadow Cabinet. Dr. Edith Summerskill totters on the margin, and although in times past she has been a member of both groups, she was not elected to either one of them in 1959 and rated fifteenth in the parliamentary poll. Miss Bacon, Mrs. Braddock, Miss Lee (Mrs. Bevan), Miss Herbison, and Mrs. White were successful candidates in the Women's Section of the National Executive but did not stand for the Parliamentary Committee.

The left-wing zealots in the party show little strength in the parliamentary poll, but they may exercise influence by other means. Mr. Swingler, who was Chairman of the Victory for Socialism group within the Labour Party, ranked twenty-eighth in 1959, with thirty-nine votes. Mr. Zilliacus, another left-wing leader, was expelled from the Labour Party in 1949 for persistent opposition to the Government's foreign policy but was re-admitted in 1952; drawing thirty-eight votes, he ranked just below Mr. Swingler in the 1959 election.

There is a certain incompleteness, a non-representative quality, in the composition of the Shadow Cabinet, and one notes that certain names are missing, including those of Members who have held ministerial posts. One does not find the name, say, of Mr. Chuter Ede, a former Leader of the House of Commons; Mr. Emanuel Shinwell, former Minister of Defence; or Mr. Creech Jones, a former Secretary of State for the Colonies. In the younger group, the name of Mr. Geoffrey de Freitas is conspicuously absent.

The Party Committee (Shadow Cabinet) and the Parliamentary Labour Party meet at least once a week during a session to discuss policy, strategy, and the obligations of membership. There has been controversy within the party over the extent to which the caucus should control the membership, but the general principle is that decisions are made collectively and are binding on the individual. The Standing Orders of the party were suspended in the early days of the Attlee Government, but they were reintroduced in March 1952, when fifty-seven Labour Members abstained from voting on a party motion relating to national defence. Following the General Election of 1959, new rules were adopted which emphasized co-operation rather than command and stated the obligations of party membership somewhat more politely than the stern phrases of the old Standing Orders. Rule 1 permits the party to withdraw the Whip from a party member and lays down procedures for doing so. Rule 2 states the general principle that if the party is to be an effective force politically 'its activities must be co-ordinated and collective decisions taken'. The Members of the party 'are expected to observe those decisions'. Under Rule 3, members are obliged to vote with the party, although abstentions are permitted 'on matters of deeply held personal conscientious conviction'. It was on this point that Earl Attlee once remarked that conscience spoke with a still, small voice and not with a loudspeaker. Under rule 4, members are 'requested' to consult the party officers when tabling motions or amendments 'so that confusion, misunderstanding, and contradiction can be avoided'. The former rule, making consultation mandatory, was not always obeyed. In the final rule, the 'honour' theme is stressed. Membership in the party, it says, involves responsibilities and obligations as well as rights and opportunities. 'We are relying now', it states, 'not on formal standing orders but on a spirit of good friendship, co-operation and comradeship for the acceptance of these responsibilities and obligations.'[1]

LABOUR SUBJECT GROUPS

The party committees in the Parliamentary Labour Party have a less well-defined part to play than in the Conservative Party, and there is a prevailing suspicion that the committees were set up initially to provide a kind of occupational therapy for frustrated Members on the back benches. They were to have no real power and seemed a harmless contrivance for keeping impatient Members busy and out of harm. There are some fourteen subject groups, as they are called, organized along departmental lines, but there is no subject group bearing the title Defence or Labour. Committee membership is voluntary, but the subject groups tend to have definite membership. The secretariat is provided by the Party Headquarters at Transport House. The influence of these various committees varies considerably, and there is no general understanding on the function they should perform or on their relationship with the National Executive of the Party or with their own Front Bench. There have been occasions where the chairman of a subject group has been co-opted by the National Executive to serve on one of their own policy committees, but it could not be said that the subject groups normally have an important part in developing Labour Party policy. In some cases, however, the party committees give Private Members the chance to become independently well-informed on policy questions, and there are opportunities for discussing policy questions with expert witnesses.

The relationship between the subject groups and the Front Bench raises some basic questions of the location of power, for the groups represent a trend away from the highly centralized leadership in the

[1] The text of the Standing Orders is found in the Annual Reports of the Party Conferences.

party. In some cases the subject groups attempt to keep the Front Bench informed of their attitudes through the services of liaison officers, but in other cases the subject groups are the recipients, not the promulgators, of ideas. In 1960, five chairmen of subject groups were themselves elected members of the Shadow Cabinet. They included Mr. F. T. Willey (Agriculture, Fisheries and Food); Mr. L. J. Callaghan (Commonwealth and Colonies); Mr. Harold Wilson (Economic); Mr. Aneurin Bevan (Foreign Affairs); and Mr. Patrick Gordon Walker (Home Office Affairs). With this type of relationship the tendency may be for the chairman to convey his views to the committee, rather than the other way round. In Mr. Bevan's case, however, this relationship was not of great importance inasmuch as Mr. Bevan did not convene his Foreign Affairs group with any frequency.

In addition to the party committees, there are also many transient, informal parliamentary committees, organized to bring pressure on the Government or to influence public opinion; some of these committees are bipartisan in composition and may also include members from the general public.

THE COMMITTEE SYSTEM IN PARLIAMENT

The development of a committee system for Parliament, with bipartisan membership, presents something of an intellectual quandary. If parliamentary government is identified exclusively with ministerial responsibility, the final decision on all subjects is placed with the Government; but if it is considered that Parliament is a balance to the Government, able to criticize, revise, initiate, and investigate, then Parliament requires some independent means for carrying out its functions, and the committee system can serve a useful purpose in this regard. This quandary is not unique for Parliament and is inherent in any system of control: the controlling unit requires some independent source of power but not so much that it is always the master. In the parliamentary system, Parliament supports the Government, yet it requires some measure of independence so that its criticisms may be effective. This duality of roles—of support on the one hand and criticism on the other—has to some extent been resolved by the development of the party system, wherein one party has a propensity to support, the other to oppose. However, there are other types of balances at work also, and one may distinguish the work of the various committees. There are, in particular, the debating committees consisting of the Committees of the Whole and (in the House of Commons) the several Standing Committees.

Administrative committees are of no importance, for Parliament no longer attempts to govern through committees, as it did under Cromwell, or as many legislative bodies still do—such as the London County Council and many local councils. However, Parliament has taken a step or two in the direction of administrative scrutiny by creating a limited number of committees whose function it is to examine specific phases of Government policy. Because composition of these committees is relatively stable, fluctuating little from year to year, they tend to develop a corporate identity. Some have the authority to send for persons, papers, and records, and we can envision in this area some of the routine functions of Parliament being carried on quietly, efficiently, and without very much public notice given to their activities. The committees' deliberations tend to be confidential, although their reports may be published, but members of the public are not normally permitted to attend their meetings. The major control committees are concerned with Statutory Instruments, Public Accounts, Estimates, and Nationalized Industries. There are also several committees (under a proliferation of names) for considering private bills. In the House of Lords there is the special judicial committee, and both Houses have committees for internal administration.

The parliamentary committees do not introduce legislation, and they make no independent demands for time; whatever legislation they may recommend has no special status as such and must be sponsored by the Government or by a Private Member. Nor is there any assurance that the reports of the Select Committees exercising control functions (Public Accounts, Nationalized Industries, Estimates, Statutory Instruments) will be debated.

Membership on a Standing Committee—that is, one which considers the details of legislation previously approved in principle by the House of Commons—is not necessarily coveted, and it is not the main road to a successful parliamentary career. Unless the subject under consideration has some compelling interest, many Members would prefer to be excused from service. During the 1957–8 session, approximately two-thirds of the membership served on at least one Standing Committee, the other one-third having been able to persuade the party managers that their services were more urgently required elsewhere. In a recent session, for example, there were 174 who were not summoned to service on Standing Committees, 34 who were summoned but did not attend,

207 who were summoned and attended from one to ten meetings, and 208 who were summoned and attended a minimum of eleven to a maximum of seventy meetings.[1]

The selection and persuasion of committee members is the job of the Chairman of the Committee of Selection, although the Party Whips are consulted. The Standing Committees have no permanent membership extending beyond a session, and, save for the Scottish Standing Committee, no exclusive jurisdiction over special types of legislation. The Committee on Selection is able to discharge Members and appoint others, but this power cannot be used when a Bill is before the committee, except to replace the sick, and is not used to enforce party discipline.

The arrangements regarding the Scottish Standing Committee are slightly different. The jurisdiction extends to all public bills, estimates, or other public business relating exclusively to Scotland, and membership is more constant than in other committees. The membership consists of the seventy-one Members from Scottish constituencies together with not less than ten or more than fifteen other Members, to whose appointment due regard is taken so that the balance of power in the committee approximates that in the whole house. The Scottish Standing Committee is empowered to consider bills at their second reading as well as at the committee stage of the proceedings.

Several committees are concerned with the internal operation of the House of Commons, but there is no super-committee comparable to the House of Lords Offices Committee which has general charge of internal arrangements. There is a Select Committee on Kitchen and Refreshment Rooms; on Publication and Debates Reports; on Public Petition; and on Privileges. There is also a House of Commons Offices Commission, which regulates the pay and conditions of service of officers and officials. There is some accountability of these committees to the House of Commons and the chairman may have to answer questions in much the same fashion as a Minister; the Chairman of the Kitchen Committee, for instance, was recently asked by a querulous Member to explain why a second (unnamed) Member has been permitted to entertain more than his quota of guests in the dining room!

The question whether Parliament should create bipartisan committees on policy (on transport or colonies, for instance) is sometimes debated, but the weight of opinion is against their creation because it is believed that they would conflict with the doctrine of ministerial responsibility.

[1] Compiled from Report, 'Standing Committees, Return for Session, 1957–58,' 23rd October 1958, H. C. 309.

At the present time, the need for specialized information is met in several ways. It has been mentioned that both major parties have created their own policy committees, and there are some bipartisan attempts to secure information, such as the Parliamentary and Scientific Committee. The House of Commons has a Select Committee on Nationalized Industries, a solution which is not entirely satisfactory, and a proposal to create a specialized committee for considering colonial questions was recently rejected. The Library of the House of Commons offers some assistance and there are pressure groups, often anxious to help, although from the nature of their work their information may be selective.

The desirability of Parliament's having greater research facilities was emphasized by Mr. Wedgwood Benn (Lab.) in December 1959, in opening a debate on traffic congestion in the urban areas. 'I have often complained in the past about the facilities for research arrangements available for Members of Parliament in this House,' he said. 'I have never been more conscious of this than in the last few weeks when I have been trying to get a grip of some of the elements of this problem of transport. The House of Commons Library, and its staff, within their enforced limits, extend every courtesy and help that are available to it to Hon. Members. But it is still true that all the information and research facilities that are required are in the hands very largely of the pressure groups.' The previous day in the Grand Committee he had seen a colour film put out by the Roads Campaign Council which, he said, must have cost the Council at least £15,000. 'It is a very poor thing', he said, 'that Members of Parliament should be less well equipped to cope with this problem than are the pressure groups which exist.'[1]

PARTY ORGANIZATION IN THE HOUSE OF LORDS

The political organization of the House of Lords is similar to that in the House of Commons, but it is less formal and more permissive and the trend is towards individual freedom in debate and in voting. Partisanship is frequently muted in the actual deliberations, but the parties work out the agenda, keep in touch with their members, and carry on the traditional arrangement of a Government Front Bench and an Opposition Front Bench.

In terms of numbers, the Conservatives have a great preponderance,

[1] House of Commons Debates (London, H.M.S.O.), 10th December 1959, col. 754-5.

although many Lords are somewhat casual about their party identity. The Lords, moreover, are tolerant of political deviants, and the accommodations on the 'cross-benches' are normally used by those who wish to be considered independent and spatially removed from the partisan clusters. However, party identity may be of considerable importance to some of the Peers, and in 1959 there was a reshuffling of seats when some of them changed their political affiliations. Lord Boothby came to the House of Lords as a Life Peer in 1958 after a thirty-four year career in the House of Commons as a Conservative, but he soon decided that he wasn't a party man after all and moved over with the Independents on the cross-benches. On the other hand, Viscount Montgomery came to the conclusion that he was a partisan, and he left the cross-benches to join the Conservatives. Lord Ogmore, who as a Member of the House of Commons had been a Minister in the Labour Government, became disenchanted with his party (among other things he thought the membership was excessively quarrelsome) and joined the Liberals.

In these latter days, when a Peer has practically no chance of becoming Prime Minister, the main stream of political activity flows through the House of Commons. The Leaders of the Conservative Party and of the Labour Party are found in the House of Commons, and their pre-eminence is accepted in the House of Lords. The Earl of Home was appointed Leader of the House of Lords by Mr. Macmillan in 1957, following the resignation of the Marquess of Salisbury who had disagreed with the Government over the release of Archbishop Makarios.[1] The Leader of the Labour Peers, Viscount Alexander of Hillsborough, is a former Member of the House of Commons; he is also one of the three Labour Peers who are *ex-officio* members of the Committee of the Parliamentary Labour Party. The Leader of the Liberal Peers is Lord Rea. The Lord Chancellor (Viscount Kilmuir) and the Chairman of Committees (Lord Merthyr) have specific functions to perform in carrying on the business of the House of Lords but they are not a part of the formal party organization.

Each party has its Whip organization, which is responsible for the conduct of business and for keeping Peers informed thereof. There is some partisan co-operation in sending out Whip notices, however, and after the proposed agenda has been agreed to by the party leaders, notices of the public business for the ensuing week are prepared in the

[1] The Earl of Home resigned in 1960 when he became Secretary of State for Foreign Affairs.

The Pattern of Power

office of the Leader of the House of Lords and made available to all Lords for the asking. The parties will inform their members, confidentially, what degree of significance is placed on the various events. The Conservative Peers may be informed, for example, that an Opposition motion may be pressed 'in a critical sense', and, with two-line underscoring, it will be suggested that the attendance of their Lordships in support of the Government, not later than 6.00 p.m., is urgently requested.

The Government Whips of the House of Lords, but not the Opposition Whips, are paid, and they also have offices, or at least titles, in the Queen's Household.[1] The parties in the House of Lords also have subject-matter committees, much like the House of Commons, which meet infrequently.

The House of Lords Offices Committee, composed of fifty-nine Peers from all parties, has special responsibilities for the internal administration of the House of Lords. The Committee is representative and comprehensive in its membership, and its members may be considered to be the *élite* corps, the inner circle, of the House of Lords. It contains the Leader of the House of Lords; the Leader of the Opposition; the Liberal Leader; the principal Whips of the three parties; the Earl Marshal of England (the Duke of Norfolk), who performs certain ceremonial functions; the Lord Great Chamberlain (the Marquess of Cholmondeley), who has nominal custody of the Palace of Westminster. It also contains twelve of the fifteen members of the Committee for Privileges; thirteen of the fifteen members of the Committee on Procedure; and nine of the ten members of the Committee on Selection. The full committee approves personnel appointments and salary scales; considers the estimates for the House of Lords; recommends the allocation of space in the Palace of Westminster; and in general makes certain that the entire organization runs smoothly and efficiently. There are subcommittees on Library, Refreshment Department, Windows in the Prince's Chamber, and the Housing of Historical Documents in the Victoria Tower. There is no similar committee in the House of Commons.

---

[1] The Chief Government Whip is the Captain of the Gentlemen-at-Arms, £2,200 annual salary; the Deputy Government Whip is the Captain, Yeomen of the Guard, £2,200 annual salary; the three Assistant Whips are Lords in Waiting, £2,000 annual salary.

The Pattern of Power

STAFF AND ACCOMMODATION

STAFF

The permanent staff of Parliament not only performs functions that are essential to the parliamentary process, but it also supplies an element of continuity and rigour in the process itself. The permanent officers may be said to strengthen the framework within which Parliament operates; they primarily act as custodians of the procedures and the organization in which parliamentary action takes place. The partisan struggle, the developments of policy, the enactment of law, all proceed within well-established lines of permissible conduct, and the parliamentary officers see to it that the requirements of Parliament itself are met. In the proceedings of Parliament, there is a sense of purpose and achievement, and action is taken in an ordered way towards a specific end. To a considerable extent, it is the work of the trained and dedicated staff which makes it possible for Parliament to maintain its freedom and to organize its business in such a way that essential and pertinent debate is possible.

One category of staff provides assistance in the normal work of Parliament: keeping records, preparing documents, offering technical and procedural advice, and supplying information. The set of traditional officers responsible for this type of work includes the Clerk of the Parliaments (Sir Victor Goodman, whose parliamentary career began in 1920), the Clerk of the House of Commons (Sir Edward Fellowes, whose parliamentary career began in 1919), and other officers of the clerical departments. Another category of staff deals with physical comfort and order, with the need for habitable surroundings and sufficient tranquillity that the assembly can carry on its functions. This work falls within the province of such officers as the Sergeants at Arms, Doorkeepers, and the ceremonial Officer of the House of Lords who bears the quaint title of Black Rod. The control of the Palace of Westminster, which is still a Royal Palace, rests with the Lord Great Chamberlain (the Marquess of Cholmondeley) who has the assistance of the Ministry of Works in the care of the building. Another category of officers, drawn from the membership of Parliament itself, is especially concerned with deliberations, although they perform other functions as well. The Speaker of the House of Commons and the Speaker of the House of Lords (the Lord Chancellor) are in turn assisted by deputies, panels of chairmen, and their own staff. (For the election of the Speaker, see Chapter IV.) The permanent staff is non-political and the principal officers hold royal appointments. The initial appointment is normally made after competitive examinations, and promotions to the higher ranks are greatly coveted.

THE PALACE OF WESTMINSTER

The life of Parliament is conditioned by the physical environment found in the Palace of Westminster. The general appearance of the building is well known, and the commanding exterior has become a symbol of parliamentary government itself. The Palace has an extensive neo-Gothic façade, flanked on each end by an impressive tower; Victoria Tower stands 330 feet high and guards the House of Lords, and the great Clock Tower, 320 feet high, which houses Big Ben, guards the House of Commons. The roof design follows a broken pattern and is ornamented with crockets, gargoyles, small spires, and pinnacles. Westminster Hall, with its ancient ties, abuts the Palace on the north-west.

The building has many interesting historical associations, growing as it has from a palace, court, and chapel to the current dimensions, but the present building (exclusive of Westminster Hall) was built for the purpose in the nineteenth century, and there has been some reconstruction in the postwar period. The interior of the Palace gives an impression of spacious grandeur, with its long corridors and large public rooms, but it is not always a comfortable place for Members. The Palace contains, foremost, the debating chambers, and it is well known that the chamber of the House of Commons is constructed along the lines of a church choir; there are procedural as well as architectural reminders that the Commons once met in a chapel. The Palace also contains committee rooms; various public rooms; office space, primarily for Ministers and parliamentary staff (Private Members have no offices, although more recently special rooms for dictating and interviewing have been provided); and extensive corridors and passages. There are stores and changing rooms; bedrooms and living quarters; kitchens and canteens; and rooms for relaxation. There is considerable space in the basement and in the towers, but it is not readily adaptable for offices and is used primarily for storage.

The part of the building most used by Members is reminiscent of a large, well-furnished club, containing lounges, libraries, dining rooms, and other accoutrements (the facilities are similar for the Commons and for the Lords). The Members live very much together, eating, drinking, talking, grousing, and endlessly gossiping, and the arrangements contribute to the social life of Parliament: friends can be entertained; hospitality can be extended, say, to visitors from the Commonwealth; private groups (with the sponsorship of a Member) can have meals and receptions in special dining rooms. Once inside the restricted area, Members of both Houses are protected from strangers by a cordon of police who go about their job as eagerly as if Guy Fawkes were still at large. However, such close relationships where one lives constantly with his colleagues may pall at times, and some Members find it taxing to spend most of the day, and every day, in the close environment of parliamentary politics. Other Members are more leisurely in attendance, regarding Parliament respectfully as another kind of club to be visited occasionally or even frequently but not to be attended routinely. The physical structure of Parliament tends to encourage the amateur aspect of membership.

The problem of securing enough space in the Palace of Westminster for all legitimate claimants has been most vexatious, and Select Committees have considered the issue without finding a solution. There are many claimants for space, but even though the Palace of Westminster is a very large building indeed, containing some 1,100 rooms, all of the space is not necessarily adaptable or usable, and the diffuse system of control over the building makes it difficult to allocate space on the basis of the respective needs of the two Houses. Nominally, each House is assigned approximately half of the building, but control in the House of Commons is not centralized, and the Lord Great Chamberlain, however royal his prerogative, has limited power in fact. The Minister of Works allocates some of the space and the ministry itself occupies about 10 per cent of the total floor space. The Ministry is responsible for the custodial care of the Palace and the upkeep of the fabric and employs a parliamentary staff of about 340. Expenditures of the Ministry of Works are in turn controlled by the Treasury. When Parliament is actually sitting, control of the building is delegated to the respective Sergeants at Arms, who are in turn assisted in keeping public order by one police inspector, one police sergeant, and sixty-two police constables. Thirty-five of the constables are on the Vote of one or the other House and twenty-seven are on the Vote of the police fund. This division of payment occurred in 1933, when it was thought that Ministers should be given greater protection, and the additional force of police were charged to the police fund. When the House rises during the weekend, the police go off duty, and the control of the building reverts to the Lord Great Chamberlain; during this period the Palace is patrolled internally by custodians employed by the Ministry of Works. In former days there was an official known as the Keeper of the Palace, but when his function was taken over by the Minister of Works, the title disappeared; nevertheless, the Minister retains the title of Keeper of Westminster Hall.

There are many claimants for space, and some, perhaps all, would like to be close to the physical centre and conveniently located to their work. Some claims were staked out many years ago, and the pattern of claims reminds one of an ancient feudality, where old rights are not extinguished but linger on from one era to the next. A Select Committee was not able to identify all users of space, and one Member remarked that there were 'all sorts of odd people up in those rooms on this floor above'. Another Member stated that a whistle was blown when the House adjourns, 'and the place vomits people. I want to know who they are. It is nothing to do with Members of Parliament.' He didn't find out.[1]

It is difficult to say how many people, or how many families, actually live in the Palace of Westminster or in the adjoining premises. In the various shifts of power, some high officials of Parliament have lost the accommodations once possessed by their predecessors; they may nurse a silent grievance, hoping as some banished prince to regain their lost heritage. Accommodations are provided for the Speaker of the House of Commons, the Lord Chancellor, the Sergeant at Arms of the House of Commons, and the Yeoman Usher and Secretary to the Lord Great Chamberlain. The Clerk of the House of Commons has sleeping rooms; the Clerk of the Parliaments has none. The Librarian of the House of Commons has two bedrooms, one of which is used as a mess room for his staff. In 1953 three office keepers had household accommodation in the Palace. Sleeping rooms in the several buildings on Abingdon Street, across the road, are used by doorkeepers, many of whom are naval petty officers from the coastal area, and there are accommodations for five or six members of the kitchen staff.

Some space is required for cooking and serving food. In addition to the listed accommodations, the Special Committee found a score of staff rooms and canteens where meals were cooked, or food warmed on a hot ring. A whiff of smoking sausage may float into the Central Lobby from the Hall Keeper's mess room adjoining, and there is a canteen opening on to the New Palace Yard for the use of cabmen and friends.

The Lord Chancellor, enlarging his office space after the war, took

[1] Report from the Select Committee on House of Commons Accommodation, 27th October 1953, H. C. 309.

over about twenty additional rooms and moved in a large staff from the Law Courts. There is a special room for painting, used by the Lords. There is a shooting gallery in a sub-basement and (no necessary connection) a mortuary. The Lobby Correspondents have a private, unnumbered room where Members and especially Ministers can be whisked away to be interviewed in strict privacy. The Special Committee also discovered the existence of three typing rooms, theoretically available for the use of Members, which the Committee, in any event, was unaware of. There is also a room assigned to the Second Church Commissioner.

Claims for space on the part of Members have increased. Members would like more public rooms, dining rooms, and working rooms, all conveniently located, and the staff, also, would like more space. 'What puzzles us,' said the Chairman of the Special Committee, 'is the number of rooms in the Palace and the paucity of accommodations for Members and Ministers.' But will there be any reform? 'Everything goes against change in the Palace,' the Chairman concluded ruefully.[1]

[1] Ibid., pp. 4, 57.

CHAPTER IV

Deliberations: Government, Opposition, and Mr. Speaker

THE POLITICS OF PROPINQUITY
IN THE HOUSE OF COMMONS

The great political drama is unfolded on the floor of Parliament. This is where the game is played. This is where the leading partisans clash, the topics are debated, the policy explained, and the decisions recorded. In the two chambers, British political life is dramatized, and one may witness for himself the political cleavages, the contenders for power, the proposals of Government, the alternative solutions, the questions, the probings, and the indications of discontent.

When the House of Commons is in full battle dress, as it were, it makes an imposing spectacle of political virtuosity, and although the seating arrangement does not provide for the subtle shadings of political belief as in the French Chamber, it is a visible expression of current status, political propensities, and former glories. In the seating arrangements of the House of Commons, the question of precisely where one sits has certain symbolic meaning. First, there are the Front Benches, one on each side of the Speaker, which are reserved for the exclusive use of the Government Ministers and the Opposition Leaders. The Private Members who strongly support their leaders, who are 'bucking for promotion', one might say, fill up the benches behind the hierarchy. The third bench below the gangway on the Government side is the home of the party patriarchs, those who have once held high office and who may have resigned because of a disagreement over policy. On the Opposition side, the first bench below the gangway is occupied by the more radical members of the party: in 1960, Mr. Sidney Silverman took the first seat, followed by Mr. Emrys Hughes, Mr. Zilliacus, Mr. Swingler,

Deliberations: Government, Opposition, and Mr. Speaker

and Mrs. Braddock. Mr. Jo Grimond, the Liberal Leader, sat behind Mr. Silverman and behind Grimond was Mr. Chuter Ede, the former Leader of the House.

Party faces party. Under the Gaitskell régime of Labour leadership, the pairing off of minister and potential minister, the matching of the substance with the shadow, reached a fine peak of perfection. For purposes of deliberation the Labour Front Bench is a stolid emulation of Government.

At the beginning of the new session of Parliament, following the General Elections in 1959, the following office holders, and potential office holders, were designated:

GOVERNMENT		OPPOSITION
Prime Minister	*Harold Macmillan	†Hugh Gaitskell
Deputy		†Aneurin Bevan
Admiralty		
Civil Lord	C. I. Orr-Ewing	Thomas Steele
Agriculture, Fisheries and Food		
Minister	*John Hare	†F. T. Willey
Jt. Parl. Sec.	J. B. Godber	T. F. Peart
Air		
Secretary of State	George Ward	Geoffrey de Freitas
Parl. Under-Sec. of State	W. J. Taylor	
Aviation		
Minister	*Duncan Sandys	G. R. Strauss
Parl. Secretary	Geoffrey Rippon	G. R. Chetwynd
Colonies		
Secretary of State	*Iain Macleod	†James Callaghan
Parl. Under-Sec. of State	Julian Amery	A. Creech Jones
		George Thomson
Commonwealth Relations		
Minister of State	C. J. M. Alport	Hilary Marquand
Parl. Under-Sec. of State	Richard Thompson	
Defence		
Minister	*Harold Watkinson	†George Brown

Deliberations: Government, Opposition, and Mr. Speaker

GOVERNMENT		OPPOSITION
Duchy of Lancaster (Information)		
Chancellor	*Dr. Charles Hill	Christopher Mayhew
Education		
Minister	*Sir David Eccles	†Anthony Greenwood
Parl. Secretary	Kenneth Thompson	Mrs. Eirene White
Foreign Affairs		
Secretary of State	*Selwyn Lloyd	†Aneurin Bevan
Minister of State	D. Ormsby-Gore	†Denis Healey
Minister of State	J. D. Profumo	Philip Noel-Baker
Jt. Parl. Under-Sec. of State	R. A. Allan	
Health		
Minister	Derek Walker-Smith	Dr. Edith Summerskill
Parl. Secretary	Miss Edith Pitt	Kenneth Robinson
Home Department		
Secretary of State	*R. A. Butler	†P. C. Gordon Walker
Jt. Parl. Under-Secs. of State	David Renton	Miss Alice Bacon
Jt. Parl. Under-Secs. of State	Denis Vosper	Eric Fletcher
Housing and Local Government		
Minister	*Henry Brooke	Michael Stewart
Parl. Secretary	Sir Keith Joseph	Cledwyn Hughes James MacColl
Labour		
Minister	*Edward Heath	†Alfred Robens
Parl. Secretary	Peter Thomas	R. E. Prentice
Law Officers		
Attorney-General	Sir Reginald Manningham-Buller	†Sir Frank Soskice
Lord Advocate	W. R. Milligan	Sir Lynn Ungoed-Thomas
Solicitor-General	Sir Jocelyn Simon	
Solicitor-General for Scotland	William Grant	

Deliberations: Government, Opposition, and Mr. Speaker

GOVERNMENT		OPPOSITION

Pensions and National Insurance

Minister	John Boyd-Carpenter	R. H. S. Crossman
Jt. Parl. Secretary	W. M. F. Vane	Douglas Houghton
Jt. Parl. Secretary	Miss Patricia Hornsby-Smith	

Post Office

Postmaster General	J. R. Bevins	Ness Edwards
Asst. Postmaster Gen.	Miss Mervyn Pike	Roy Mason

Power

Minister	Richard Wood	†Fred Lee
Parl. Secretary	J. C. George	Harold Finch

Scotland

Secretary of State	*John Maclay	†Thomas Fraser
Jt. Parl. Under-Sec. of State	Niall Macpherson	Miss Margaret Herbison
Jt. Parl. Under-Sec. of State	Thomas Galbraith	
Jt. Parl. Under-Sec. of State	Gilmour Leburn	

Trade, Board of

President	*Reginald Maudling	(Combined with Treasury)
Minister of State	F. J. Erroll	
Parl. Secretary	John C. Rodgers	

Transport

Minister	*Ernest Marples	A. Wedgwood Benn
Jt. Parl. Secretary	John Hay	R. J. Mellish

Treasury

First Lord	*Harold Macmillan	†Hugh Gaitskell
Chancellor of the Exchequer	*D. Heathcoat Amory	†Harold Wilson Douglas Jay
Financial Secretary	Sir Edward Boyle	†G. R. Mitchison
Economic Secretary	Anthony Barber	Roy Jenkins

War

Secretary of State	Christopher Soames	John Strachey

Deliberations: Government, Opposition, and Mr. Speaker

GOVERNMENT		OPPOSITION
Welsh Affairs		
Minister	*Henry Brooke	James Griffiths
Works		
Minister	Lord John Hope (M.P.)	Mrs. Barbara Castle
Parl. Secretary	Harmar Nicholls	
Whips		
Chief Whip (and Parliamentary Secretary of the Treasury)	Martin Redmayne	†Herbert Bowden

* Member of Cabinet
† Member of Parliamentary Committee—'Shadow Cabinet'

THE GOVERNMENT

The Government has two primary duties in debate: it must defend and explain its position, and it must produce enough supporters at the right time to win the division. The Government is obliged to put its case and to have a point of view. In debates on legislation, it must propose, explain, and defend; in policy debates, it must state its position; during question time, it must give a reasoned answer and if possible a reassuring response. The Government dominates most debates and, except in the case of a free vote, the position taken by the Government determines the nature of the decision. The influence of the Government is such that its consent is usually required at all stages of the proceedings where a decision will be made. Attempts are made to persuade and influence the Government at the various stages of the proceedings, so that in a very real sense the Government itself may be considered the major issue of many debates.

The Government keeps a watchful eye on all of the deliberations in Parliament, wherever they occur and whatever the topic, and it may be able to anticipate the areas of policy where controversies will occur and to know which Members will be most concerned. The extended Government, if it may be so called, operates much like a sensitized nervous system. Information on the attitude and the reaction of Members is gathered, collated, and evaluated; the Whips play a part here, and so do the Parliamentary Private Secretaries as well as the Ministers themselves and the party committees. The Government must make up its mind on the significance of the information and set its sails accordingly, and the attitude of the membership may help the Government to decide what legislation to introduce, what amendments to accept, and even what bills to withdraw.

The programme for a session of Parliament is planned well in advance, perhaps as early as May for the following session beginning in October or November, and the number of controversial items must be somewhat restricted if the programme is to get through Parliament in the time available. In planning for the annual legislative programme, there is some flexibility in the length of recesses permitted and in the total length of a session, but in recent years the programme has been so heavy that there has been little relaxation in pace. Since the days of the First World War, increased attention has been given to planning a session; the co-operation of the ministries is required so that proposed legislation will be prepared on time and its consideration will be properly spaced during the session. Although the Government has the primary responsibility for developing the legislative programme in Parliament and for sponsoring the major public bills, the Opposition is always consulted on the order of business. They are not taken by surprise.

Generally speaking, only those bills are introduced which are almost certain to be approved, and there is the assumption that once Government legislation has been introduced it will proceed through the various stages until final passage. Legislation sponsored by the Government has a preferred status, one would almost say a charmed existence, for its passage through Parliament is seldom resisted to the point where it might be withdrawn or seriously amended, much less defeated. In the 1957–58 session, to take a recent example, the fifty-two bills sponsored by Government passed all stages of the parliamentary process and received the Royal Assent. This record is a tribute to the Leader of the House as well as to the Whip organization; considerable planning and co-ordination were necessary and the exercise of more finesse than simply 'whipping the Members into line'. Bills not sponsored by Government met with less success. Of the forty-seven public bills, twenty-four received the Royal Assent, twenty-one were introduced but not passed by the Commons, and two were passed by the Lords but not by the Commons.

In introducing legislation, the Government may anticipate the difficulties that lie ahead, and, to soften the shock and allay the resistance, a Minister may hint that he might possibly accept some amendments. Sometimes the Government has second thoughts, and legislation, once introduced, is permitted to languish. This was the case with the Shops Bill, which met opposition within the Conservative party after it was introduced in 1957 and was not enacted into law. The harmony of the Government's party, and of Parliament as a whole, may be advanced if Members see that their criticism is effective, but the Government may be reluctant to give in too easily, to swing like a weather-vane at every puff of criticism, and it may conclude that it cannot go too far in mollifying special groups without losing control over policy and over the party too. The appearance of party solidarity is worth something, and to give in too frequently might encourage the belief that proposals had been made recklessly. The Government would rather appear to be farsighted and omniscient, thus giving the impression that criticism raised in debate had previously been considered and rejected.

However, the appearance of omniscience may belie the facts, and it has been suggested that the flow of legislation since the war has been so great that Ministers have not always had time to master their subject. They stick too closely to the proposals made by the departments and show too little resiliency in debate. The leading speakers on both sides of the aisle may be guided by briefs prepared for them. None of his own comments on the Amendments would deserve 'the compliment of masterly authority', said Mr. Douglas Houghton, talking from the Opposition Front Bench on the Finance Bill of 1959. He, like the Financial Secretary, was 'speaking from a brief which has been put in my hands', and he had not had long to study it.[1]

On some issues the Government expresses no interest and a free vote is permitted. It may adopt a neutral attitude towards bills sponsored by Private Members, but the Government will be implored to offer some assistance, at least to the extent of providing the necessary time, and it may express an opinion in committee. It may also express an attitude on private legislation. On these occasions the traditional roles are curiously reversed inasmuch as the Ministers appear as interested parties before the committees and the Members act as impartial adjudicators.

[1] House of Commons Debates (London, H.M.S.O.), 10th June 1959, col. 1,024.

Deliberations: Government, Opposition, and Mr. Speaker

THE PRIME MINISTER

The Prime Minister does not attend every session, and the general responsibility for the conduct of the Government's business rests with the Leader of the House of Commons. In the more leisurely past, some Prime Ministers were sedulous in their attendance, and it is said that Stanley Baldwin gained an acute knowledge of the ability of Members and their reaction to Government policy by listening to debates during the odd hours of a session when his presence was not normally required.

The Prime Minister is ordinarily present for the important debates and divisions; he makes statements on policy from time to time; he may make the opening or the closing speech in an important debate; and he will undertake to answer personally some of the questions on the order paper. The Prime Minister may be questioned, as any other Minister, and it may be a glorious day for the Private Member when he can cross swords with the Prime Minister. The general rule is that, on certain days, the Prime Minister will answer Question Number 45 and subsequent questions addressed specifically to him. This places him at the very end of question time, and if there has been a surfeit of discussion on the earlier questions the name of the Prime Minister may not be reached before the time for questioning has expired. The Opposition may be indignant if their quarry escapes so easily, and they may complain against the tedious Members who prolonged their supplementary questions and against the Speaker who permitted them to be asked.

It is necessary for the Prime Minister to establish effective mastery over the House of Commons, and the various Prime Ministers have developed their own technique for doing so. Mr. Harold Macmillan gives the impression of personal confidence—or of 'unflappability', as the newspapers call it—combined with a zealous attempt to persuade the Opposition, as reasonable men, of the wisdom of his policy. He treats the Opposition frankly and politely, an attitude less of deference than of flattering blandishment, and the impression is conveyed that had the Opposition been in his place they would have acted precisely as he did (being the intelligent men that they are). The Prime Minister is quick and resourceful in debate, a polished product of parliamentary experience extending back to 1924. He is often witty and at times playful and is not above engaging in the particular brand of humour enjoyed in Parliament. Some of his witticisms have a fragile quality; they are amusing enough at the time in the tense parliamentary atmosphere but tend to lose point in retelling. Mr. Macmillan apparently collects quaint expressions or homiletic quotations as some people collect string, hoping some day to find use for them. However, his wry retorts often raise a laugh and serve to blunt the force of the opponent's argument.

The Opposition does not always accept Mr. Macmillan's own picture of himself, and he may have to put up with harsh words. Mr. Harold Wilson once told the House that 'The right hon. Gentleman is the only statesman of this century to claim . . . to embody all that is best in both Disraeli and Gladstone. In fact, of course, he is wrong. He has inherited the streak of charlatanry in Disraeli without his vision, and the self-righteousness of Gladstone without his dedication to principle.'[1]

In needling the Prime Minister, the Opposition leaders attempt to draw him out, hoping that he will lose his aplomb and perhaps show his claws; and with provocation Mr. Macmillan can be sharp and deflating. In the winter of 1959, there was general elation when the Government could at last inform Parliament that agreement had been reached with Greece and Turkey on the future of Cyprus. Now the fighting was over. In the House of Lords, the news was warmly received by all parties. In the House of Commons, Mr. Macmillan, expecting general approval of the announcement, called the agreement 'a victory for reason and co-operation', but Mr. Gaitskell, speaking as Leader of the Opposition, was neither jubilant nor charitable. Her Majesty's Government, he said, deserved 'particular credit for eating so many words and even inviting Archbishop Makarios to the Conference'. Past criticism had been well deserved, and it was 'extremely satisfactory' that at long last the Government members 'have seen the light'. Mr. Macmillan came back with his own deflating retort. The expressions of Mr. Gaitskell, he said, 'were of the tone and temper that I expected from the narrowness of his outlook. He never has been, and never will be, able to rise to the level of great events.'[2] Mr. Gaitskell flushed perceptibly.

THE LEADER OF THE HOUSE OF COMMONS

The Leader of the House of Commons acts as Deputy to the Prime Minister and, in a general way, is in charge of Government business in the House of Commons. Until the days of the Second World War, this formidable job was assumed by the Prime Minister himself, but since 1942 it has been filled by appointment. Mr. R. A. Butler became Leader

[1] H. C. Deb., 3rd November 1958, col. 628.
[2] Ibid., 19th February 1959, col. 523–24.

106

of the House in 1955. One cannot define with any precision the obligations of the Leader, for the element of personality may be important. Some aspects of the job, however, are fairly conspicuous. The Leader must arrange the business of the House; he must protect and to some extent define the position of the Government; and he must appraise the reaction and the competence of the Members. Mr. Herbert Morrison, who was Leader of the House of Commons in the Attlee Government, has said that 'the Leader should possess an intuitive instinct about what is going on in the minds of Members on both sides, and if some trouble blows up he should be able to estimate in a flash what the nature and extent of the commotion is.'[1]

The Leader of the House is perhaps the most influential figure in the entire legislative process; he helps to determine the scope of the legislative programme for the session as well as the business of the week; he also influences the content of legislation and may have the final decision as to what amendments will be acceptable, whether a free vote will be permitted, and what Private Member's Bills will receive Government support. It is an exacting job requiring a wide command of facts and the ability to interpret correctly the mood of the House. He must accommodate the wide variety of demands to the extent that he can, and he must attempt to carry the House along with him with the minimum amount of discontent and obstruction. The Leader must show some force in advocating the Government's programme; he must hold the party in line; and although some resilience may be necessary he cannot appear to be weak or indecisive or to cave in under pressure. He can usually count on the support of a majority, but the rights of the Opposition and of the House must also be respected, and the co-operation of the Opposition may count for a good deal. He is constantly importuned to find time for debate or to give his coveted approval to proposed legislation. An instance of the pressures brought on the Leader of the House of Commons is found in the following series of questions which were put to Mr. Butler following the announcement of the business of the House for the following week:

Mr. Gaitskell: May I ask the Leader of the House whether he will make arrangements for an early debate, if possible the following week, on the Central African Federation Constitution . . .

[1] Herbert Morrison, *Government and Parliament: A Survey from the Inside* (London, 1954), p. 118.

Sir G. Nicholson:	Will my right Hon. Friend consider the possibility, fairly soon, of devoting a day to the discussion of the important subject of Treasury control of expenditure?
Mr. Patrick Maitland:	Would my right hon. Friend bear in mind the desirability of a debate on the Montreal Conference? . . .
Mr. Iremonger:	Has my right hon. Friend given any consideration to the Motion standing in my name in connection with the Fourth Report of the Committee of Privileges?
Mr. H. Wilson:	May I also ask the right hon. Gentleman whether he is aware that we are now approaching the time when it is urgent to have a debate on the Free Trade negotiations?
Mr. Ernest Davies:	In view of the important statement made by the Minister of Transport and Civil Aviation last week on the affairs of the British Transport Commission, which is now, at the instigation of the Opposition, rather belatedly to be published as a White Paper, can the Leader of the House say what arrangements are being made for a debate? . . .
Mr. Usborne:	Could the Leader of the House say how soon we may expect to debate the Report of the Wolfenden Committee? . . .
Mr. Grey:	Is the Leader of the House aware of the great concern there is about open-cast mining? . . . Can he say whether we shall have a debate on the matter shortly?

Mr. Butler replied to these and other questions: 'It is natural, at this time of the season, that all claims should be staked. I will take note. . . .'[1]

In addition to being Leader of the House in 1960, Mr. Butler was also Secretary of State for the Home Office, a department which sponsors numerous bills, and Mr. Butler has himself been directly involved in a good deal of controversial legislation: mental health, street offences, aid to religious schools, obscene publications, and gambling. In carrying

[1] H. C. Deb., 13th November 1958, col. 572–579.

out his parliamentary functions, he is assisted by the Chief Whip and his competent organization.

Mr. Butler is an effective and influential politician and yet, withal, an unusual one in that he combines his obvious love of politics (he became Chairman of the Conservative Party following the 1959 General Election, thus achieving 'a lifelong ambition') with scholastic erudition (he received a double First at Cambridge and was president of the Modern Language Association in 1946). He is a politician in the grand manner, erudite, polished, urbane, who smoothly blends politics with his many other interests. He works with a fine brush, and there is a subtlety to his character which may not be readily apparent. Even when debating partisan legislation, Mr. Butler is able to take a detached view of the proceedings, often giving them a philosophical perspective, wryly expressed, which must be puzzling to the out-and-out political animal in the House of Commons.

In his relations with the House, Mr. Butler is bland, polite, and considerate, yet his manners are not warm or effusive and he is not what would be called jovial. A friendly colleague might take his elbow in an intimate conversation, but Mr. Butler would surely wince if he were cordially clapped on the back. He is deliberate and clear in debate, as if he had mastered every detail and thought through every argument, and he attempts to explain and persuade by a careful mobilization of facts and logic. He gives the appearance of having mastered his subject and established such self-control over himself that he could not easily be unnerved. Yet there is a sensitivity in his approach, and he seems aware of the nuances of opinion on any subject with which he is concerned. In answering questions, he is not evasive and he does not shut off inquiry with a petulant answer, although in the Guenter Podola case he showed some embarrassment. Podola was accused of killing a police officer, and Labour Members threw down a barrage of questions on the conditions of Podola's arrest. Mr. Butler believed the case, which was then before the courts, to be *sub judice* and not debatable in Parliament, and he was somewhat taken back by the flood of questions and comment which he was constrained from answering.

Mr. Butler's humour is never far from the surface, but it is a dry variety, specialized, selective, and amusing; pungent without being funny. On Mr. Eden: 'The best Prime Minister we've got.' On the pending week's business: 'We always live in hope and announce what we hope to achieve.' On party loyalty: 'Some degree of stupidity and docility is vital to our affairs, as I am sure the Patronage Secretary would agree.' On procedures: 'There must, and will always be, in a properly free assembly, surprises, ambushes, and jostling together, with tedious waiting, as there are in war and in love.' On the House of Lords: 'Members of that place happen to have debates on the most inconvenient subjects at the most extraordinary moments.'

The Front Bench is also occupied by various Ministers, who may show up in strength for an important debate, but for the most part Ministers appear only occasionally, to take care of the business at hand, and then return to their work. When a Minister is debating legislation, he will be assisted by his faithful Parliamentary Private Secretary, sitting in the second row, who will supply him with the necessary document or fact or misremembered date. Civil Servants from the department, occupying the box at the end of the benches, will be prepared to offer further comfort and assistance.

THE OPPOSITION

The part played in the deliberations by the Opposition is now highly organized, and the debate is bifurcated between the Government and the Opposition. Under this type of sponsorship, the debate may have more than a tinge of partisanship, but partisanship does not crop out on all occasions and a wide range of attitudes may be expressed beneath these party canopies.

The Opposition, like the Government, has the opportunity for developing its own point of view, and it will be expected to state its own position even where it is in agreement with the Government. This obligation to have a point of view requires some internal planning, and the Shadow Cabinet, or the Parliamentary Labour Party, or even party committees or various groups of Members (as, for instance, the Miners), will discuss in advance the line to be taken in deliberations. The principal speakers will be designated to give the party's point of view, and when issues are discussed on which a partisan appeal may be made, debaters will be selected to 'ginger up the debate', as the phrase goes, thus forcing the Government to explain its actions under bleak conditions. Some Ministers must surely feel surprised and chagrined when their speech, seemingly reasonable and convincing, is answered by a withering torrent of scorn by a voluble Member from the opposite side.

The Opposition Front Bench may be used as a proving ground for developing new talent, and promising Members from the back benches may be invited to join the party *élite* on the Front Bench, but on the whole, the chasm between the Front Bench and the back benches seems as wide on the Opposition side as on the Government side. Complaint will be made at party meetings if Members on the Front Bench engage in debate on subjects beyond the scope of their designated field of competency, and it will be held that time is consumed which properly belongs to the back benches. The custom of recognizing Privy Councillors first also causes resentment, and some Private Members believe that their time is snatched from them by their own colleagues.

THE LEADER OF THE OPPOSITION

Mr. Hugh Gaitskell became Leader of the Labour Party in December 1955, and had previously been a Minister in the Attlee Government. Mr. Gaitskell is personally attractive, with kind, thoughtful manners, and he gives the impression of sincerity, integrity, and ability. He smiles readily, though not effusively, but his words are too carefully chosen, even too pedantic, to permit indulgence in levity, jokes, or witticisms. Because his speeches tend to be solemn, often other speakers on the Opposition Front Bench can more easily arouse the emotional support of the back benches or the resentment from the opposite side. This solemnity of Mr. Gaitskell is converted into a somewhat brittle and petulant reaction when he is annoyed and frustrated by Government Ministers, or when they appear to be too lighthearted, and the perpetual gayness of the Prime Minister seems to nettle him no end.

Despite his reactions in moments of tenseness, Mr. Gaitskell is a person of charm, intelligence, and character and a considerable asset to his party and to Parliament. As Leader of the Opposition, he receives a salary of £3,000, in addition to £750 of his parliamentary salary, and he has his own Parliamentary Private Secretary.

The steady, relentless probing in debate is left to other occupants of the Opposition Front Bench (and of the back benches also), those who can stir the party with a rousing speech and taunt the Government with their censorious quips. For giving the hard knocks, for pursuing a point, or a Minister, relentlessly, tenaciously, determinedly, the talents of such others as Mr. Wilson, Mr. Callaghan, and Mrs. Castle will be called on.

There is no formal, well-established pattern for the Opposition to follow, and indeed this is an area where the Leader of the Opposition can be inventive and imaginative. Mr. Gaitskell's strategy is to keep the party united on all major questions of policy and to organize the Front Bench, with its tendrils and extensions, as if it were an alternative

Deliberations: Government, Opposition, and Mr. Speaker

Government. In following such a policy, the Parliamentary Labour Party appears to be concerned with the major problems of the day and it is seriously concerned with achieving power. This is a policy of happy anticipation, as if the willing bride kept her gown in the closet just in case she received a proposal. It also contains risks. The party itself is not agreed on some of the main political issues—the H bomb tests, further nationalization of industry, German armament, and European cooperation; and the splits and rifts within the party are dramatized for all the public to observe. Moreover, the leadership does not always have full support or exercise a free hand in determining the party strategy, and at times it may have to yield to testy Members on the back benches, some of whom would like to engage in a tendentious verbal war with the Government. Although the Opposition is organized as if it were an alternative Government, the party Leader lacks the control over party appointments and over policy that he would have as Prime Minister. In short, Mr. Gaitskell does not always have very much room to manoeuvre.

DEPUTY LEADER

Mr. Aneurin Bevan, long a controversial figure in British politics, became Deputy Leader of the Opposition following the General Election in 1959 and died the following year. (He was succeeded by Mr. George Brown, a more conservative name in the Labour party.) During his parliamentary career, Mr. Bevan gained a reputation as a debater skilled in quick, barbed repartee, with a penchant for the biting phrase. When he was about to join in a partisan debate, he sat somewhat crouched on the Front Bench, ready to intervene with a sharp question or a rebuke, and there was an element of physical dynamism in the vigour of the attack. He was on his feet at the slightest opening, rushing in like a driver finding a hole in a traffic jam, and by the force and suddenness of the charge he seemed to compel his opponents to give way. Although his phrases were often expressive and colourful, his effectiveness rested also on the pungency of the thrust, his ability to seize a point quickly and exploit it, and a scornful voice which imputed evil design and pronounced a condemnatory judgment.

When delivering a speech of substance, Mr. Bevan sometimes gave evidence of mental laziness, of not having prepared himself fully, and he showed unexpected vistas of ignorance in colonial and foreign affairs. Once when taunting the Government, he surprisingly accused the Conservatives of having once put Dr. Nkrumah in gaol. This gaffe was followed by reproachful head shakings on his own bench (and laughter from the opposite side), and he attempted to cover up his error by saying, 'Well, we shoved him in gaol.'[1]

PRIVATE MEMBERS

The Private Member on the back bench participates in debate under certain handicaps. He is less certain of being recognized than his colleagues on the Front Bench, and if there is competition for recognition he may require patience and a degree of physical agility. To catch the eye of the Speaker, he must rise to his feet when no one is holding the floor, and he must anticipate, by a split second, the precise time when the Member currently holding the floor will finish his speech. Even so, he may fail to attract the Speaker's attention. When the Private Member is at last able to catch the Speaker's eye, he may find that the chamber is no longer crowded, the debate unexciting, the point now irrelevant, and the press gallery empty.

It is difficult to satisfy everyone, and proposals have been made to extend the opportunities for debate by providing that during certain periods of the week the speeches should be limited to five minutes in length. Even a short speech, or a speech given to a relatively empty chamber, may have its satisfactions: the speech may be reported in the regional press; it will appear in *Hansard's Debates*, and thus be available in departments and libraries; and the Government will be apprised. Somewhat curiously, however, there are occasional flat periods of debate when no Members plan to speak and the Whips may be compelled to stir up interest so as to keep the debate running for the allotted time.

The facile references to Private Members sitting on the back benches may give the impression that Private Members are an inarticulate mass, devoid of personality or interest. Far from it. Individualism can shine on the back benches. The Private Members have considerable freedom in expressing their opinion, far more than the occupants of the Front Benches, who are hedged about by the restriction of subject matter and the expectation of party conformity. Nor is it necessary for back-bench Members to participate in debate in order to be influential; Members who sit so inscrutably silent in the great chamber may in fact exercise considerable influence within the confines of their own party. Private Members may also combine to bring pressure on the Government, or on the Opposition Front Bench, as illustrated by the following news item:

[1] H. C. Deb., 19th March 1959, col. 660.

Deliberations: Government, Opposition, and Mr. Speaker

The Times of 10th December 1958 reported that Mr. Watkinson, the Minister of Transport, attended the joint meetings of the Conservative back-bench Finance and Transport Committees, which were held privately. 'Discussion gave the Minister some inkling of the line that Conservative back-bench speakers will take when the Commons debate tomorrow the Transport (Borrowing Powers) Bill. . . . The critics are expected to make it clear that the railways cannot continue to look to Parliament for millions of pounds to meet deficits and that they must take action to make the system more profitable, even if it means drastic closing down of uneconomic lines and selling off some of the railway properties.'

The privileges of a Private Member may be restricted, but within the system of values of the House of Commons the Private Member has an honoured place. It is the normal status of most Members at any one time, and it is also the status to which Ministers return after relinquishing power. Once, in a philosophical mood, Mr. Butler expressed the view that politics was a profession 'in which the reward is precisely that life, and not the honours that sometimes come from promotion to ministerial rank or anything else.' He did not think 'that one of us here who has ever seen a man retired from his position will disagree when I say that it is one of the most dignified spectacles to see him take up his normal part in the House of Commons.'[1]

Some of the Private Members, like the Perpetual Curate of Hogglestock, have made a career for themselves on the back benches, and although inwardly they may yearn to be a powerful Minister whose words are quoted by all the newspapers, they have in the meantime taken advantage of opportunities closer at hand. Their intervention in debate is anticipated, although their views may not always flow in the mainstream of party conformity, and within the broad world of politics they have laid hold of a circumscribed area in the House of Commons where they can exercise influence. Some of these inveterate back-bench Members have acquired distinctive eccentricities which amuse and charm and sometimes annoy.

Among the successful and influential Private Members, the name of Mr. Sidney Silverman may be noted. Mr. Silverman is a vocal, visible, and active member of the left-wing of the Labour party who has used his parliamentary skills with singular effectiveness. He sits on the first bench below the gangway, the traditional home of parliamentary rebels,

[1] H. C. Deb., 13th July 1959, col. 39.

ready to offer his opinion on a complicated procedural point or to protect the rights of Private Members or simply to make a comment. A smallish man, with a sleek beard and a head of creamy-yellow hair, Mr. Silverman commands considerable attention as he stands near the very centre of the chamber when he speaks. His performances are polished, executed with skill and verve, and he speaks with such delicate assurance, such overweening finality, that one may imagine that the speech was practised some hours before a mirror. His greatest parliamentary feat was his sponsorship of the Bill abolishing the death penalty. In this debate he was adroit and skilful, combining moral courage with the tactical expertness of a parliamentarian. Mr. Butler once referred to him as a *justum et tenacem propositi virum*.[1]

A Private Member on the other side of the aisle who is able to draw attention to his views and to himself is Mr. Gerald Nabarro, a person who looks like a caricature of John Bull, or the well-fed clubman, and whose views on many topics are suitably exaggerated. Mr. Nabarro has the stylish long hair, much cultivated in Parliament, appearing always to be just in need of cutting, and a magnificent R.A.F. moustache, drooping and curvilinear, and undeniably striking; and if there is any doubt of his identity, the signature that identifies him absolutely as Mr. Nabarro is the boutonnière in the lapel. He has a loud, throaty, and booming voice, which is greatly to his advantage when he tosses out his numerous asides not necessarily meant for the record but loud enough to be heard by the Opposition, whose foibles cause him no end of pleasure. The Opposition is never certain whether to be provoked or amused, whether to answer back or to ignore temptation, but Mr. Nabarro, with his constant prodding, can generally provoke some Labour Member into answering back.

In addition to baiting the Opposition, he also teases his own Front Bench, pleasantly and wittily and without malice, and over a period of time he put down 199 questions on the purchase tax for the Chancellor of the Exchequer to answer. He is a member of the Institute of Directors, which to many Labour Members is a fearsome Chamber of Horrors, full of faceless men, and this identification in turn makes Mr. Nabarro the target of the taunts of the Opposition. These personal encounters may be dangerous and highly explosive, as if one were lobbing hand grenades from trench to trench and back again, always hoping that they would explode on the other side and not in one's own hand. Mr. Nabarro seems to enjoy these personal encounters. His general volubility once led a

[1] Ibid., 6th February 1957, col. 455.

Labour Member to wonder 'whether the hon. Member for Kidderminster has sworn to eternal loquacity by some sort of inverted Trappist vow.'[1]

Although Mr. Nabarro appears to be the champion of opulent display, and is now the director of several companies, he has had an unusual background for his present career. He was born in 1914 and left school at the age of fourteen. After serving at sea for a short while, he was in the Regular Army for eight years, during which time he rose to the rank of Staff Sergeant Instructor; he also held a commission in the Second World War. In 1937 he entered industry as a labourer in sawmills and worked as a machine hand, charge hand, foreman, cost clerk, and eventually Works Manager, General Manager, and Managing Director. Now he is a member of the Institute of Directors. He entered Parliament in 1950.

THE SPEAKER

The Speaker now plays an indispensable role in debate, for he holds the balance between the opposite sides and sees to it that debate is full, free, and fair.[2] So important has his role become that when new legislatures are created in the colonial territories, the first essential task is to find a suitable Speaker. There is no satisfactory book on the speakership; none which describes the historical development of the office as well as the part played in modern times. However, it is well understood that the speakership has been modified over the centuries from that of spokesman for the monarch to an impartial presiding officer of the House of Commons. The assessment of his position given by Speaker Lenthall to Charles I in 1642—that he had 'neither eye to see, nor tongue to speak in this place, but as the House is pleased to direct me, whose servant I am'—is often quoted to show the growing independence of Parliament from the influence of the King.

There are certain characteristics which a Speaker is now expected to have. He should be good humoured but firm; impartial and neutral but sufficiently co-operative to enable the Government to complete its business; he needs to understand the moods and petulances of the House,

[1] H. C. Deb., 11th June 1959, col. 1,313.
[2] The functions exercised by the Speaker are also performed (with slight modifications) by the Chairman or Deputy Chairman of Ways and Means. These play a subdued role in partisan politics; they do not participate in debate and they do not vote.

and he must be able to cope with the intervention of tiresome Members. Physical presence and a commanding voice are desirable adjuncts in presiding over the House of Commons inasmuch as the Speaker shuns the gavel and relies on his voice alone to keep order; he secures silence and attention by rising in his seat.

Although the position of the Speaker is at the vortex of political conflict, an attempt is made to immunize the Speaker from competitive partisanship and to exalt his position so that his basic loyalty is towards the House of Commons itself. This is not always easy, however, for the Speaker remains a Member of Parliament and must wear the party label when standing for election. There is also a degree to which the Speaker must assist the Government in getting through its business. Moreover, the Speaker may face opposition in the General Election, and there is no firm convention that his seat should be unopposed. One Speaker is said to have met the challenge of remaining technically neutral during the course of a partisan election by making a single campaign speech in which he read a selection from Sir Erskine May's *Parliamentary Practice*.

The part played by the Speaker in the deliberations of the House of Commons extends beyond that of a moderator or presiding officer, and although the Speaker presides in the sense that he keeps order during debates, he also has considerable authority in shaping the form of the deliberations. He sees to it that time is allocated fairly, that the debate is relevant, and that waggish and assertive Members are duly admonished. On some occasions he is the conscience of the House, making certain that the rights of Members and of the House of Commons are respected. He is not the kind of chairman who leads the discussion so as to produce a meeting of minds of the Members. Rather, his function is to see to it that the process itself is working without his influencing the decision.

The Speaker has considerable, almost unlimited, authority within a narrow jurisdiction. He is answerable only to the House for his actions, and although his decisions can be overruled, this seldom happens. He has the power to permit Members to speak and he has some discretion in selecting topics and amendments for discussion and in permitting divisions. He sees to it that there is adequate discussion before a decision is made and that the essence of the proposal has been discussed with fair play all around. The most important guide line for the Speaker is 'the sense of the House', and the ability to interpret this particular mystery is acquired from association and experience, not from written rules. It is not too far wide of the mark to say that the Speaker has to ascertain the sense of the House for every debate, knowing what issues and interests are involved and the possible contribution of the various Members.

Even dull debaters may have their place, and a former Member has suggested that the Speaker may deliberately call a bore to speak after a stormy scene 'in order that he or she may empty the House and give Members a chance of cooling down.'[1] Earl Winterton, who served in the House of Commons from 1904 to 1951, found that the Speakers had their personal reactions to the speeches they were compelled to hear. 'Mr. Speaker Lowther told new Members, in private, whether they had spoken well or badly. Speaker FitzRoy mumbled to himself, "What a speech," "When is this boring fellow going to sit down?" Mr. Speaker Clifton Brown drummed angrily and repetitively with his fingers on the sides of his chair when he thought a speech had lasted too long.'[2]

The Speaker is given some indication of the course the debate will take; Members will write a note suggesting they would like to speak; party Whips, sitting at the Speaker's feet, may suggest names of partisans who wish to catch his eye; and Members who are known to represent the opinions of special groups or who have a point of view different from that of their colleagues or who may have some special competence may expect to participate. The Speaker will attempt to permit a variety of points of view to be heard, a practice which is a boon to the fringe elements of both parties. However, these informal suggestions and presumptions are not binding, and the Speaker alone determines who is to speak.

The Members are normally recognized alternately, by parties, a procedure which ensures fair play and adds to the fullness of the total debate, but at the same time it may break the continuity of the argument. A Member, perhaps gaining the floor after waiting for some hours, or even days, may decide to proceed apace with his prepared speech and ignore the points made by his predecessors.

Although treating each party equally, the Speaker has some discretion in determining which of several claimants from the same party is to speak. A Privy Councillor has priority over a non-Privy Councillor, and if both claim the floor simultaneously, the non-P.C. is expected to sit down. This is a sensitive point with many of the back-bench Members who do not approve of the custom. (There are sixty-three Privy Council-

[1] Earl Winterton, *Orders of the Day* (London, 1953), p. 96.
[2] Ibid., pp. 95–96.

lors in the House of Commons: thirty-seven Conservatives, twenty-five Labour, and one Liberal).

The debate is not full in the sense that all Members who wish to talk have the opportunity to do so but it is usually representative in the sense that a variety of points of view may be heard. The deliberations appear to develop smoothly and naturally, an appearance which is perhaps more obvious to the observer than to the back-bench Members who are unable to catch the Speaker's eye.

There is no procedural limit on the length of a speech, and some of the speeches of Private Members may be quite short, often less than ten minutes in duration. The rule of brevity is enforced by the understanding that the scarce commodity of time is not to be abused. The time consumed by one Member decreases the time available for others and it is considered bad form to make lengthy speeches; the offending Member will, in some fashion, be reprimanded for his thoughtlessness, perhaps by his own colleagues. Time is further conserved by the rule permitting a Member to speak only once on a given subject, and this rule prevents the development of a round-robin type of filibuster, where a small clique is able to monopolize the time.

There is sanction, also, in the memory of Mr. Speaker, and a Member who has made a long, boring or repetitious speech may have to do penance for some time by sitting in silence, ignored by the Speaker. Moreover, the Speaker can bring debate to an end by calling for a vote on the previous question, although this is a power he would rather not use if debate will terminate otherwise. Normally, it is possible to fix an end to the debate by prior agreement, but extraordinary procedures are permitted. One procedure is the guillotine, the popular term for 'closure by compartments' or 'allocation of time order', wherein a specific amount of time is allocated to a Bill or parts of a Bill; when the time has expired, questions on Government amendments are put without debate. Another procedure is the so-called kangaroo closure, which empowers the presiding officer to select some amendments for consideration and to jump over others. Debates may be brought to a close if the motion 'that the question be now put' is supported by a majority and at least one hundred Members. However, the Speaker need not accept the motion if it appears 'that the motion is an abuse of the rules of the House, or an infringement of the rights of the minority.'[1]

On some occasions, the Speaker may be treated somewhat dis-

[1] *Standing Orders of the House of Commons* (London, H.M.S.O., 1956), Standing Orders 29 and 30.

courteously by Members who do not accept his decisions, and under such conditions the Speaker may be without recourse to make his decisions effective. One method of showing displeasure while remaining within the bounds of parliamentary decorum is to raise numerous points of order; this delays proceedings and may even offset the effect of the Speaker's ruling. One incident of this nature occurred in November 1958, in connection with the proposal made by Mr. Francis Noel-Baker (Lab.) to create a Royal Commission for considering safeguards against the influence of advertising. Mr. Noel-Baker and friends, carried away with their subject, talked too long and ended by taking up approximately 65 per cent of the time available for the debate. The Speaker said that he could not permit a division because the topic had not been adequately discussed, and he admonished the proponents that 'In opening up a subject of this complexity they ought to leave more time for other Hon. Members.'[1] Labour Members (Messrs. Stonehouse, Dugdale, Callaghan, Noel-Baker, Lindgren, Willey, Skeffington, J. Hynd, Mitchison, and Orbach) received the Speaker's ruling with poor grace, and for the next thirty minutes they showed their displeasure by raising points of order. The Speaker protested that raising points of order continually was 'not playing very fair with the Chair'. It was not playing fair, either, with the Member who was to have made a speech on the adjournment during the thirty minutes in which the points of order were raised.[2]

THE SELECTION OF A NEW SPEAKER

The Speaker of the House of Commons from 1951 to 1959 was Mr. W. S. Morrison, a former Minister, but inasmuch as Speaker Morrison did not stand for re-election in 1959, it was necessary for the House of Commons to elect a new Speaker following the General Election. Once elected, the Speaker is transformed into the neutral guardian of the rights of the Commons, but before this transformation takes place and the neutrality is achieved, it is necessary to reach agreement within the parties and between the parties on who the next Speaker will be. Indeed, the selection of the Speaker may cause a degree of political tension in the House of Commons, as was the case in 1959. Somewhat surprisingly, considering the long tradition of the speakership, some of the conventions which govern the selection of the Speaker are unclear, and in 1959 there was controversy on the following points: Should the outgoing

---

[1] H. C. Deb., 21st November 1958, col. 1,611.
[2] Ibid., 21st November 1958, col. 1,503–1,620.

Deliberations: Government, Opposition, and Mr. Speaker

Speaker retire at the end of a session, during a session, or at the beginning of a session? What are the mutual claims of the parties over the selection of a Speaker? Is a party obliged to continue in office a Speaker inherited from the prior Parliament? What procedure should be followed in canvassing the opinions of Members?

The Speaker is customarily selected from the majority party, which gave the Conservatives some claim to the new Speaker in 1959, but Labour also felt that it had a strong claim inasmuch as there had never been a Speaker from the Labour Party and the office of Speaker had not fallen vacant during any of the three occasions when Labour had organized the Government. In 1945, when Labour had a clear majority, Mr. Clifton-Brown, a Conservative, was retained as Speaker, and upon his retirement in 1951 the Conservatives were again in power and supported Mr. Morrison. Labour opposed Mr. Morrison, partly on the grounds that he was a former Cabinet Minister, partly because they wished to 'promote' their own Member, Major Milner, who was Chairman of Ways and Means. (After his defeat in the contest for Speaker, Major Milner was given a peerage).

The Labour Party may have considered itself both generous and unlucky, but at an earlier period the Conservatives had on several occasions failed to secure the Speakership on organizing the Government. In the seventy years between 1835 and 1905, during which time the Conservatives formed five Governments, all of the Speakers were either Whigs or Liberals (Abercromby, Shaw-Lefevre, Denison, Brand, Peel, and Gully). In 1905 a Conservative Speaker (Lowther) was elected, and he served from 1905 to 1921 during a period in which the Liberals were normally supreme. A Liberal Speaker (Whitley) was elected during the Lloyd George Coalition Government and served from 1921 until 1928, during which time both Labour and the Conservatives were in power. Then followed a series of Conservative Speakers: FitzRoy in 1928; Clifton-Brown in 1943; Morrison in 1951; and, finally, Hylton-Foster in 1959.

Mr. Morrison was in many ways the prototype of the ideal Speaker. Wearing his full-bottomed wig and dark robe, he was majestic and somewhat awesome in appearance as he sat brooding in solitude under the canopy of the Speaker's chair. He had a rich, melodious voice, clear and succinct, and his impromptu decisions, cogently expressed, gave the impression of careful, premeditated thought. He was good humoured and considerate, although at times under considerable pressure from recalcitrant Members.

Deliberations: Government, Opposition, and Mr. Speaker

Whatever the equity of the case, however, some Labour Members began to develop a grievance on the question of the Speakership after Mr. Morrison became Speaker. They reasoned that they had retained a Conservative Speaker when they were in power and they were now compelled to accept a Conservative Speaker when out of power. The relations between Labour Members and Speaker Morrison were respectful but not always cordial, and a Labour candidate contested Mr. Morrison's seat at Cirencester and Tewkesbury in the General Election of 1955.

During the 1958–59 session, a number of Labour Members grumbled about the Speaker's actions. It has been mentioned that some Members were discourteous to the Speaker in raising pointless points of order, and they disputed his decisions. It was even rumoured that the Labour Party would drop Mr. Morrison and select a Labour Speaker if it won the next election. Complaints were made that the Speaker was unimaginative in selecting topics for adjournment debates, and on one occasion an angry Mr. Delargy (Lab.) told the Speaker: 'You decided that certain questions, like Scottish horticulture, were much more grave and urgent than the shooting of Cuban citizens with British guns. Does not this throw a peculiar light on your common sense and responsibility?'[1] There was also complaint that the Speaker was too lax in permitting supplementary questions to be asked. Back-bench Members normally like to raise supplementary questions, for it gives them a chance to match wits with a Minister. Now, however, it was said that the Speaker had another motive. He permitted supplementary questions to be asked as a device for protecting the Prime Minister, who would normally be expected to answer questions personally after Question Number 45 was reached.

The vendetta terminated when the Speaker announced in February 1959 that he would not be a candidate at the next General Election. Medical examination, he said, had shown that he was 'sound in wind and limb' but that he was personally conscious of a slight difficulty in hearing. 'I am aware', he added, 'that a certain degree of judicious deafness is not an unmixed evil in the occupant of this Chair, but I could wish that mine were sometimes more selective and less fortuitous.'[2]

After Speaker Morrison announced his plan to retire, the discussion of his successor was put off until after the General Election, and opinion on a logical successor did not crystallize in either party. If Labour won

---

[1] H. C. Deb., 15th December 1958, col. 765.
[2] Ibid., 19th February 1959, col. 549–550.

the election, there would surely be a Labour Speaker. The most persistent demand for a Labour Speaker came from the rank and file, who wanted their party to reflect in the refulgence of the office. On the other hand, some former Ministers in the Labour Government have commented that their relations with Speaker Clifton-Brown were excellent and that there was much to be said for selecting a Speaker from the opposite party, inasmuch as questions of party favouritism were less likely to arise. However, this attitude was not fully shared by the mass of either party.

As it happened, however, the Labour Party was defeated in the General Election and was in no position to make the commanding decision on the new Speaker. If Labour were now to have a Speaker, it would be due to the grace and favour of the Conservatives, and to some this would be galling indeed. However, many Conservative Members had no objection in principle to selecting a Speaker from the Labour Party, although some of the back-bench Members were more inclined to adopt the spoils-of-office theory of selecting a Speaker.

There was limited time available for the delicate negotiations required in a manœuvre of this sort. It was necessary to reach an agreement between the parties in the short period following the General Election on 8th October and the reconvening of Parliament on 20th October. Moreover, if there was to be a Labour Speaker, it was necessary for the Conservative Party to agree to support a Labour Member, and the Labour Party had not yet indicated a preference or drawn up a short list of candidates. As things progressed, the Conservatives discussed the problem among themselves, in their own fashion, and it became apparent that the name of Sir Frank Soskice would command general support. Sir Frank had been Attorney General in the Attlee Government and was currently engaged in the practice of law. Alternatively, the Conservatives favoured one of their own group, Sir Harry Hylton-Foster, who was at that time the Solicitor General.

The leaders of the Parliamentary Labour Party were informed of the Conservative position, and the information was passed on to the full Party, which met on the morning of 20th October, the day on which the Speaker was to be selected. The reports state that the meeting was noisy, belligerent, and bad tempered. The Conservative plan fell apart, for Sir Frank Soskice bowed out, saying that he could not accept the office. Labour was left with nothing, for the Conservatives were now committed to Sir Harry Hylton-Foster, and there was no further possibility of selecting a Labour Speaker.

Deliberations: Government, Opposition, and Mr. Speaker

Time had run out. The Conservatives had acted; the House of Commons was to reconvene that afternoon; and there was now no opportunity for suggesting alternative names or even for discussion. Labour Members were angry and indignant, flushed with pride and self-pity, and they thought they had been treated badly. They directed their anger against the Conservative Party, which was held responsible for the embarrassing predicament in which they now found themselves. The Conservatives were said to be high-handed in attempting to dictate the choice that Labour should make, and the gesture of goodwill in supporting Sir Frank Soskice was distorted to imply that only one Labour Member was competent to be Speaker. In the end, the Party decided not to offer a candidate for Speaker, who in any event would be defeated, but to express disapproval of the methods by which the choice had been made.

When the House met on the afternoon of 20th October 1959 the chamber was tense and crowded. Following custom, Sir Edward Fellowes (the Clerk of the House) rose from his chair and solemnly pointed a finger at Sir James Duncan, who then moved that Sir Harry Hylton-Foster 'take the Chair of this House as Speaker.' Sir James Duncan's speech was designed for a normal ceremonial occasion but the event turned out to be noisy and irreverent, and the Labour Members brought to the meeting the bickerings, anger, heartaches, and frustrations that had been expressed earlier at their own party meeting.

Sir James proceeded calmly, not suspecting the ambushes that lay ahead. His fine-mannered attempts to provide a touch of sedate humour and pompous dignity were mocked by the scornful Opposition, who formed a Greek chorus as they answered Sir James's remarks with derisive, ironic cheers.

'The office of Speaker is the highest office that we can offer to any man,' Sir James said solemnly. 'It is most important, therefore, that we should deliberate together . . .' and there was a wild outburst of abusive groans from the side Opposite. There was an attempt at pawky humour. 'We Scots' had hogged the important jobs too long, but now there would be an English Speaker. 'We are content to have a Highland Prime Minister . . .', and an impudent voice came back from the other side of the chamber: 'We are not.'

Sir James had no better success when he delved into history. 'As time went on,' he explained, 'the office of Speaker tended to become a party matter,' and there were more groans and cheers, and his reference to 'our strange way' of electing a Speaker provided hoots and laughter. The mysterious process of selecting a Speaker, he went on, 'can never be understood by foreigners,' and there were now dark grins in the Commonwealth gallery. It was in all a luckless speech, unchanged from the original script to a quicker tempo and a nimbler wit, and Sir James met heavy weather throughout.[1] The seconder (Sir Robert Cary) also suffered moments of discomfort, and his observation that 'Anyone outside, uninstructed and uninformed, may think that this is a mere formality' brought clamorous agreement from the Opposition benches.[2]

At last the embarrassing speeches were over, and after having heard the debate—'a misery for a candidate in my circumstances to have to listen to'—the Speaker-Elect addressed the House. Sir Harry was pleasant, good humoured and obviously sincere; he knew his audience and his touch was sure. There was a time, Sir Harry told the House, when the Speaker's Chair was considered a kind of prequisite for the office of Solicitor General. However, all that came to grief in 1601 when one of his predecessors 'was said to be too lawyer-like and uncouth for the Chair, and the House was advised to find someone more presentable.' The remark helped to ease the tension, and the House appeared anxious to hear the new Speaker.

Sir Harry then went on to pledge his service to the cause of Parliament. It would be his whole ambition in life to serve the House faithfully, 'to maintain in full vigour those traditions that have made this House at once the origin and the example of parliamentary institutions throughout the world.' These words were well received, and they reaffirmed in the heart of every Member the identity he feels with Parliament as a glorious institution which binds the present with the past and with the future. They were proud to be Members of Parliament. The traditional ceremony then followed, and with mock resistance a reluctant, protesting, and unco-operative Sir Harry was conducted to the Speaker's Chair.

There was now a new Speaker; he had charmed the House and had made the Members feel that they were part of a great tradition. It was an electric moment as, for the first time, Sir Harry Hylton-Foster stood before the Members in front of the Speaker's Chair; spontaneously, as in a flash, it seemed that doubts were resolved, wounds healed, and anger forgotten, and the Members knew for themselves they had selected 'a very good Speaker indeed.' The speeches, the boorish behaviour, the selection procedures, were forgotten; were now in fact meaningless. The Speaker had the confidence of the Members, they had his, and everyone knew it.

[1] H. C. Deb., 20th October 1959, col. 2–4.   [2] Ibid., col. 4–6.

CHAPTER V

Free Speech and Public Policy

THE DEBATES IN THE HOUSE OF COMMONS

In the life of Parliament, many important events take place in some secrecy off the floor that are designed to influence events within the chamber itself. The public deliberations recorded in Hansard are but part of the whole process, the final product of the constant planning and plotting and preparation that takes place elsewhere. The strong undercurrent of secrecy concerns many affairs of Parliament; there are proscribed topics, meetings, and decisions that are not discussed publicly. The public is largely cut off from this other world of Parliament, and it has no direct access to the meetings of parties and their committees or of Select Committees, and vast areas of Westminster are not accessible to the public. It is true that other public bodies have what may be called a public and a private life, but what is of interest here is the nature of the distinction made by Parliament between what is public and what is not public and the effect of this distinction on its deliberations.

One of the factors leading to secrecy is the principle, mentioned earlier, that on questions of public policy, Parliament should be informed first; and it follows that the deliberations in Parliament should not be impaired by premature disclosures. It may therefore be argued that the confidential development of policy and of political tactics helps to preserve the autonomy of Parliament and sustains its right to make the final decision. There is another result of the operation of this principle: activities designed to inform, interest, or influence Parliament may be considered to be confidential, not to be discussed openly or published prematurely. The presumption of secrecy is found in many of the actions, records, and proceedings of the Government; in the meetings of Select Committees; in the activities of political parties and the negotiations carried on among Government, political parties, and private groups; in the activities of interest groups; and even in political reporting. One could include the proceedings of Parliament itself, which are open to the public by courtesy only and not by right. As Erskine May solemnly reports, 'By the ancient custom of Parliament and by the orders of both Houses, strangers are supposed not to be admitted while the Houses are sitting' and then lists the regulations governing the attendance of strangers.[1]

The confidential nature of many governmental activities directly affects Parliament. As a general proposition, when the Government submits legislation to Parliament for its consideration, a considerable amount of preparation will already have been made. The Government will have conferred with many interested groups; inquiries will have taken place; and adjustments will have been made in the proposals in order to secure all-round agreement. Although reports of these proceedings may later be printed, the preparation of the legislation may be carried on confidentially, without public awareness or participation at the time. In other words, the process of political compromise for securing consent may actually be pushed back a stage, from the legislative chambers into the confidential labyrinths of the bureaucracy.

The control of information by Government also affects the deliberations in Parliament. Much of the information on public policy is supplied by Government, and only rarely does Parliament attempt to mobilize information on its own. The Government not only supplies Parliament with a considerable amount of information but also controls its scope and flow, with the result that Members are constantly seeking information from Government on topics ranging, say, from weapons research to the authenticity of the Casement Diaries. Normally the consent of the Government is necessary if inquiries or investigations are to be undertaken, and part of the task of the Opposition (and of Private Members, too) is to force the Government to disclose information which it might not have disclosed otherwise, without this extra prodding.

The rule of secrecy also applies to the actions of the Select Committees of Parliament, and the rule here is that 'no act done at any committee should be divulged before the same be reported to the House.'[2] This restriction may help to preserve the autonomy of the committees, for it shields them from external influence in their deliber-

---

[1] *May's Treatise on the Law, Privileges, Proceedings and Usage of Parliament,* Fellowes and Cocks, eds., 16th ed., (London, 1957), p. 239.
[2] Ibid., p. 119.

ations, and it also reserves to Parliament the right to be informed first. However, the fact that the committees meet in camera means that neither the Members of Parliament nor the public hear the testimony of experts or the questioning of witnesses; they are unable to follow the proposals of the various groups and the defence made thereof. The committee reports, together with minutes of evidence, are ordinarily published in due course; however, the reports are not necessarily reported fully in the press; they are expensive to purchase, rarely accessible, and seldom debated. In short, the excellent work of Select Committees does not necessarily become a vital part of the life of Parliament or the discussions of the public.

The general air of secrecy surrounding the activities of political parties also has some bearing on the partisan manœuvres as they are unfolded in Parliament. The notices sent out by the Whip's Offices in the House of Commons are marked secret, for they may indicate the strategy of the party, the proceedings which the Whips believe to be particularly important, and the crucial times when Members are urged to be present. The parties play the game of secrecy with each other, and in a way this also adds to the zest and even the uncertainty of public deliberations. In theory the party meetings are also secret, although news does seep out. The element of privacy may help to preserve party solidarity since the internal discords of the party are to some extent concealed from public view. But the privacy of party meetings has another effect. Party committees on the Government side may question Ministers privately and one can argue that one of the more effective controls over Government takes place in private within the party. It may also be the place where the most effective influence can be exercised. Another by-product of secrecy is that it is not always easy to discover where the effective power lies, and the formal structure of the party may not in fact reveal the important influences within the parties.

The secrecy of party meetings may actually be protected by parliamentary rules applicable to official committees, where violations of secrecy are contemptuous actions and punishable as such; however the legal position of party meetings is not entirely clear. In any event, the Speaker once admonished a Member for disclosing events that had occurred at a private meeting of the Parliamentary Labour Party, and the House of Commons declared that it was a breach of privilege for a Member to profit financially by selling confidential information obtained from such a source.[1]

[1] The cases are those of Mr. Evelyn Walkden and Mr. Garry Allighan, 1947.

Free Speech and Public Policy

In the development of public policy, the normal avenue of approach is to consult the various interest groups concerned. However, the relationship between Members and the agents of interest groups is also affected by the secrecy that prevails over much of the extracurricular life of Parliament. In a debate on the Baking Industry Bill in February 1959, it developed that two Members had discussed the Bill with employers and the union in an attempt to reach an agreement between them. However, due to the general assumption of secrecy, the nature of the talks was not revealed. 'What happened at the negotiations?' Mr. Pannell asked. 'I do not think that those negotiations need be so private. We have been dragged on the Floor of the House (on a Friday morning), but we cannot say what took place in the presence of hon. Members.'[1]

The secrecy surrounding the other world of Parliament has led to special arrangements for reporting. The proceedings of Parliament are covered comprehensively by the regular reporters who sit in the press galleries and watch the proceedings below. There is also a special type of reporter known as the lobby correspondent, who has been given special rights to fish for news in parts of Westminster not open to the public and otherwise reserved for Members only. Information may be revealed confidentially to lobby correspondents, and news may also be leaked to the press in general. Secrecy, yes; but there is also constant gossip in corridors, lobbies, and reception rooms; and news, although not officially divulged, may nevertheless get around through the network of grapevine rumour and unofficial channels of communication that are part of the private life of Parliament.

THE CONTROLS

In the course of its history, Parliament has developed certain specific controls for influencing the action of Government and holding it responsible, for regulating society, raising issues, giving directions, and discussing policy, all of which give Parliament its pre-eminent position in British politics. Not only that. These methods of control and regulation are also used, with modification, by other legislatures, even where the relationships with Government are somewhat different, and everywhere they are now considered to be functions that Parliaments or legislatures should perform.

The debates on public policy are an example where Parliament has

[1] H. C. Deb., 13th February 1959, col. 1,536.

extended its interest into once forbidden areas and in so doing it has created new instruments for controlling the Government. These controls also include legislation; the various instruments of finance; the scrutiny of personnel; and, as a measure for maintaining its autonomy, the preservation of privileges. In practice, the emphasis in Parliament may move from one form of control to another: if it is inconvenient to change policy by legislation, there may be a debate on the major issues of the policy itself, or perhaps there will be criticism of the Minister for the way in which he is administering the law. Criticism of spending may take place during Question Time rather than during the formal consideration of the Estimates.

The trend during the present century has been for Parliament to establish influence over policy through debates and through ministerial responsibility, and there is less direct control over money and less reliance on the independent acquisition of facts. Parliament has shown considerable resiliency in establishing its supremacy, and it is not unlikely that new forms of control will be developed and that older forms now somewhat muted may be reasserted. One may note in particular the growing vigour of party committees in attempting to influence policy, personnel, and legislation; the search for more effective controls over nationalized industries; the desire on the part of some Members for Parliament to resume its function of criticizing the Estimates in detail; and the proposals for increasing the effectiveness of Special Committees and for making it possible for individual Members to become better informed.

In considering the historic development of some of these functions (as will be done here briefly and in subsequent chapters as well), one must be cautious in applying contemporary concepts to an earlier period, but with this disclaimer having been made, there is perhaps some advantage in taking a backward look to see how the controls have developed within the parliamentary system. In an earlier period, Parliament, bound by parochial interests, was not bold in expressing its opinion; and it was restrained from discussing the King's prerogative or the nature of judicial decisions or the policy of foreign governments. The timidity and deference of the Commons is shown by an incident occurring in 1323, when they demurred from advising Edward III on the conduct of the French wars. 'As to your war and the equipment necessary for it,' they said in answer to his request for advice, 'we are so ignorant and simple that we know not how, nor have the power, to devise.' Others should be consulted instead, and 'whatsoever shall be thus ordained by assent and agreement for you and your Lords we readily assent to.' This deference was not permanent, and later the Commons plucked together enough courage to debate the causes given by the King for summoning Parliament into session.[1]

Queen Elizabeth I objected to parliamentary debates on her marriage, on the succession to the crown, and on economic reform, but on one occasion a Member by the name of Peter Wentworth replied to these strictures in vigorous terms. 'There is nothing so necessary for the preservation of Prince and State as free speech,' he said, 'and without this it is a scorn and a mockery to call it a Parliament House, for in truth it is none but a very school of flattery and dissimulation. Two things, Mr. Speaker, do great hurt in this place: the one is a rumour that the Queen's Majesty liketh not such a matter—whosoever preferreth it, she will be offended with him; or the contrary. The other is a message sometimes brought into the House, desiring that this or that complaint should not be mentioned. He wishes such rumours and messages were buried with the father of them in hell!' Wentworth was punished by the Privy Council for his bluntness and committed to the Tower, but he was soon pardoned and reappeared in the House within a month.[2] The issue of freedom in parliamentary debate was not settled at this time, and the conflict continued under the Stuarts and under Cromwell. The Bill of Rights, however, contained a forthright assertion of the rights Parliament believed it should have, and the Ninth Article proclaims 'that the freedom of speech, and debates and proceedings in Parliament, ought not to be impeached or questioned in any court or place out of Parliament.'

The primary concern of Parliament is perhaps found in discussing policy; the major decisions may be made elsewhere and Parliament is not required to develop new legislation, but Parliament does insist on discussing the great issues of public policy and calling the attention of Government to specific discontents. It can be said in general that the restrictions on what Parliament may now consider are procedural, not topical. Procedures have been developed for raising specific questions or for discussing broad public policy, for interrupting the regular order of business so that immediate issues may be discussed, and for securing additional information through special inquiries. In all, Parliament spends about half of all available time in discussing policy with topics

[1] J. R. Green, *A Short History of the English People* (London, 1915 ed.), vol. 1, p. 218.
[2] G. Barnett Smith, *History of the English Parliament* (London, 1894, 2d ed.), vol. 1, pp. 341–43.

ranging in scope from those of general importance, which are given a so-called full-dress debate, to those exciting local interest only.

THE DEBATES: TECHNIQUE AND SUBSTANCE

The debates are the glory of Parliament, and one may conjure up in imagination the dramatic speeches made in a political crisis, or resounding clashes between partisan giants, or a vigorous, stinging debate which humiliates a Minister and defeats a Government. Some of the debates in the House of Commons live up to these stereotypes, and at their best the debates in Parliament are very good indeed. But the debates are uneven in quality, and they may vary also in the degree to which they attract the interest of Members and of the press. Deliberation in some form is carried on during the long hours of a daily session, but the nature of the deliberation changes considerably during this period. Members also carry on their own routine tasks during the deliberations; they talk to constituents and to each other, gossip and plan, secure information from the departments and attempt to influence their action, attend meetings and make speeches, and perhaps even make a living independently of Parliament.

A full and tense House of Commons may be enthralled in discussing a topic of compelling political interest and then, with a change of topic and speaker, it will pass quickly to a gentler, quieter period where only a score of Members are present and there are no forensic displays and no raised voices. In the first instance, the chamber may resound with the emotions and vituperation of partisanship, as rebukes and even insults are hurled across the aisle, but in the second instance there may be unity between the partisans, with sweet serenity everywhere.

In unravelling the strands of parliamentary debate, one can identify the topics, the personalities, and the occasions that call forth such uneven responses. The proceedings might be compared to a day's viewing of television, in which some of the performers and some of the programmes are more compelling than others. But the comparison soon ends, for the significance of parliamentary action is not always observable on the surface. What Parliament does is part of a broader scheme of action, and each topic considered is the continuation of an unfinished tale.

The speeches in the House of Commons tend to be conversational, and resort to the stentorian tones of an orator would be frowned upon. However, good speaking habits are prized, and a Minister is often judged by his behaviour when appearing before the House. In general, the House does not like to be lectured or treated in a disdainful or contemptuous manner. When the House is aroused and excited, a skilled debater may be able to command the chosen response; he may utter words which he knows will provoke the Opposition into a frenzy of protest and bring his own side up cheering, or alternatively, he may talk persuasively and convincingly and secure the support of the whole chamber. There may be hidden dangers in arousing the opposite side: an unhappy phrase may be pounced upon and given an embarrassing political twist, and even party colleagues may react coolly to some gaffe. If a Minister is seen to falter, part of the sport is to get him on the run, perhaps forcing him to withdraw in confusion with confessions of ignorance. The House shows little mercy in hounding out an irritating colleague, but the Member may save the day and his own reputation by a clever sally or by turning a phrase to his own advantage. The compelling and somewhat stylized deliberations in the House of Commons are enticing to observe for their own sake, regardless of the effect they may have on Government or the public or the careers of Members or the fate of the parties.

There has developed within Parliament a consensus of the relative significance of the various issues considered; of the weight to be attached to the words of those who take part in debate; and of the occasions when partisan attitudes should be expressed and when they should be muted. Pre-eminent attention is given to the major policy debate; where the party leaders participate, and the chamber is usually crowded. These debates are, in a way, 'staged' in the sense that the routine in the events, the persons concerned, and sometimes the arguments used, can be anticipated. The big debates are given wide publicity and often excite the emotions, but there are also quieter periods when the topics are of interest to fewer Members although the standard of debate may nevertheless be high. However, events cannot be planned with finality in a free legislature and there may be surprise revelations, interventions, or performances.

The debates in the House of Commons give an overall impression of spontaneity, and at the same time the debates are conducted so that some concrete action is taken. The impression of spontaneity is enhanced by the fact that speeches are not read; discussions are primarily conversational, with oratory roundly discounted; short interruptions are freely permitted; and the Member must be prepared to speak whenever he can catch the Speaker's eye. A high premium is placed on an interesting and lively speech, containing perhaps a quip or two to amuse one's colleagues and annoy the party opposite, and one test of an effective Member is his ability to hold the attention of the House. There is often an underlying structure of the debate which gives point to the deliberation. The debate is focused on a particular topic for which action must be taken; the debate does not simply consume time without leading anywhere.

In debate the Opposition has perhaps the greatest opportunity for flexibility and a change of pace. An Opposition speaker may rally the support of his own side by taunting the Government, and he may take seriously the bromide that the duty of the Opposition is to oppose; Government speakers will also wish to carry their own side enthusiastically, and this can often be done by making a partisan appeal, but it is incumbent on the Government also to try to carry the whole House on some issues. There are perils in irritating the Opposition.

Debates may be used strategically, as part of a broader plan of tantalizing the Government or outwitting the Opposition. There are a variety of techniques for delaying action, which make it difficult or, at most, uncomfortable to carry on deliberations, and one lengthy session in 1881 went on for two nights and lasted in all 41 hours and 30 minutes. The utility of the all-night session is abetted by the provincial customs of the London public transport system which comes to a halt at midnight when taxicabs increase their fares. If debate continues until midnight, the dread of walking home (for those without cars) may provide the necessary spur to continue the debate until the trains start running again. Mr. Chuter Ede, the former Leader of the House, claims to have participated in more all-night sessions than any other Member of Parliament. He finds that they serve a useful purpose and even claims to enjoy them! They act as a catharsis, he says, during a period of bad blood between the Government and the Opposition. The Opposition believes that the Government has acted in a high-handed fashion and the Government insists that it will have its way. The session proceeds in a predictable fashion, according to Mr. Ede. Between 2:00 and 4:00 a.m., there will be a political row; by six o'clock each side will think that it has made its point. Adjournment will come at eight or nine o'clock in the morning, with good will all around. Some of the clerical staff have (at some remote time in the past) anticipated the need to provide for their own comfort during an all-night session, and there are various beds and bedrooms scattered through the Palace and reserved for their use. There are no beds for the Members!

Deliberations are also used to further the ends of the political parties, and the influence of the parties over proceedings is so considerable that debate normally occurs under the aegis of the parties, or may be given a partisan slant. The parties may use the deliberations for strengthening their own solidarity, or weakening the opposite side, or appealing to the public. A ringing partisan speech may do less than justice to the subject under discussion, but it may succeed in binding the party to a common cause. During the 1958–59 session of Parliament, for instance, there was a prolonged debate over the Government's proposal to remove the restrictions on the number of cars that could be used in elections. The facts of the case were scarcely developed in the debate, and the issue would seem to have been the virtue of one party and the duplicity of the other.

The control of debate by two strong partisan groups, and the competition between them, adds a sporting touch to many of the deliberations and gives the debates in the House of Commons much of their thrust. Party leader faces party leader; party mass faces party mass. The fervour of partisanship sometimes leads to sallies and sounds not recorded (or recordable) in *Hansard*; taunts and rebukes may be tossed across the aisle, perhaps in the zest of good sport, but sometimes they are cutting, derisive, and insulting. The noises of the House of Commons are sometimes disconcerting, and I once noticed the bewilderment of two Indian girls in the gallery as, puzzled and embarrassed, they listened to the parliamentary roars coming up from the floor below. There is a strong sense of approval and disapproval within the House, and outrageous or simply unpopular statements may be given a noisy reception. At times, it seems as if a speaker must hold the floor physically against the mass of sounds which confront him.

People hold different views on the value of partisan debate and the extent to which its use is defensible. All Members are partisan, to a degree, but the harshness of partisan debate is more pronounced on some issues and with some Members and on some occasions. This exhibition of strong, unrelenting partisanship may, in fact, limit the usefulness of Members and make it less likely, say, that parliamentary commissions would be created to gather facts.

The unity of the partisans does not prevent the expression of differences within the party, and parties are more tolerant of defections in this regard than in voting. Under the broad aegis of parties, a variety of views are expressed, and Members speaking as nominal partisans can advance independent ideas of their own or the views of special groups. Sometimes they criticize the policy of their party although supporting it in the division lobby.

Free Speech and Public Policy

A disparity between one's expressed opinion and one's vote may suggest that the requirement of party loyalty makes it difficult for Members to be sincere. However, such an ambiguity is inherent in the democratic procedure of adjusting political conflict through debate. In the parliamentary process, Members are required to perform different functions; they not only are expected to speak up for their point of view but are also expected to come to a conclusion. The essence of the process within Parliament is the skill, judgment, and balance with which these various roles are played. If there were nothing but support and Members always agreed with the Government, it would be a very dull show indeed; and if there were nothing but criticism, leading to the withdrawal of support, Parliament would be ineffective.

The debates are a means by which views can be exchanged between the Government and its critics or supporters, and Members may attempt to influence Government policy by their speeches even though Parliament does not make any concrete decision on the issue. Some debates merely restate former positions, and Parliament does not always make a fresh appraisal every time an old topic is debated. One looks for subtle changes in attitude, or slight shifts in position, not necessarily some penetrating new analysis. Policy is clearly associated with personnel and ministerial responsibility, and the Opposition may shift the focus of its attention from one policy to another, and from one Minister to another, as it attempts to discover some weakness in the conduct of the Government.

In the various areas of public policy, a coterie of Members will normally have some specialized knowledge of the topic, and the policy committees of the parties also assist in promoting and developing this interest. Some debates are better informed and more illuminating than others; and some topics arouse considerable interest, particularly if they are spiced with a dash of partisanship: Suez; unemployment; pensions; nationalization; schools (grammar or multilateral). Labour relations are often contentious. When the subject of coal mines and coal-miners is up for discussion, some Members become effusive and sentimental, and their voice takes on a mellifluous quality.

In considering foreign policy, there are perhaps fewer parliamentary experts than one might expect, but increasingly parliamentary delegations are being sent to meetings of the Inter-Parliamentary Union, the Commonwealth Parliamentary Association, and the various European conferences. On the subject of defence, there is the constant problem of acquiring sufficient information to make an intelligent evaluation of Government policy, and in certain technical areas of defence, particularly relating to aviation, Mr. de Freitas, on the Labour benches, always seems to be remarkably well informed. In the realm of scientific and technological development, the Parliamentary and Scientific Committee attempts to keep up with developments. Legal debates, more frequent in committees than on the floor, are popular with some Members and are boring to others.

So-called constituency debates have an uneven popularity, but many Members like to participate in them and contribute their own specialized knowledge. In view of the extensive control exercised by the Central Government, one may learn a good deal about British local government from such debates. Regional interests are expressed in debates on cotton manufacturing, coal-mining, fishing, shipping and ship-building, agriculture, and the like, and the badgering often suffered by the Government when such topics are discussed, is administered with bi-partisan impartiality. The Scottish fishing industry seems to be without political bias and willingly seeks the aid of whatever Government will lend a hand or whatever Member will lend an ear. Herring always gets a hearing!

Debates initiated by Private Members may be used to dramatize a political issue: for example, for several years Mr. Norman Dodds, a Labour Member, and Dr. Donald Johnson, a Conservative, acted as a team in calling Parliament's attention to the procedures followed in committing patients to mental hospitals. Many of the minor debates are concerned with charges of administrative shortcomings, and occasionally, as in the Crichel Down case, such a topic will command wide public interest. There is considerable concern in Parliament that rights be respected and correct procedures followed, and in this area of action Parliament has a strong conscience and a free voice.

QUESTIONS

One of the easiest and most popular methods of raising a point is found in question time, and a question may in some cases lead to further discussions and debates. Every day five or six Ministers are interrogated, in rotation, and about 130 questions are set down, of which about half are answered. Much of the information disclosed at question time could be produced in a letter, but the question period also provides an opportunity for Members to observe the behaviour of the Minister when he is under some pressure.

Free Speech and Public Policy

Considerable preparation goes into the first hour of a daily session of the House of Commons, when questions are answered. Complaints may flow into Parliament from all sections of Great Britain, and from the colonies as well: the Members sift the complaints and prepare the questions, which are then vetted by the parliamentary staff; the departments review their policy and prepare an answer; the Minister is briefed, with suggested answers for any supplementary questions that may be anticipated. During the time for asking questions the chamber is usually crowded, for the period is informative and engaging; it gives rise to interesting exchanges and arguments, and the supplementary questions often provide the occasion for a witty observation or a deflating partisan thrust. The practice of asking and answering questions, pertinent and impertinent, is a developed art. Strict rules govern the form of the question and the nature of the subject matter, and it may be a test of skill to phrase the question, or the supplementary, in such a fashion that a Minister reveals more than he intended to. Some Members have developed their own technique for getting under the skin of a Minister, and Ministers have also perfected certain protective devices for defending themselves. For example:

'That point will not be overlooked.'

'That is a separate Question, which I should like to see on the Order Paper.'

'I cannot yet add to the statement made on 20th January by my right hon. Friend.'

'I indicated that in an Answer last week.'

'I have nothing new to say on this subject at present.'

'I am not in a position to make a statement today.'

'No, Sir.'

And Members can protest:

'In view of the unsatisfactory nature of the Answer to this very serious Question, I propose to take steps to raise this matter on the Adjournment as early as possible.'

'On a point of order. He tries to avoid supplementary questions by asking for other Questions to be put down, simply because he is totally unaware of the answers. Is not this most unsatisfactory?'

'(Members: "Answer!")'

'(Members: "Resign!")'

Free Speech and Public Policy

Earl Winterton tells in his parliamentary memoirs how, as Minister, he once choked off a persistent questioner.

'My principal Conservative opponent was a charming and genial, if not highly intelligent, old gentleman called Colonel Yates, M.P. for Melton Mowbray. He enjoyed a reputation in the House, where he was very popular, as an expert on Indian affairs—a qualification denied him by some of his contemporaries in the Indian Army. Knowing that his constant denigration of Lord Reading and the Government of India was doing harm, I decided to put him in his place and gave a very offensive but effective reply to one of his supplementaries. Almost the whole Conservative Party roared its disapproval, the Press criticized me next day, and Colonel Yates sat red, gasping and at a loss for any retort. From henceforth he tackled me more warily.'[1]

NATIONALIZED INDUSTRIES

The creation of nationalized industries, which have special independent status, has posed the problem of the extent to which their administration can be debated in Parliament. Mr. Butler once made the laconic remark that 'The relationship of Parliament to the Nationalized Industries has always been a difficult one. It perplexed the serene intelligence of one of my predecessors as Leader of the House, Mr. Morrison, who is still interested in it, and it has perplexed me, and I think it perplexes the House.'[2] There is the fear that parliamentary interest, or interference, as some would call it, would break down the present relationship with nationalized industry by unfair criticism or restrictive controls, and there is general (but not universal) agreement that day-to-day operations of the industry should not fall within the competence of Parliament. On the other hand, Parliament has a legitimate concern with the actions of the nationalized industries inasmuch as they involve questions of prices and price-fixing, of the effects of the industries on the economy, and of the desirability of extending or contracting the scope of their activities.

One reaction of Parliament has been to create a Select Committee on Nationalized Industries, composed of thirteen Members, and the Committee has interpreted its function primarily in terms of securing in-

[1] Earl Winterton, *Orders of the Day* (London, 1953), p. 113.
[2] H. C. 276 (1959), p. 38.

formation of value to the House and of investigating 'certain points which seemed to be of importance.'[1] Its reports have dealt with Treasury Control of the Nationalized Industries; the North of Scotland Hydro-Electric Board; the National Coal Board; the British Overseas Airways Corporation, and the British European Airways Corporation.

The committee would like to have additional assistance for making economic and statistical studies of the industries, but there are parliamentary (and constitutional) difficulties in employing even a small research staff for the committee. It is thought to be undesirable to employ Civil Servants, in view of the principle that separation between Parliament and the Executive 'should be clear and complete',[2] and neither the Clerk of the House nor the Librarian employs specialized talent of the kind required. In the old days, Mr. Butler reflected, Members were competent to deal with political matters or (with the aid of the Clerk of the House) with procedural matters. 'Now we are attempting to combine politics and economics and we find . . . that the new demands on the human brain have outstripped the panoply of clerks which was provided for us. . . . So that it is the new world which is catching up with the old, and we therefore have to think very deeply.'[3]

Parliamentary criticism of the nationalized industries is sometimes resented, and in a later chapter there is a discussion of an extraordinary controversy which developed between the London Electricity Board and Mr. G. R. Strauss (Lab.). There was also an incident in 1957 when Mr. Gerald Nabarro (Cons.) criticized what he termed the 'endless extravagance of the State boards, headed by the N.C.B. (National Coal Board).' Mr. Wilfred L. Miron, the deputy chairman of the Coal Board's East Midlands Division, took umbrage at these words and had some hard things to say of Mr. Nabarro personally. 'This gentleman, this political hoodlum, this Kidderminster carpet bagger,' he said, 'thinks that in the rarified atmosphere of Whitehall he can conduct the affairs of the coal-mining industry.' However, Mr. Nabarro held his fire and did not answer back: 'This is the first time any ministerially-appointed representative of a nationalized undertaking has personally attacked a Member of Parliament for views he has expressed on the ministerial conduct of the undertaking,' he said. 'It seems to me that as these people are ministerially appointed they are largely in the same position as civil servants. Constitutionally, I would be quite wrong in replying to this attack by direct reference in a speech or Press statement

[1] Ibid., p. iii.　　　　[2] Ibid., p. 45.　　　　[3] Ibid., p. 43.

to what has been said about me.'[1] The Minister, Lord Mills, wrote a reprimanding letter to the Coal Board.

THE DEBATES IN THE HOUSE OF LORDS

One hears a considerable amount of good talk in the debates in the House of Lords, and although it would be going too far to say that everyone who participates in debate is necessarily an expert, the competence of the participants is nevertheless very high, and those Peers who may have nothing in particular to contribute are awed or shamed into silence. The routine business of the House of Lords does not consume much time, and as a result there is considerable time available for the leisurely consideration of public issues. The House of Lords has accepted its constitutional position and it permits the House of Commons to exercise the greater impact on legislation: to determine its content, to propose amendments, and to put the legislation in final shape. However, the Lords fulfil the function of a revising chamber by amending some legislation, but they are rarely headstrong in insisting on having their own way. The general docility of the House of Lords in going along with the Government is such that on an occasion in 1959 when Mr. Bevan wanted a free vote on the Gambling Bill, he argued that if the Government were defeated in the House of Commons, everything could be put right in the House of Lords! Sometimes, however, the Lords do take a strong stand, and in 1956 they defeated the Death Penalty Abolition Bill by a vote of 238–95. The Bill had been passed by the House of Commons on a free vote and against the wishes of the Government. The fact that an unusually large number of Peers voted on this measure has helped to create and preserve the popular (and to a considerable extent, fallacious) image of 'backwoodsmen' pouring into the House of Lords when occasion demands to vote against progressive measures. The House of Lords occasionally asserts its authority on minor matters, but on the whole it is not a troublesome and irresponsible body which creates special problems for the Government to sort out.

The House of Lords has developed a role which, in many ways, is complementary to that of the House of Commons. In gathering power unto itself, the House of Commons has become enmeshed in all types of political activity, including the struggle of power to form the Government. It supplies most of the Ministers; it is the centre of the network

[1] *Daily Telegraph*, 22nd, 23rd July 1957.

of partisan politics; and it has exclusive control over finance. The deliberations of the House of Lords, by contrast, are less restricted by the cumbersome details of the execution of policy or legislation, and the Peers are less affected by the exigencies of political competition. The House of Lords has more freedom to consider questions of public policy, to the envy of some Members of the Commons who themselves would like the House of Commons to spend more time on debates of this nature. Some might argue that the House of Lords is without influence because its political power is restricted, but this thesis would be difficult to prove.

Primarily the House of Lords provides a forum where public questions are discussed, and the membership is large enough to provide a cluster of interested specialists on the various topics considered. One may note, for example, the debate in 1959 on a motion introduced by Earl Jellicoe, proposing that the Western nations develop 'a definite, long-term and consistent policy towards those countries which lie outside the Atlantic Community. . . .'[1] The topic was discussed by a number of Peers who could claim some special knowledge on the topic: a former Minister in the Colonial Office and the Commonwealth Relations Office; a lecturer on international affairs; the editor of an international journal; the head of an international group for aiding refugees; a former Secretary of a British Embassy; several high-ranking military officers with experience in the underdeveloped areas; and a Government Minister. Earl Jellicoe, the son of the former Admiral of the Fleet, has himself spent a number of years in the British Foreign Service.

The debates in the House of Lords tend to be structured. A Lord who wishes to speak on a motion will drop a note to the Secretary of the Leader of the House of Lords indicating his intentions; the order of the speakers will then be arranged by the Whips and a list of the proposed speakers will be circulated in advance of the meeting. There is normally time enough available for all who wish to speak to do so, and if there is an unusually long list, the session will usually continue until everyone has spoken. The rule that a Lord cannot speak more than once on a topic means that debate is automatically terminated when the supply of Peers is exhausted.

On the whole, the debates in the House of Lords are good tempered, and there is a certain elegance of courtly expression which raises even a tedious debate above the level of the humdrum and serves as a shield against political vituperation. The gentle admonitions in Rule 29 of the

[1] H. L. Deb., 20th July 1959, col. 225.

Standing Orders ('Asperity of speech to be avoided') are delicately phrased: 'To prevent misunderstanding, and for avoiding of offensive speeches, when matters are debating . . . it is for honour sake thought fit, and so ordered, That all personal, sharp, or taxing speeches be forborn, and whosoever answereth another man's speech shall apply his answer to the matter without wrong to the person: and as nothing offensive is to be spoken, so nothing is to be ill taken. . . .' Similar admonitions are found in Rule 30, 'for avoiding of all mistakes, unkindnesses, or other differences which may grow to quarrels, tending to the breach of peace, it is ordered . . .' One finds in the House of Lords a practised deftness of speaking which may disarm an opponent with a compliment, and one new Life Peer, a veteran of the political wars of the House of Commons, where meanings are less disguised, said that it was 'a totally new experience . . . to sit and listen to debates without being aware that blows have been struck until I read the same speeches in *Hansard* the next morning.'[1]

However, it should not be implied that there is no partisanship, no emotion, and no anger, and that all speeches fulfil the expectations of Rules 29 and 30. Men grate on each other's nerves, as in other public assemblies, and some Noble Lords irritate other Noble Lords.

Lord X. After accusing Lord Y of misreading figures on unemployment, said: 'But perhaps he likes worrying people and causing anxiety among the people.'

Lord Y. 'It is about time you stopped being insulting.'

After Lord X had finished his speech, Lord Y said he should like the Noble Peers to know 'how thankful I am now, looking back, for my membership at birth of the working class and how I did not have to go to Oxford University to be a bully.'

Several Noble Lords: 'Order, order!'[2]

The Lord Chancellor performs several functions in the deliberations; although he also bears the title of Speaker of the House of Lords, his functions are quite different from those of his opposite number in the House of Commons. At times he is a moderator, merely granting the floor to the various Lords who wish to speak, but he is also permitted to address the chamber. When making a motion, for instance, he steps two or three paces forward from his seat on the woolsack and a step to the

---

[1] Lord Stonham, H. L. Deb., 11th November 1958, col. 648.
[2] H. L. Deb., 11th March 1959, col. 1,104, 1,111, 1,112.

left, then turns around and addresses the empty woolsack which he has just vacated. When the House of Lords transposes itself into the Committee on the Whole, the Lord Chancellor again changes hats, or at least removes his wig, and joins his colleagues on the Government Front Bench.

An interesting characteristic of the House of Lords is that the discipline over the debate is provided by the Peers themselves, not by the Lord Chancellor. The discipline takes the form of a stern, persistent call of 'Order' which may develop such volume and so great an intensity of feeling that the offending Peer is forced to withdraw. On one occasion in 1959 when Viscount Malvern (formerly Sir Godfrey Huggins, the Prime Minister of the Federation of Rhodesia and Nyasaland) was speaking, his reference to the actions of a former Colonial Secretary displeased the late Viscount Stansgate, who attempted to intervene. Viscount Stansgate was a short, brusque man with pronounced views and a mercurial temper, and it could be said of him (as of another person on another occasion) that the underdog held him on a short leash. He was born in 1877 as William Wedgwood Benn and elected to the House of Commons as a Liberal in 1906; he transferred his allegiance to the Labour Party in 1928 and was called up to the House of Peers in 1941. On this occasion he did not like what he heard, but Viscount Malvern would not give way. Here was a contest between two political veterans, and both had very strong wills indeed. Viscount Malvern kept the floor. Viscount Stansgate persisted in intervening, trying to force Viscount Malvern to give way. The chamber was crowded, and loud shouts of 'Order' came up from the back benches.

Lord Home, then the Leader of the House of Lords, attempted unsuccessfully to re-establish harmony, but Viscount Stansgate kept on talking. Only snatches of his remarks could be heard above the general uproar and the cacophonous calls for Order. At the end of the noisy interchange, the official debate records the following:

Viscount Stansgate: 'A gross breach of the practice of the two Houses.'
Viscount Alexander of Hillsborough: 'Hear, hear!'
A Noble Lord: 'Do not take any notice. It is quite irrelevant.'[1]

And then Viscount Malvern was permitted to continue his speech.

The political organization of the House of Lords is neither so formal nor so structured as that in the House of Commons. There is a Govern-

[1] H. L. Deb., 24th March 1959, col. 256–257.

ment Front Bench and an Opposition Front Bench, but the membership is not highly organized nor is it thrust into a constant competitive struggle for status and recognition and achievement. Considerable emphasis is placed on individual performance and competence, without these achievements being necessarily or directly associated with the struggle for political power.

Following the General Election of 1959, the political structure of the House of Lords was as follows:

	GOVERNMENT	OPPOSITION
Admiralty		
First Lord	Lord Carrington	
Agriculture, Fisheries and Food		
Joint Parliamentary Sec.	Earl Waldegrave	
Colonies		
Minister of State	Earl of Perth	
Commonwealth Relations		
Secretary of State	*Earl of Home	
Foreign Affairs		
Jt. Parl. Under-Secretary of State	Marquess of Lansdowne	
Lord Chancellor	*Viscount Kilmuir	
Lord President of the Council	*Earl of Home	
Lord Privy Seal	*Viscount Hailsham	
Minister without Portfolio	Earl of Dundee	
Paymaster General	*Lord Mills	
Scotland	Lord Craigton	
Transport		
Joint Parliamentary Sec.	Lord Chesham	
Welsh Affairs		
Minister of State	Lord Brecon	
Floor Leaders		
Leader	*Earl of Home	Viscount Alexander of Hillsborough
Chief Whip	Earl St. Aldwyn	Earl of Lucan

*Member of the Cabinet

The legislative restrictions are such that, in effect, a certain number of Lords must be included in the composition of the Government. However, there is no specific quota for the House of Lords. The restrictions, rather, are on the total number of Ministers who are eligible to sit in the House of Commons. If all appointments were filled, the number of Ministers and junior Ministers who would be eligible to sit in the House of Commons would be roughly seventy-two out of a total of seventy-eight. The Lord Chancellor, alone among the Ministers, is expressly barred from sitting in the House of Commons.

CHAPTER VI

The Controls: Legislation

Legislation is now one of the chief instruments for expressing policy and regulating the internal relations of society, and this particular control has played such an important historic role that the derivative word legislature is used to describe some types of parliamentary assemblies. However, the function of Parliament is not now, and historically has not been, restricted to making law, and the fact that Parliament has other techniques in its arsenal of control gives it great resiliency and strength. There are limitations on the extent to which some types of policy can be formulated in terms of law, and legislation is often a cumbersome method for expressing purpose. Once granted power, the Executive becomes the effective agency for making rules, and delegated legislation, in turn, may also be a difficult object to control.

The reign of the Tudors marks the period when Parliament began consciously to create new law; this specific function, newly recognized, developed from Parliament's more traditional practice of presenting petitions to the King for his approval. As a high court, Parliament was interested in clarifying the law, and petitions for changes in the law could be submitted by Parliament to the King. The petition thus clarified and to some extent modified the common law of the land. If one now substitutes a written Bill for an oral petition, it can be seen how easily the transition was made; how the purposeful creation of legislation, in the modern sense of the term, developed from the earlier period when Parliament was an agent in securing the King's consent.

The consent of Parliament to a petition was required, as well as that of the King, and a petition of 1465 uses the phrase, 'advis and assent of the Lordes Spirituell and Temporell and the Commons in this youre present Parliament assembled.' (There is an echo of this phraseology in the American Constitution, where the President is required to secure

The Controls: Legislation

'the advice and consent of the Senate' in making treaties and appointments.) The principle developed that law could be changed only on request of Parliament, although the King was not obliged to make every change requested by Parliament ('but that it stand in the freedom of your prerogatives to grant which of those that you please and to pass over the remainder').[1] As a matter of prerogative, however, the King might make decisions on other matters without asking Parliament.

The place of the petition in Parliament (once the making of law had been regularized) has had an uneven history. If one thinks of petition in a general sense, then it can be said that thousands of people besiege Parliament annually with their grievances and that Members take up the grievances with the Ministers. The more modern terms are lobbies and pressures. Used in the formal, procedural sense, petitions have fallen into desuetude as a method for calling the attention of Government to grievances. Petitions are still used, however, in private Bill legislation, and they play an integral part in the process. Lord Campion has written that in the early part of the nineteenth century the presentation of petitions 'offered a convenient method of raising any subject desired' and 'threatened to become the sole business of Parliament.'[2] But such is not the case now. Strict rules control the form and presentation of public petitions, and after presentation they are deposited in a large cloth bag hanging conveniently on the back of the Speaker's Chair. From there, they are referred to the Committee on Public Petitions, and hence to the relevant Ministry. Petitions may, however, be used for propaganda schemes, where the shape or size of the petition, or the number of

[1] A petition of the Commons presented to Henry V in 1414 describes the ideal relationship that should exist between the King and his Commons in making law and calls attention to some of the irregularities in current practice. The following extract contains modifications in spelling: 'Our Sovereign Lord, your subjects that have come for the Commons (Commune) of your land beseech you: That inasmuch as it has ever been their liberty and freedom that no statute nor law should be made unless they give their assent thereto, considering that the Commons of your land, that which is and ever has been a member of your Parliament, and have been Assenters as well as Petitioners, that from this time forward by complaint of the Commons of any mischief, seeking remedy by mouth of their Speaker for the Commons or else by written petition, that no laws be made and engrossed as Statute and Law, neither by additions, diminutions, or any manner or terms which would change the sentence and intent . . . without the assent of the aforesaid Commons. Considering, our Sovereign Lord, that it is not in any way the intention of your Commons . . . but that it ever stand in the freedom of your Prerogatives to grant which of those that you please and to pass over the remainder . . .' From H. L. Gray, *The Influence of the Commons on Early Legislation* (Cambridge, Mass., 1932), pp. 261–2; R. P. IV, 22.

[2] Campion, *An Introduction to the Procedure of the House of Commons* (London, 1958, 3d ed.), p. 38.

petitioners, or the method of transferring the petition and conveying it to Westminster is stressed instead of the legal form in which it is couched.

The division that developed in Parliament between public legislation and private legislation still survives, and the latter is concerned with special powers for private groups, such as municipal corporations. A distinction is also made between public Bills sponsored by Government and those sponsored by Private Members, although from the point of view of public law they are the same. The right of Private Members to sponsor legislation, with some hope that it might be enacted, is a contentious issue; parliamentary time is required as well as the helpful assistance of the Government, and the Government is often niggardly on both counts. One also suspects that the departmental bureaucracies would not approve the extension to Private Members of what they often consider to be their prerogative.

The general process for considering legislation has now been highly stylized. There is the introduction and First Reading, followed by the Second Reading (debate of principles); the Committee stage (amendments considered); the Report stage (consideration of amended Bill), and Third Reading (final approval or disapproval). In considering public Bills, the general theory prevails that the two Houses should discuss the main principles of the legislation, permitting committees to consider the legislation in greater detail. With minor exceptions, the procedure in both Houses is similar, although in the House of Lords public Bills are not referred to a small committee but to the Committee of the Whole House. In considering private legislation, however (and in considering judicial appeals in the House of Lords), the committee system is especially important.

Considerable attention is given to the form of the final legislative document inasmuch as the law must give unambiguous directions and must also be enforceable by the courts. An effort is made to bring all legislation up to an acceptable standard of uniformity and conciseness, and there are procedures for rejecting amendments that are not procedurally correct. In preparing legislation, the Government is assisted initially by a Cabinet Legislative Committee and, at the technical level, by the Parliamentary Counsel. Private Members and Peers have no drafting service, although in special circumstances the Clerk of the House of Commons and the Lord Chancellor may offer assistance.

Parliament has some control over rules made by Government departments and a restricted category of regulations must be laid before Parliament before they go into effect. Additional control was developed in

1944 when a Select Committee on Statutory Instruments was created. The Committee has limited powers, however; it cannot consider questions of policy and it has no sources of information independent of the Government. Parliament spends comparatively little time debating administrative rules.

THE REPEAL OF THE RESTRICTIONS ON THE USE OF CARS IN ELECTIONS

For an example of the manner in which Parliament considers legislation, we have selected the Bill repealing the restrictions on the use of cars in elections, which was enacted in the early weeks of the 1958–59 session of Parliament. This legislation is not necessarily representative or typical, but the partisanship so obvious in this particular debate is a facet of parliamentary life; it is sometimes muted but always present and may flare up dramatically on some occasions. The legislation also illustrates the manner in which attempts are made to secure bipartisan understanding and co-operation on the more prickly partisan topics (and what happens when this procedure fails).

Legislation is frequently debated in Parliament with partisan vigour, but on some topics, where the partisans themselves are directly involved in the legislation, or where the issue might split the society into bickering factions, an attempt is made to remove the nettle by securing an agreement between the parties before the issue is debated publicly. An instance of this nature was the agreement reached by private conferences in 1959 on the extent of state aid to be provided for religious schools. Public controversy over the topic, it was thought, might revive old antagonisms and create a feeling of bitterness between religious groups, and many of the important agreements on the legislation were reached in private. There seems to be a tendency in British political life to draw away from the precipice, the point of no return, and to keep political discussions within tolerable bounds.

When Parliament considered electoral legislation in 1958, there had been no prior agreement between the parties and, indeed, the restrictions which were repealed had been added to the law at an earlier period by a partisan majority. The issue in 1958 was of relatively minor significance, and as a political issue it seems to have been soon forgotten and was not a controversial topic in the General Election which took place within a year. However, when the legislation was debated in Parliament, there were many tense and angry moments, and some political tempers were at fever heat.

The 1958 episode was a sequel to the events of ten years earlier when the Labour Government sponsored the Representation of the People Bill. This legislation grew out of proposals made by the Speaker's Conference on Electoral Reform and by the Committee on Electoral Reform under the chairmanship of Sir Cecil Carr, and in both instances there was bipartisan representation and consultation. As it happened, neither of these preparatory groups recommended restrictions on the use of cars in elections (although the opinion was not unanimous), and the Labour Government itself did not recommend any limitations when it presented the measure to Parliament. However, pressure began to develop from the Labour back benches to limit the number of cars that could be used on polling day. It was argued that otherwise the Conservatives would have an advantage, and some Labour Members objected in particular to the special arrangements made by Conservatives for conveying old people to the polls. 'These cars would go to the local hospitals and old people's homes,' Mr. John Hynd (Lab.) explained, and 'bring in the halt, the lame, and the blind all day long.' It was generally believed, he said, that the preponderance of cars used by the Conservatives 'was one of the greatest weapons which that party had on polling day.'[1] The Labour Government capitulated to the back-bench pressure, and amendments were added which restricted a candidate for Parliament to the use of one car for every 1,500 electors in a country constituency and one for every 2,500 electors in a borough constituency. All cars so used had to carry a placard indicating that they were duly registered. A contravention of the provisions was an illegal practice.

In applying these restrictions, Mr. Gordon Walker explained, 'We were creating equality by taking away party advantage from the Conservatives.'[2] And Mr. Diamond, another Labour Member, developed the principle that no party should have any advantage over other parties, 'even though that may mean that some voters are inconvenienced or even prevented from getting to the poll.'[3]

The restrictions created special problems for the party managers, who were compelled to secure and register the requisite number of cars and to use them exclusively for transporting voters on Polling Day. In operation, the restrictions worked unevenly and sometimes capriciously.

[1] House of Commons Debates (London, H.M.S.O.), 18th November 1958, col. 1,044.
[2] Ibid., col. 1,068.
[3] Ibid., 25th November 1958, col. 277.

People who customarily rode to work in a car pool might find they had broken the law if the car stopped at a polling booth to permit the occupants to vote. It was also suggested in the debates that it was possible to get around the law by various ruses; for instance, voters could be transported to a spot near the polling booth, then permitted to walk the remaining distance. Detection of violations was difficult and convictions few, and in one by-election, there was insufficient evidence to warrant prosecution in any of the thirty-one complaints which were investigated. In fourteen of these cases, the complainants withdrew their allegations on discovering that they had made charges about the conduct of a member of their own party.[1] The casual, even anomalous, nature of the proposal was shown by the failure of the Labour Government to apply similar restrictions on the use of cars in municipal or county elections.

The new legislation also irritated many Conservatives who thought that, in the name of equality, Labour had attempted to gain partisan advantage, and the law was branded by Sir Henry d'Avigdor-Goldsmid, a Conservative M.P., as 'a piece of manufactured class indignation.'[2] The restrictions were irritating and vexatious, a symbol of partisan spite which should be repealed now that the Conservatives were again in power. Resolutions to repeal the provisions were submitted repeatedly at Conservative Party Conferences, but they were resisted by the party leaders who said that it was desirable to secure an agreement between all parties when changes were made in the electoral law. In the summer of 1958, Mr. Butler approached the leaders of the Parliamentary Labour Party and proposed that the restrictions be repealed, but he was unable to get their consent. The minutes of these conversations have not been published, but the Labour leaders may have been held to their position by the same elements in the party who advocated the restrictions initially. The focus can now be shifted to the Conservative Party Conference, held in Blackpool in October 1958, where it was again proposed that the restrictions be repealed. Mr. Butler now consented. It was still desirable, he said, that the parties should agree on such a course of action, but failing that, Parliament would be asked to remove what he later called 'an excrescence on the electoral law.'

The Government was now prepared to repeal the restriction, but the Queen's speech at the opening of the parliamentary session did not include this proposal. Later, during the more partisan phases of the debate, the Government was criticized for this omission, and Mr. Rich-

[1] Ibid., 5th November 1958, col. 1,070.
[2] Ibid., 18th November 1959, col. 1,053.

ard Crossman (Lab.) said that the proposal 'was too dirty and shameful to put into her Majesty's mouth.'[1] The Prime Minister shortly announced the Government's plan to repeal the restrictions during the Debate on the Address, and he chided the Labour Party for having held on to an old-fashioned attitude towards the motor car. Messrs. Gaitskell and friends, he said, were backward looking and out of date; 'they seem to regard a motor-car as a kind of perquisite of rich men, the things we used to go about in, with ladies in veils and all the rest of it.' And then he mimed, making a gesture as if describing a ride in a surrey with the fringe on top.[2]

Mr. Butler presented the Bill to the House of Commons, giving a reasoned defence for repealing the restrictions, which he found to be 'misconceived in principle and unsatisfactory in practice.' He regretted that it had not been possible to reach agreement with the party opposite on the topic. He found that the law was out of accord with present conditions; that it was not necessary in order to secure fair play between the parties; that it caused inconvenience to candidates of all parties and to the electorate; and that it brought the law into contempt. On one occasion Mr. Butler wryly teased the Opposition, saying that of the twenty persons who had been convicted for breaking the law, eighteen would appear to be Labour; the figures suggested to him that the party opposite was 'finding it more difficult than any other party to live with the restrictions which itself invented, and we may be doing what is really in its best interest by repealing the Section.'[3] In all it was a clear and unemotional speech, with Mr. Butler in command of his topic and his audience.

The calmness of the debate did not last long. Mr. Ellis Smith, a Labour Member, made a surprising interjection which could be interpreted either as a veiled threat of violence or as an example of heavy-handed humour. He proposed that Mr. Butler should use his influence with the police 'to acquiesce in the workers on Election day taking the same action as students take on their rag day.' He was not threatening disorder, he said, but 'if it is correct for the police and the Home Secretary to acquiesce in what the students do on rag day, then it will be correct for the working class to take certain action in regard to the cars being used against the people on Election day.'[4]

The debate was shortly given an unexpected turn by Mr. Gordon

[1] Ibid., col. 985.
[2] Ibid., 27th October 1958, col. 28.
[3] Ibid., 5th November 1958, col. 960–961.
[4] Ibid., 5th November 1958, col. 961–2.

Walker, and the new issue temporarily diverted the attention of the House of Commons from the cars-in-election topic. He announced that he had evidence showing 'that the facilities of Government Departments are being used for party political purposes.'[1] A pamphlet entitled *A Nation of Council Tenantry*, published by the Rented Homes Campaign, had been distributed, he said, 'with the direct aid of government official facilities.' Two envelopes were displayed, one sent out in the normal course of business by the Ministry of Housing and Local Government and one which had contained the pamphlet. Both envelopes bore stick-on labels and, according to Mr. Gordon Walker, having an identical address, identical type, and produced by the same addressograph with identical code references.[2]

Mr. Gordon Walker enlarged on his topic, proceeding from the label story to an attack on the publicity activities of the Conservative Party. A public relations firm whom they had employed had turned the Prime Minister into a 'varnished man', he said, and the Prime Minister was now in the curious company of other commercial products, 'rubbing shoulders with Chocolate Penguins, Lyons Ready-Mixes, Munch-mallows, Payne's Poppets and Amplex.' This process of Americanization had been carried to the completion by the Conservatives. 'No decent person in Britain wants to see us brought down to the level of American electioneering with all its high-pressure salesmanship.'[3]

There was now a question whether Labour had discovered some indiscretion on the part of Government. If the evidence were authentic, what did it mean? Could the Government have blundered so badly as to permit the facilities of the departments to be used by propaganda agencies and pressure groups? There had been coy hints for several days that the Labour Party knew more than it would reveal, and some people appeared to be playing a tantalizing game with the Government. The *Daily Herald* had published an article on the misuse of envelopes, but according to statements made in Parliament it had not published the Government's denial of misdoing. Mr. Mitchison (Lab.) had put down a question on the use of envelopes, but it had been taken off the Order Paper before it had been answered.

The sticky label incident, as it was named, was investigated at once by Sir Norman Brook, the head of the Civil Service, and an explanation was soon printed as a Government White Paper.[4] The incident had occurred in the following fashion: A former civil servant, now working

[1] Ibid., col. 971. [2] Ibid., col. 972.
[3] Ibid., col. 977. [4] Cmnd. 583, 1958–59.

for the Association of Land and Property Owners, had asked an officer in the Press section of the Ministry of Housing and Local Government for a copy of the mailing list used by that section for sending out official material to those who were interested in housing questions. He was furnished with the material, partly in the form of a duplicated list, partly in the form of pre-addressed economy labels. Subsequently the list was made available to Rented Homes Campaign, and, to save time, an employee had used about one hundred stick-on labels after cutting off the top portion, 'On Her Majesty's Service'. No pamphlet had been sent out by the Government. The report said that the press officer had acted unwisely and had been reprimanded; the former civil servant had been less than frank and should have been more scrupulous. This was the end of the case, and it played no further part in the debate on the use of cars in elections.

Now another stratagem was employed, this time by Colonel George Wigg, who during the debate succeeded in a parliamentary manœuvre of 'spying strangers', which had the result of clearing the public galleries. The ancient procedure for spying strangers developed in the days when proceedings were secret in fact, and it is now used as a device for enabling the House of Commons to go into a secret session. In spying strangers, Colonel Wigg apparently acted impetuously, without the advice or approval of the leaders of his own party, and his strange move surprised the House. The public was forced to leave the galleries and neither observers nor press and shorthand reporters were permitted to hear the debate. The Official Reports contain the laconic notation:[1]

8.27 p.m.
    Strangers withdrew—
    The House rose at twenty-nine minutes past Ten o'clock.

The incident, according to one journal, was a bit of Wiggery Pokery. Ironically, with the galleries cleared, the House finished debating the Bill more quickly than anticipated.

During the debate, the Labour Members 'played poor', and it was implied that the Labour Party had no money and no cars and no newspapers to support them. The Conservatives were roundly abused. To Mr. Crossman, the Bill was 'a crooked and dirty measure', and Labour would 'see that the electors know the type of people they have in Government, dirty little cardsharpers.'[2]

[1] H. C. Deb., 18th November, col. 1,118.
[2] Ibid., 25th November, col. 282, 285.

The Controls: Legislation

The partisan attack continued in the House of Lords, although milder and more restrained, and Earl Attlee's brusque comments were amusingly expressed. It was quite obvious to Lord Attlee that the Conservatives 'have to snatch at any chance whatever in order to try to scramble home.' In the country constituencies, 'it will give the Conservative Party a pull.'[1] Whether or not the measure would give the Conservative Party 'a pull' in the country constituencies, as Lord Attlee suggested, it was apparent that many Members in Parliament believed that any change in the election laws might affect party fortunes. In all, some 78 Members of the House of Commons participated in the debate; 47 Labour and 29 Conservative. The leaders on either side of the aisle said relatively little or did not participate at all; it was primarily a debate for the Private Members from the back benches—lively, vitriolic, and thoroughly partisan. The Members knew that the Bill would be passed; perhaps most of them were actually in favour of the Bill; but in the debate itself, the partisans could not let such a superb opportunity go by without putting in a lick or two for their own side.

Once the debate ended, the topic was dropped in Parliament as a conversation piece, and it did not develop into a controversial issue in the General Election. The evidence on whether the new legislation affected the results of the election would be difficult to acquire, but in discussions with campaign workers and party agents of both parties during the election, one found considerable satisfaction that the provisions had been repealed. One Labour Member, who had opposed repeal in 1958, said that Labour appeared to have had sufficient cars to get its supporters to the polls, but that car ownership had had another unexpected effect: many voters on whom the Labour Party had relied for support, now driving cars of their own, had voted Conservative!

THE CONSIDERATION OF LEGISLATION IN THE STANDING COMMITTEES

One of the main functions of the committees in the House of Commons is to give detailed consideration to legislation and in this sense the deliberating committees are an extension of the House itself, with the debate carried on under a system of party controls in much the same fashion as in the parent chamber. The Committee of the Whole is, as is well known, merely the name given to the whole House when it is

[1] H. L. Deb., 9th December 1959, col. 112.

transacting business under a somewhat relaxed set of procedures. Any Member is free to attend, although specialists may be primarily attracted, and the decisions of the committee are subject to review and confirmation by the full House, acting in its corporate capacity.

The function of the Standing Committees is essentially to continue the deliberations of Parliament in another setting; there is opportunity to debate legislation more leisurely and in greater detail, but the organization, procedures, and activities of these Committees are similar to those of the House of Commons itself. The number of Standing Committees varies with the business before the House, for it is not necessary to submit Bills to Standing Committees for further detailed consideration, and during the Second World War the committees were suspended. In 1959 there were six Standing Committees: A, B, C, D, E, and Scottish.

As a general rule, the deliberations in the Standing Committees are not greatly unlike those of the parent chamber. The debate is not of a different kind, with partisanship suspended as the Members consider the effect of technical amendments on legislation. Only occasionally does a committee break away from the traditional pattern and take independent, assertive action in reframing legislation. Normally, the debate is organized on partisan lines, with an impartial chairman presiding; and even the physical arrangement of the committees, where rectangular masses of partisans face each other, is similar to that of the House of Commons.

The Standing Committees are not autonomous and cannot defeat legislation by refusing to report it back, and in all but one of the Standing Committees, Government Bills have precedence. They have no authority to take testimony or to hold hearings or to make an independent inquiry into the effects of the proposed legislation.

The chairman of a Standing Committee is selected by the Speaker from a Chairman's Panel, which is appointed for each session, and it contains Members from both major political parties. The function of the chairman is similar to that of the Speaker of the House: he is the impartial presiding officer who, in the midst of party competition, sees to it that the rights of the participants are protected and that the business at hand is considered. He does not attempt to lead the committee towards a particular conclusion or to steer the deliberations in such a fashion that the sense of the meeting is developed.

The debate in the Standing Committees proceeds in much the same fashion as in the larger chamber. The Minister in charge of the deliberations is the key figure; he will explain and defend the legislation and he decides whether to accept proferred amendments. In some cases the Minister may be opposed to considering any amendments, an attitude which may indicate that the Minister is not in complete control of his department: that, in fact, the permanent civil service is controlling him rather than the other way round. A Government Whip will be assigned to the Committee to provide the Government with political support; the Opposition will also have its chief spokesman on policy and its Whip to encourage party solidarity.

There may be a good deal of pressure group activity associated with a Standing Committee; the groups may suggest to Members certain issues to be stressed and they may also propose amendments. The topic before a Standing Committee is often of interest to one of the party policy committees, and such a committee may, for instance, invite the Minister to a meeting for a discussion of proposed amendments. The activity of the pressure groups and party committees is not necessarily secret or covert but it is a phase of the process that is not part of the public record.

The activities of the Standing Committees are fairly routine and standardized, but the pattern occasionally varies and there may even be surprises. During the debate on the Obscene Publications Bill in 1959, for instance, the Government Whips were not applied inasmuch as the Bill had been introduced by a Private Member. Nevertheless, the Government presented its attitude towards the legislation. The Committee was closely divided (eighteen Conservatives, sixteen Labour, one Liberal); and without the Whips seeing to it that the party line was followed, the Government was frequently defeated.

From time to time, special techniques of obstruction are found in Standing Committees, and, just occasionally, it may be possible to defeat Bills by such procedural devices as a filibuster. In considering a Private Member's Bill in 1957, Committee C encountered an unusual situation. The Bill, on Local Government Polls, had been introduced by a Private Member on the suggestion of the Government, but once the Bill had been referred to the Committee and the public became aware of its contents, opposition developed on a very considerable scale. The parties appeared to change sides. Labour Members tended to support the Bill, perhaps because it seemed to increase the power of local Councils, whereas, for a variety of reasons, many Conservative Members either opposed the Bill or expressed reservations concerning it. It now became the task of the Conservative Members to defeat a Bill which had been

introduced by a colleague at the request of the Government they otherwise supported.

A type of filibuster developed within the Committee, and there were
prolonged and frivolous discussions concerning the question of when
the Committee would next meet: amendments would be proposed to
amendments, with subsequent divisions of the committee:

Motion: 'That during the further proceedings . . . the Committee do
meet on Wednesdays.'

Amendment proposed: 'To leave out Wednesdays and to insert Wednesday 29th May.'

Question again proposed: 'That Wednesdays stand part of the
Question.'

Member: 'On a point of order . . . Let us suppose that we reach 29th
May without bringing the discussion to an end. What is the position
about the Amendment? Do we then go on, assuming that it is 29th May
1958, or do we then table another Amendment, if we wish to do so, in
order to have a further delay . . .'

The tables were turned in yet another fashion. The Labour Whip now
had to keep a sharp eye on the attendance of his own Members; if
Labour attendance fell below fifteen, the Conservatives would absent
themselves, and the Chairman would be forced to suspend the proceedings for lack of a quorum. If the Labour Members reappeared and a
quorum was re-established, the Committee would resume sitting. On
the fifth and last meeting, the Committee met briefly, with nineteen
Members present, thirteen Labour and six Conservative. Apparently
some few Members left the meeting, and the last item in the official
report reads: 'The Chairman's attention having been called to the fact
that fifteen Members were not present, he adjourned the Committee at
sixteen minutes to eleven o'clock till Thursday next.' The Committee
did not meet again, and the Bill was subsequently withdrawn.[1]

A situation may also develop where the Opposition wishes to prolong
the debate by speaking fully and effusively on every amendment, engaging in a kind of concealed filibuster to embarrass the Government
and discomfort its supporters. The Members on the Government side
are compelled to remain in the committee room to retain a majority, and
there they sit, bored and annoyed, a captive audience which must listen

[1] Official Report, Standing Committee C, 17th April, 1st May, 8th May, 15th
May, 21st May 1957.

to the Opposition and refrain from speaking themselves lest the proceedings be further prolonged.

Item: Member X was waiting impatiently for the committee to adjourn: sometimes he was in the committee room, looking at his watch, but neither he nor his party colleagues were participating in the debate; sometimes he was in the lobby, talking or telephoning, but remaining near enough to return to the committee room for a division. He said that he found it difficult to serve on the committee because of his legal work: he knew very little about the Bill, was not especially interested, and had apparently been added to the committee because he had made a speech on the floor during the second reading. He had been in the House until after midnight the prior evening, when there had been a late division; the Government's majority was small because Members from Scotland and the North of England had not yet returned from the week-end with their constituencies. Now he was waiting for the Opposition to finish talking so that the committee could report the Bill and he could get back to his own work.

Parliament has practically abandoned the former practice of creating a Select Committee to sift facts and prepare legislation, although occasionally the procedure is still followed. In 1957, for instance, a Special Committee was created to consider the Obscenity Bill in greater detail, and to report back. The Committee heard the testimony of a number of expert witnesses during its deliberations. In March 1958 Mr. Denis Howell attempted to secure consent for creating a Special Committee to consider Sunday observance legislation, but his motion lacked the support of the necessary one hundred Members and was defeated 54–31. In general, the acquisition of specialized information has been relegated to the Government, although the Government may in turn create a commission to make further inquiries.

DELEGATED LEGISLATION

One of the constitutional problems that has troubled Parliament for some years has been the control it should exercise over delegated legislation. Parliament has traditionally claimed the right to make law, but in modern times the rules and regulations made by the Government exceed in quantity the legislative output of Parliament. In the nineteenth century, Parliament was still able to enact most of the legislation required, but laws were frequently full of detail and the practice began of delegating power to the departments to make rules and regulations based on the parent statute. Delegated legislation became more extensive during the First World War and again during the Second World War and the subsequent period of expanding nationalization and control.

The delegation of legislative power raised the question of the proper function of Parliament in making law or in controlling its delegation, and some lawyers voiced the fear that the power of the Government to make binding rules, not reviewable by the courts, was a threat to the common law tradition of Great Britain. This latter point of view was forcefully expressed by Lord Hewart (then Chief Justice) in his controversial book, *The New Despotism*, published in 1929.

In subsequent years, Parliament has attempted to rationalize its con- · stitutional position and to develop new procedures for asserting its authority over delegated legislation, without, at the same time, destroying the advantages of specialized regulation. A step towards redefining the position of Parliament was taken in 1929 when the Committee on Ministers' Powers (the Donoughmore Committee) was appointed to examine questions raised by delegated power. The committee report, published in 1932 (Cmd. 4060), defended the system of delegated legislation and found that the charges of abuses had been exaggerated; but it also recommended safeguards to protect the supremacy of Parliament and of the courts.

Special procedures are now followed which permit Parliament to review the Statutory Instruments (the general name given to rules and orders made by the departments) and Special Orders (relating to private legislation affecting municipalities and corporations). Certain categories of Statutory Instruments must lie before Parliament for a specific length of time (generally standardized at forty days); some Instruments require the further consent of Parliament before they take effect; others come into effect automatically unless they are specifically annulled by Parliament. A list of Statutory Instruments, published weekly, informs Members of the status of the various Instruments currently before Parliament.

To assist Parliament in its work, a Select Committee on Statutory Instruments, consisting of eleven members, was created in 1944 and is charged with the task of scrutinizing all Statutory Instruments laid before Parliament. The Committee does not consider questions of policy or merit, but it can draw the attention of the House to Instruments which impose a charge on public revenues or which show an 'unusual or unexpected' use of statutory power. The actual procedure of approving the Statutory Instruments may take very little time, but the reports of the Committee, Lord Campion has said, 'wave a red light' to which the House of Commons may, or may not, pay attention. However, a Member who objects to the Instruments, or who otherwise may wish to discuss them, can raise his point in the normal ways which are available to him.

The House of Lords also has a committee (a Special Orders Committee) for considering all Ministerial orders requiring the further consent of Parliament; it consists of twenty-one Peers and the Chairman of Committees. The reports of the Committee contain comments on whether the orders raise important questions of policy and principle; whether they are founded on precedent; and whether special attention of the House is required. The reports may be critical, as in 1958 when the Committee criticized the continuation of powers that were originally granted for the war period only.[1]

PRIVATE BILLS AND APPEALS

Private Bill legislation receives the attention of a limited group of dedicated Members, Peers, and parliamentary officers, but it lies beyond the interest of most Members and normally beyond the scope of party politics also. For its consideration, Parliament has created a complex structure of rules and procedures, and it is in this area that parliamentary influence is so considerable compared with that of the Government; and within Parliament the influence of the Lords is often predominant.

The consideration of private Bills is relatively independent of the main streams of political controversy within Parliament. The smaller world of private legislation is the domain of municipalities and other public corporations who want to have changes made in existing law. Although this conflict is in a minor key, there is often a sharply disputed issue at stake, and the conflict is expressed and resolved through well-developed procedures. In some respects the process of private Bill deliberation, in which alternative choices are made, is even more precise than that followed in the parent chamber, and the committees have considerable scope for exercising an independent judgment. Rather than being extensions of the debate on the floor of the House, the committees

[1] House of Lords Journal, 12th November 1958, p. 13. For a further account of the procedures followed by Parliament in considering delegated legislation, see May, op. cit., pp. 847–54.

are autonomous, and the controversies are brought to them for settlement without having first been considered in the parent chamber. The committees can consider evidence, take testimony, and make an independent decision. An attempt is made to eliminate the influence of special interests in the composition of the committees, and the Bills are considered in an atmosphere of judicial decorum. Some of the participants are different from those that consider public Bills, and special status is given to private individuals and parliamentary officers; these include the promoters (who must present a petition and otherwise advertise their intention); the parliamentary agents (who are employed as professional experts for shepherding the legislation through Parliament); the Lord Chairman of Committees, and the Chairman of Ways and Means.

In the House of Commons, the general control over private Bill legislation is in the hands of the Chairman and Deputy Chairman of Ways and Means and of a Committee of Selection composed of eleven Members. Smaller committees chosen by the Selection Committee consider opposed private Bills, and committees drawn from a panel, appointed by the Committee of Selection, consider unopposed Bills. Before a Member joins a committee considering an opposed private Bill, he must sign a declaration 'that my constituents have no local interest, and that I have no personal interest, in the said Bill or any Bill included in the said group; and that I will never vote on any question which may arise without having duly heard and attended to the evidence relating thereto.'[1]

Control over private Bill legislation in the House of Lords rests primarily with the Lord Chairman of Committees, the Committee of Selection, and the professional staff of the House of Lords. The Lord Chairman of Committees must be a man of many talents: he takes the chair in all Committees of the whole House and in all other Committees as well, unless otherwise directed by the House, and he also 'sits Speaker' from time to time in the absence of the Lord Chancellor. He receives an annual salary of £3,250.

Lord Merthyr became Lord Chairman of Committees and Deputy Speaker in 1957, bringing to the job considerable experience in public service and local government. He was born in 1901, attended Eton

[1] House of Commons, Standing Orders 120. Special committees are set up for the consideration of each private bill. Opposed bills are sent to a committee of four Members, 'not locally or otherwise interested in the bills referred to them' (S.O. 109); unopposed bills are sent to a committee of five, composed of the Chairman and Deputy Chairman of Ways and Means and three Members drawn from a panel; Consolidated bills are sent to a Joint Committee, consisting of six Lords and six Commoners.

College and Oxford, and succeeded to his father's title in 1932. Trained as a lawyer, he has been chairman of Pembrokeshire Quarter Sessions and a Justice of Peace and Deputy Lieutenant of County Pembroke. He has also been active in the work of various local government organizations; Magistrates Association; Central Council of Magistrates Courts Committees; Rural District Councils Association; and National Association of Parish Councils. In addition, he has served on several Royal Commissions, including one on local government, and he has been a member of constitutional commissions for Malaya and for Nigeria.

The Committee of Selection of the House of Lords (appointed in effect by the Whips, with all parties represented) is composed of twelve Members: five Conservative Peers, three Labour Peers, two Liberal Peers, the Lord Chancellor, and the Chairman of Committees. Although most committees in the House of Lords have specific and exclusive membership, the Standing Orders state that 'any Lord, though not on the Committee, is not excluded from coming in and speaking, but he must not vote.'[1]

Several Committees on Opposed Private Bills are appointed each session, and as in the House of Commons an attempt is made to secure an impartial and judicial atmosphere in the meetings. The Standing Orders provide that 'Lords shall be exempted from serving on the Committee of any Private Bill wherein they have an interest, and Lords shall be excused from serving for any special reasons to be approved of in each case by the House.'[2] The Committee on Unopposed Private Bills consists of the Chairman of Committees only, and although the word 'unopposed' refers to the actions of another petitioner, the Bill (or parts thereof) may actually be objected to by Government departments. The Chairman of Committees has the services of his Counsel in presiding over such committees.

Before 8th January of each session, the Chairman of Committees (or his Counsel) holds a conference with the Chairman of Ways and Means (or with the Counsel to the Speaker), for the purpose of determining in which House the private Bills should be first considered. Petitions and Bills are deposited in the Private Bill Office of the House of Commons and in the Parliament Office of the House of Lords, following which a document known as 'The General List of Petitions for Private Bills' is prepared. According to Sir Erskine May, 'The petitions are numbered,

---

[1] House of Lords, Standing Orders 57.
[2] House of Lords, Standing Orders 96.

The Controls: Legislation

and arrangements are made for them to be heard by the Examiners, the convenience of the parties being the primary consideration in arranging the order in which they are heard.'[1] The petitions and Bills are then examined by two Examiners (parliamentary employees, one from each House), who certify whether the Standing Orders have been complied with by the promoters in preparing the legislation. The recommendations of the Examiners are considered by the Standing Orders Committee of each House, who consider the question whether Standing Orders 'ought to be dispensed with, and leave given to introduce the Bill.' Some half dozen certificates of this category are considered annually, and agreement to permit the noncompliance, which is often of a technical nature, is normally given.

The consideration of Private Bills is closely associated with two other procedures, known as Provisional Orders and Special Procedure Orders. Abraham and Hawtrey comment: 'Procedure by way of provisional order was introduced with the object of reducing the expense incurred by parties in promoting private Bills and at the same time lightening the burden thrown on Members by delegating the duty of considering the application to a government department and holding the inquiry locally.'[2] Under provisional order legislation, Parliament is requested to confirm an order previously made by a Minister. The provisions are similar to those followed in considering Private Bills; they are examined by Examiners, with Certificates sent to the Standing Orders Committee, following which they are sent to a Select Committee. In 1958, some twelve Provisional Order Confirmation Bills were considered.

In the Special Procedure Order, orders made by Ministers may be annulled by a resolution of either House, and individuals affected by the order may file a petition against the order. The petitions follow a prescribed form and must be presented within thirteen days. They are examined by the Lord Chairman of Committees and the Chairman of Ways and Means and 'if they are satisfied that a petition is in order and discloses a substantial ground of objection to the order, they certify it as "proper to be received" as a petition of general objection or a petition for amendment, as the case may be.'[3] A report of each House follows. A petition for the amendment of the order may be referred to a joint committee consisting of six members, three drawn from each House, and the subsequent procedure is similar to that of an opposed Private Bill.

[1] May, op. cit., p. 888.
[2] L. A. Abraham and S. C. Hawtrey, *A Parliamentary Dictionary* (London, 1956), p. 30.
[3] Ibid., p. 188.

The Controls: Legislation

The House of Lords also appoints annually a Personal Bills Committee consisting of six Lords and the Chairman of Committees. The Committee considers all Private Bills affecting 'the estate, property, status, or style, or otherwise relating to the personal affairs, of an individual.' In actual practice this category of legislation is practically obsolete. Special provisions are also followed when considering Scottish private legislation and Scottish personal Bills, which need not concern us here.

JUDICIAL APPEAL

There are two judicial committees in the House of Lords: the Appeal Committee and the Appellate Committee; the first considers Petitions 'in matters relating to Causes depending in this House, or to Causes formerly depending in this House; and of other matters relating thereto,' and the second hears the appeals. Membership of the Appeal Committee is theoretically open to all Lords 'who have been or shall be present this Session', but in practice attendance is restricted to the Law Lords; membership of the Appellate Committee is restricted to 'all Lords qualified under section five of the Appellate Jurisdiction Act, 1876, as amended.' The Appellate Committee submits its reports to the House of Lords, and the latter (now meeting in the chamber with only Law Lords present) proceeds to consider and adopt the reports. The following extract from the House of Lords Journal shows the procedures followed:

The House (according to Order) proceeded to take into consideration the Reports from the Appellate Committee on the Cause *Rahimtoola* against *H.E.H. The Nizam of Hyderabad and others.*

It was moved by the Lord Speaker, 'That the said Report be agreed to.' The Question was put thereupon. It was resolved in the Affirmative.

Then the following Order and Judgment was made: viz.:

It is *Ordered* and *Adjudged*, by the Lords Spiritual and Temporal in the Court of Parliament of Her Majesty the Queen assembled . . . And it is also further *Ordered*, that the Cause be, and the same is hereby, remitted back to the Chancery Division of the High Court of Justice, to do therein as shall be just and consistent with this Judgment.[1]

The wide variety of activities undertaken by Parliament in association

[1] H. L. Jrn., 7th November 1957, p. 9.

with law is a revealing reminder of the manner in which political institutions have developed in Great Britain and of the fact that, for some purposes, Parliament is still a High Court. Parliament hears appeals and determines what the law is; it regularizes the legal competence of the municipal corporations; and it debates and approves public law. Different and specific procedures are followed in performing these various functions. There is no blurring of the lines of jurisdiction and there is no confusion between the procedures requisite for expressing and resolving political competition and those for the determination of justice. Different procedures are followed and different functions are performed, yes; but all fall within a broader pattern of regulating society through a most intricate system of deliberation and representation.

CHAPTER VII

The Grievances Redressed

One of the powerful controls developed historically has been that of the purse, and this instrument, now refined in the form of an Appropriation Bill and a Finance Bill, enacted annually, still plays an important role in defining the scope and content of public policy. It is well known that the development of control over the purse was associated with the right of petition, a relationship revealed in the slogan (suggesting a touch of blackmail), 'Redress of grievances before supply'. The sanction which made petitions effective was Parliament's ability to grant funds and levy taxes, and the King was under some compunction to set things right before he got his money.

Professor Gray tells us that during the reigns of the three Edwards (1272–1377), the King expected a grant of financial or military assistance in return for the justice he administered. Sometimes, however, this appeared not to be essential, and justice was dispensed even when no grant was made. However, to increase the likelihood that the King would perform his part of the bargain, the Commons began to attach conditions, and their grants were drafted as if they were a contract stipulating the obligations of each party. The subsidy Bills were in the form of indentures, the upper half serrated, and each party apparently retained his part of the contract. An indenture from the year 1465, in the reign of Edward IV, shows that the King was granted tunnage and poundage and the wool subsidy, and there were stipulations on how the money was to be spent. The King's response, accepting the stipulations and offering his thanks for the grant, is written at the bottom of the indenture.[1]

Parliament, presumably, was able to raise funds because, with its

[1] H. L. Gray, *The Influence of the Commons on Early Legislation* (Cambridge, Mass., 1932), p. 41.

broad representation, it exercised effective control over land and other forms of wealth. Initially there was no overall control of spending: there was no annual budget; fiscal accountability was in a rudimentary state; and the King had some independent sources of supply from his own wealth and even from foreign countries and potential enemies.

The control over finance continued to be a troublesome issue in the seventeenth century. In the Petition of Rights of 1628, Parliament complained that the King had forced loans from the people against their will and it demanded that no one be compelled to contribute to any tax or charge 'not set by common consent, in Parliament'. The claims of Parliament were further asserted in the Bill of Rights of 1689 where it was declared 'That levying money for or to the use of the Crown, by pretence of prerogative, without grant of Parliament, for longer time or in other manner than the same is or shall be granted, is illegal' (Article IV).

In more recent times, Parliament's control over funds has been regularized, and the innovations include the introduction of the Consolidated Fund, where all revenue goes into a single depository and is not assigned for particular services, and the creation of an annual budget. The House of Commons now has sole authority over money bills, and every year it spends approximately a fourth of its time in considering supply or finance. It is not easy to assess the extent to which the House of Commons influences spending or taxing, however, for in this area, as in others, the influence may be indirect, subterranean, and not readily observable, whereas the public procedures often appear to be formalistic and at time arid. One major fiscal principle is that the Treasury has the responsibility for preparing the Estimates (supply) and the Budget (taxes), but different processes are followed when these subjects are considered in Parliament. Another principle is that only the Crown can initiate expenditures; or to put it another way, Parliament cannot appropriate more money or raise more taxes than the Government is willing to spend. This principle effectively restrains Parliament from increasing the estimates or from decreasing taxes. Since the enactment of the Parliament Act of 1911 the House of Lords is excluded from considering financial matters.

TAXES AND THE BUDGET

Parliament enacts a Finance Bill every year by which changes may be made in the tax rate and thus in the total revenue available for spending.

The Grievances Redressed

The consideration of Finance by the House of Commons contrasts sharply with the procedure followed in considering Supply. The tax debates are spirited, pointed, and relevant; the financial proposals are considered with care; and the Chancellor of the Exchequer listens to the arguments, participates in the debates, and just occasionally permits himself to be persuaded to modify his proposals.

Budget Day falls early in April, shortly after the beginning of the new fiscal year. This day belongs to the Chancellor of the Exchequer; he is the only star in Parliament and his name is printed in all the headlines. His words command attention because his budget proposals affect the cash position of everybody in the British Isles, relating as they do to taxes on income, purchases, and entertainment, not to mention pensions and the tax on beer. In the degree of public interest stimulated, Budget Day may be compared to a great national sweepstake, and everybody hopes for some bit of comfort when the Budget is opened and the new rates are announced. This dramatic bit of fiscal showmanship is governed by strict rules: the content of the speech must remain a secret until presented to Parliament (in 1947 the Chancellor resigned after an indiscreet disclosure); the Budget proposals are transported to Parliament in a much-photographed and tattered case, once used by Gladstone (not the Gladstone bag!); the speech itself goes into great detail and runs on for more than two hours; the new rates are announced at the end of the speech, after all exchanges are closed for the day; and the availability of a stimulant, even for a teetotaller Chancellor, receives pleasurable comment by the press. Following the speech, Budget resolutions are passed by the Committee of Ways and Means and remain in effect for up to four months; during the interim period the Finance Bill will have been enacted. The speech on the Budget leads first into a general debate, and from here into a detailed examination of the Finance Bill.

THE BUDGET DEBATE OF 1959

Mr. Heathcoat Amory, who opened the Budget in 1958, 1959, and 1960, is a debater of considerable ability with a manner so respectful and deferential that he tends to disarm his opponents. He wins his point by exuding a steady, endless flow of facts and explanations, and one gets the impression that if it were not for the exigencies of time, he could go on endlessly. His statements, or answers to questions, are rarely brief and terse; they are more like dissertations, full and wordy, and they manage to convey a sense of absolute, unchallengeable integrity. He also scores by his attitude towards the Opposition. He is polite, considerate, and kind, never rattled by an intemperate remark, and never losing his control. In his world, it would seem, there are no politics and no politicians, no designing men trying to trip him up or lead him into a trap; rather, Parliament would appear to be inhabited by men as sincere as he, people who want only to be informed, and he accommodates them.

When Mr. Amory opened his budget in 1959 there was a hushed tenseness, even restlessness, in the chamber, as the Members and the crowded gallery waited for the great speech. Question Time seemed routine and uninspiring, and the questions were over by 3:15, a quarter of an hour earlier than usual. Mr. Amory was thus forced to begin his speech sooner than he had expected, but it was still necessary to continue talking until the exchanges were closed for the day. This was an unanticipated burden. The Chancellor began to slow down after ninety minutes; he sipped his rum and milk more frequently, and paused for time.

The Chancellor may have been exhausted physically, but he had to carry on with his speech so that the new rates would not affect commodity prices that day. Moreover, the deliberative style of his delivery added to the impatience of his audience and gave the impression that he was trying hard to convince Members of the obvious point, that he was a prudent man. The speech continued on, with expected perorations and terminal sentences leading to more tenuous conclusions:

'To sum up . . .'
'The conclusion I reach is . . .'
'I turn next to the question how far . . .'
'The last, and most uncertain element . . .'
'Before recommending measures . . . I have to ask myself, on the one hand . . . and, on the other . . .'
'This conclusion raises two questions . . .'
'I have already mentioned some of the considerations I have had in mind . . .'
'I must remember two things . . .'
'These, then, are some of the considerations which I have had to weigh . . .'
'I can, therefore, now contemplate with safety some tax reductions . . .'[1]

[1] For speech, see House of Commons Debates (London, H.M.S.O.), 7th April 1959, col. 27–65.

The Grievances Redressed

At last the time arrived when the good news could be given to the impatient Members. He first took up certain minor items, important to some people but not the heart of the tax proposals, and this further added to the suspense. Having completed this explanation, the Chancellor turned to his major proposals: a reduction in the duty on beer amounting to 2d. a pint for the retail price, and a reduction in income tax amounting to 9d. in the standard rate and 6d. in each of the reduced rates. The newspapers were on the street, within minutes it seemed, bringing the glad tidings: TUPPENCE OFF BEER. INCOME TAX DOWN.

The Budget Day speech was followed by a general debate on the economy which extended for more than four days and ranged widely over various economic subjects. The Government presented two supporting documents to provide additional material for the debate: the Economic Survey and a Financial Statement.[1] The principal speech for the Opposition Front Bench was made by Mr. Harold Wilson, a man of sharp wit and some eloquence who has a special knack for translating budget figures into lyrical prose and for using colourful phrases with a stinger in them. Members on the Government side claimed to enjoy Mr. Wilson's efforts, even as Mr. Wilson enjoyed making them. In 1959 Mr. Wilson selected the treatment of old-age pensioners as the weak point in the Government's Budget; this theme was returned to again and again and later it became an issue in the General Election. Other speakers noted that the new Budget was more expansionist than that of the previous year, and Mr. John Cronin remarked that there had been no more dramatic change 'since Jupiter transformed himself into a bull.'[2]

In the general debate on the Budget, recognition was given to a number of Members who had special financial competence or who were known to represent certain attitudes and points of view: tax experts, manufacturers, accountants, miners, railway employees, specialists in co-operatives and in agriculture, and the secretary of the Inland Revenue Staff Federation. Some of the specific items in the tax bill were discussed in the general debate, but the more important controversy took place when the Finance Bill was considered for amendment.

There was considerable interest in the Finance Bill, once it had been introduced, but the debate was skewed by the principle that only those amendments could be considered which proposed to reduce taxes. Proposals for introducing or increasing certain categories of taxation, such as capital gains and winnings from football pools, could not be offered.

[1] Command Paper 708 (1959) and H. C. 132 (1959).
[2] H. C. Deb., 9th April 1959, col. 430.

The Grievances Redressed

Pressure groups were active during the debate, and Mrs. Jean Mann (Lab.) called attention in particular to the pressures brought by those representing old-age pensioners. 'They can lobby Members in the afternoon, can write out their resolution and make their threat,' she said. 'They are well organized.'[1] There were other groups also who made some claim for the consideration of their views, including those interested in beer, rural buses, musical instruments, investment allowances, a special property tax (called 'Schedule A tax'), entertainment tax, and on and on.

The proposal to reduce the tax on beer gave rise to some heavy-handed and self-conscious humour. The suggestion that a reduction in the tax on beer would help to safeguard the revenue was no doubt valid, but the favouritism shown to beer drinkers, now that a General Election was believed to be just around the corner, was certain to raise eyebrows. Were the Conservatives courting the working man? The spokesmen for the Government tended to treat the subject in a very jolly manner. Mr. J. E. S. Simon, the Financial Secretary, said that the public houses and clubs of Great Britain constituted 'a very real and valuable part of the traditional fabric of British society.' 'In them,' he went on, 'a vigorous, racy, social life is pursued with that absence of friction which scientists tell us owes much to suitable lubrication.'[2] Even the Chancellor of the Exchequer had moments of coyness, and when an amendment was before the House proposing to reduce the tax on beer sold in clubs, he said that he was uncertain whether he should declare his interest. In days gone by he had been a Territorial and also a member of a rowing club, and 'I have been trying to recollect whether I ever drank a glass of beer in either of those capacities, and I am inclined to think I did.'[3]

The Chancellor of the Exchequer held firm against most amendments, and of course he had heard many of the arguments earlier when making up the Budget. From time to time he would hint that his heart might soften at some future occasion—but without actually promising to make the proposed reform. On the Schedule A tax, for instance, which was unpopular with some of his own supporters, he said that it was not his wish 'to reject the proposal out of hand for all time'.[4] This was not a commitment but it was certainly a teaser; his party supported him in the division, naturally enough, but some of the Members hoped that the Chancellor would accept the proposal in the next Finance Bill.

[1] Ibid., 8th April 1959, col. 288.
[2] Ibid., 28th April 1959, col. 1,110.
[3] Ibid., 11th May 1959, col. 870.
[4] Ibid., 15th June 1959, col. 64.

The Grievances Redressed

If taxes were to be reduced, many groups believed that they were entitled to special consideration. The Chancellor could not satisfy everyone, but one Member suggested that it was customary for the various Chancellors to 'keep up their sleeves one or two million pounds which they propose to give away in concessions during the course of the Finance Bill debates.'[1] On Budget Day, the Chancellor did not mention the possibility of tax relief for the cinema trade and the film industry nor did he refer to the Entertainments Duty. However, the movie industry had been affected adversely by falling attendance, due in part to the competition from television, and the industry carried on an intensive campaign to secure tax relief. Eventually the Chancellor of the Exchequer relented and accepted an amendment to decrease the Entertainments Duty. Mr. Stephen Swingler (Lab.) told the following story about the lobbying which had taken place: 'As hon. Members who have taken a consistent interest in the film industry will know,' he said, 'some months ago there was an all-party meeting in the House which was attended by representatives of the industry and by some of the outstanding artists in the trade. The meeting called for the abolition of Entertainments Duty.' Following the meeting Mr. Swingler and some of his colleagues 'decided to promote a back-bench Motion calling for the abolition of Entertainments Duty. We thought that we would get some support from hon. Members opposite. However, we were unfortunate in that respect and interest in the subject seemed to have declined.'[2]

No Conservative added his name to the Swingler motion, but subsequently a motion was introduced by Mr. Geoffrey Hirst, a member of the Grand Council and of the Executive Committee of the Federation of British Industries, which was signed by some seventy Conservative Members. Mr. John Rankin (Lab.) said that 'dark hints were spread around that we did not need to worry because it was going to be all right,' and articles appeared in the *Daily Cinema* and *The Times* predicting the course of action which the Chancellor eventually took.[3] Whatever the process of persuasion may have been, during the course of the debates the Chancellor of the Exchequer decided to grant limited tax concessions to the movie industry—'giving a useful measure of help where it is most needed', as he put it.[4]

As with many other aspects of Parliament, a large share of the action

[1] Ibid., 11th June 1959, col. 1,214.
[2] Ibid., col. 1,228.
[3] Ibid., col. 1,225, 1,224.
[4] Ibid., 10th June 1959, col. 1,132.

on the Finance Bill takes place off the scene, unobserved by the general public. Taking the process at face value, one might conclude that Parliament itself exercises little influence over taxation, although in the current case the tax abatement for the movie industry was accepted. In a soliloquizing mood during the debate, Mr. Douglas Houghton (Lab.) said that he sometimes wondered about the meaning of the term 'Parliamentary government.' 'One goes through these processes hour by hour and day by day,' he said, 'but rarely ever can the House of Commons make its will effective.' Referring to an amendment then being considered, he said that he was sure 'that if it were left to hon. Members on both sides, who had listened to the debate, to decide whether or not this small concession should be given, we should, without doubt, get it.'[1]

Mr. Houghton's complaints apply also to other phases of parliamentary life, and the consideration of Finance is but another instance where Parliament gives formal approval to Government proposals and exercises influence indirectly. In the process of formulating tax policy, the Chancellor of the Exchequer makes the final decisions, although he is subject to constant pressures—before, during, and after the Budget debate. The pressures are in some cases direct, as when the discussions are held prior to the preparation of the Budget. They are also indirect: through party committees, visitations and delegations, and by speeches given in Parliament. The fact that the Chancellor is never defeated in a straight vote, that he seems always to get his own way, does not mean that he never gives in to complaints or satisfies his critics. Where fiscal control is required, there is of course much to be said for concentrating this degree of power in a single individual who, with certain checks, has the ultimate responsibility for balancing the various pressures and developing a fiscal policy. Centralized control over fiscal policy has many advantages, but one need not go beyond this and conclude that it produces a completely rationalized tax structure, free from pressures. Indeed, even under the prudent administration of the Chancellor of the Exchequer, Mr. Amory, and the innumerable questions on the purchase tax asked by Mr. Nabarro, the tax structure was shown to contain many anomalies.

SPENDING

The Estimates are submitted to Parliament in February and are debated intermittently for some months; the long process ends with the

[1] Ibid., 13th May 1959, col. 1,339.

passage of an Appropriation Act in July or August. In all, twenty-six days are allotted for considering Supply, and the debates are carried on in the so-called Committee of Supply, one of the two committees of the whole House. In order to provide the departments with funds after 1st April, when the new fiscal year begins, a Vote on Account is passed which enables the Civil and Revenue Departments and the Ministry of Defence to carry on their work until the Appropriation Act becomes law. The final transactions take place on the last two allotted days. A resolution authorizing payment from the Consolidated Funds will be agreed to by the Committee of Ways and Means and reported and agreed to by the House. Similarly, resolutions reported from the Committee of Supply will have to be agreed to. 'When the resolutions from both Committees have been agreed to, the Consolidated Fund (Appropriation) Bill is introduced. This authorizes and appropriates the expenditure contained in the Estimates, and also gives authority for the payment of the necessary money out of the Consolidated Fund, as agreed to by the Committee of Ways and Means. The Bill receives the Royal assent as an Appropriation Act.'[1]

In a technical sense, the debates are concerned with decreasing the estimates, but even in this area there is a type of play-acting where, on the face of it, the bare procedures do not reveal the significance of the action. For instance, the Government made the following motion on 30th April 1959:

That a further sum, not exceeding £20, be granted to Her
    Majesty . . . Civil Estimates, 1959–60

Class VI, Vote 9 (Ministry of Labour and National Service)	£10
Class IV, Note 1 (Ministry of Education)	£10
Total	£20

After the debate, in which Mr. Robens raised the question of Youth Employment Problems and made no argument at all for reducing the expenditures, it was moved 'That Item Class VI, Vote 9 (Ministry of Labour and National Service), be reduced by £5.' The question was put and the Committee divided: Ayes, 146; Noes, 195.[2]

[1] L. A. Abraham and S. C. Hawtry, *A Parliamentary Dictionary* (London, 1956), p. 97.
[2] H. C. Deb., 30th April 1959, col. 1,471, 1,598.

The Grievances Redressed

In keeping its eye on spending, the House of Commons is assisted by two Select Committees: the Estimates Committee, which studies proposals for spending and may also propose economies; and the Public Accounts Committees, which attempts to make certain that sums are spent only for purposes for which they are granted. The work of these committees may be debated in Parliament but normally this does not happen, and the committee reports are not included in the time allotted for considering expenditures.

In the development of procedures in Parliament, a bargain has been struck with the Opposition by which in fact they control the topics for debate. On the twenty-six days available, the Opposition may select for discussion any of the 200 Appropriation Votes or indeed any other topic of interest. As a result of this device, the figures given above on the amount of time spent in considering money bills do not give an accurate picture of what actually takes place. The procedures followed in considering money bills are complex in any event and are further overlarded with additional practices and understandings; here again is an example of convention overriding rules and rules retained for their historic or symbolic meaning. There is, for instance, some obscure symbolism to be found in the procedure for 'getting the Speaker out of the chair', and according to Abraham and Hawtrey, the procedure is popularly supposed to preserve the ancient right of the House 'of insisting on the redress of grievances before granting supply'.[1]

Debates on Supply days may wander far from the ostensible topic, and in the 1959 debates the House of Commons gave detailed consideration only to the Estimates for Army, Air, and Navy; these were the only debates where factual and relevant information about an entire department were considered. The debates on the other Supply days were concerned with a broad range of topics, most of which could have come before Parliament through some other channel, and very few contained perspicacious comments on spending. The topics selected and the ministries concerned were as follows: Attorney General: Legal Aid (1 day); Admiralty: S. G. Brown Ltd. (1 day plus); Agriculture, Fisheries and Food: Pig Production and the Bacon Industry ($\frac{1}{2}$ day); Air Ministry: Estimates (1 day plus); Colonial Office: Prisons and Detention Camps—Kenya, Central Africa, Hola Camp (1 day plus); Commonwealth Relations Office: None; Education: Youth Employment Problems (1 day); Foreign Office: Foreign Affairs (2 days); Health: National Health Service (1 day); Home Office: None; Housing and Local Government:

[1] Op. cit., p. 199.

Local Authority Housing, Housing in London (1½ days); Labour and National Service: Printing Industry Dispute, Employment of Disabled Persons, Industrial Health (1 day plus); Pensions and National Insurance: Retirement Pensions, National Insurance and Family Allowances (2 days); Post Office: None; Power: Fuel and Power, Coal Industry (2 days); Scottish Office: Industry, Employment and Roads, National Health Service (3 days); Supply: None; Board of Trade: Development Areas, Condition of Private Industry, Consumer Protection (2¼ days); Transport and Civil Aviation: Roads Programme, Traffic Congestion of Large Cities, Aircraft Production, Civil Aviation (3½ days); Treasury: Underdeveloped areas (½ day); War Office: Estimates, Defence (1 day plus); Works: None.

As one can see, the list of topics is haphazard and does not constitute a systematic review of spending. The debates on Supply are often vague, general, and rambling, and the choice of topics is sometimes determined by Private Members through the luck of the Ballot. The debate in any event would tend to be unbalanced inasmuch as Parliament is only permitted to reduce amounts. Parliament, in short, does not make the main decisions on how the available monetary resources are to be allocated; that function is left to the Government, subject to various pressures, influences, and suggestions, not all of which are found in the public record.

We may summarize our comments by saying that the debate on Supply is almost exclusively under the control of the Opposition. It is sometimes held that the proper function of the House of Commons is to debate the main principles of spending, permitting the Government to fix the details, but an examination of the process shows that this is not what actually happens. The debates on Supply are not inherently different from those on Adjournment or on Private Members' day on Friday. Although one may conclude that the Estimates are not debated in any sustained and comprehensive fashion, it is unsafe to go further and conclude that parliamentary control over finance is negligible.

If we wish to examine the areas where control is more specific and thorough, it is necessary to look at the work of the Select Committees, and in particular the Public Accounts Committee, which has a well-earned reputation for overseeing the expenditure of public funds. The Committee works in conjunction with the Comptroller and Auditor General, who audits the accounts and keeps the Committee informed on the expenditure of public funds, especially in instances where the practices followed might be questionable or might raise special issues on which Parliament should be informed. In the words of Sir Edmund Compton, who became Comptroller and Auditor General in 1959, 'the Public Accounts Committee works by examining individual instances of waste and so on, on which my report provides the facts.'[1] He went on to say that the Committee is, in essence, 'a fault-finding body who work by criticizing specific transactions. They look to me to provide them with the facts and the prima facie evidence on which they then conduct their examination and reach conclusions.'[2] Testimony is taken from witnesses on the basis of reports submitted by the Comptroller and Auditor General, and subsequently committee reports are issued with comments.

The following criticisms made by the Committee have been taken from a recent report. On the Parliament Trust:

Parliament should be made aware of the changes in the programme and the reduction in the scope of the work that will be done with the £360,000 which public funds are committed to provide. . . .

On General Dental Services:

There must be knowledge of the relevant facts, if Parliament is to be assured that the levels of remuneration in the Health Services are fair and reasonable both to those who provide the services and the taxpayers. Your Committee see no reason why it should not have been possible to obtain sufficient information about the actual earnings and costs of opticians to dispel any doubts in this respect. They trust that in the future . . .

On the Empire Cotton Growing Corporation:

Your Committee . . . consider that any future assistance should be given in a more orthodox manner.

On the Ministry of Supply:

Your Committee examined four cases where there was evidence of bad estimating and defects in the system of financial control.

On Agricultural and Food Grants and Subsidies:

[1] H. C. 276, 28th July 1959, p. 9.
[2] Ibid., p. 12.

They trust that the Ministry will continue to keep a close watch on low-price transactions, and will lose no time in applying more drastic remedies if . . .[1]

The work of the Select Committee on Estimates is placed on a somewhat broader frame and it follows somewhat different procedures, although its central interest is also the expenditure of public funds. In the words of Mr. Basil Chubb, who has studied the work of both committees, the Estimates Committee has 'tended to deal with more topical issues and with striking cases of waste and failure.' However, he concludes that their examination of expenditure 'is neither exhaustive nor professional and expert.'[2] The work of the Estimates Committee is of a more general nature than that of the Public Accounts Committee; the topics selected for inquiry relate to performance within accepted policy and are of too broad a character to be answered by a Treasury minute. Its jurisdiction is very wide indeed; it is directed to examine Estimates 'as may seem fit' and to report 'what, if any, economies consistent with the policy implied in those Estimates may be effected therein, and to suggest the form in which the Estimates may be presented for examination.' Recent topics selected for study include the police (England and Wales); food supplies for the Armed Forces; youth service grants; running costs of hospitals; power; scientific and industrial research; meteorological services; the reserve fleet; land branches of the service; Treasury control of expenditure; nature conservancy; and trunk roads.[3] In making their studies, the Committee takes expert evidence, including the testimony of departmental officials and outside experts, and it is customary for the Minister concerned to make written observations of the reports. The Committee does not have the assistance of a professional staff.

Some Ministers do not take criticism proffered by the Estimates Committee with good grace, and a case in point is the reaction of Mr. Harold Watkinson, when Minister of Transport and Civil Aviation, to a report on Trunk Roads. There had been a dramatic increase in the estimates for trunk roads, the Committee said, but it was not satisfied that there had been adequate research into traffic needs or into materials and methods. The report presented substantial evidence to support this position, and the *Sunday Times*, which had been promoting interest in highway construction and traffic regulation, upheld in general the criti-

[1] H. C. 248, 9th July 1959.
[2] Basil Chubb, *The Control of Public Expenditure: Financial Committees of the House of Commons* (Oxford, 1952), pp. 226, 227.
[3] H. C. 223, 10th June 1959.

cism of the Committee. 'The uneasy feeling remains', it said, 'that the scientific knowledge which should guide the programme is much less than it should be, in respect of traffic statistics, economic costings, technical standards and mechanical methods.'[1]

The criticism irritated Mr. Watkinson, and he answered with petulance. In a public statement (not in Parliament) he said that his plans would not be altered because of the criticism of the Committee, and the general tenor of his strident reply was that no advice was necessary. 'I do not accept their criticisms about our policy,' he said, and there was nothing to stop him from 'going on with the programme as it stands.' If the Ministry had been diverted by criticism and advice, 'we would never have had any roads at all'. He was not worrying very much about the criticism, 'because I have got the roads.'[2] Many Members of Parliament were offended by Mr. Watkinson's attitude. The point was made, in particular, that Mr. Watkinson had not made his reply directly to Parliament and had spoken slightingly of parliamentary criticism and control. A motion was put down, signed by more than a hundred Members, deprecating Mr. Watkinson's treatment of the Committee. Mr. Herbert Morrison told the House that he had added his name to the Motion 'with some regret, because it is a pity this kind of thing should happen.' There were proper procedures for a Minister to reply to a Committee which had not been followed. Mr. Butler, the Leader of the House, was pressed by the Members to exercise some discipline over Mr. Watkinson, and he agreed 'to discuss the matter of apology with him.'[3]

We would miss the main impact of parliamentary control if we limited our observations to the formal procedures only. Within the broader parliamentary process, requests are constantly being made to the Treasury to supply money for this object or that, and these requests do not go unheeded. Indeed, the Treasury is constantly making agreements with various interested groups and with Members of Parliament to award X amount of money, for example, for hospitals; or Y amount of money perhaps for schools; or Z amount of money, say, for pensions. Agreements on spending are made throughout the session, and the Treasury is under constant pressure to provide money for this and for that. Parliament is not able, on its own initiative, to increase the amount of appropriations, but its Members are constantly requesting the Treasury to do so.

[1] Issue of 19th July 1959.
[2] See *Evening Standard*, 21st July 1959.
[3] H. C. Deb., 23rd July 1959, col. 1,529–31.

CHAPTER VIII

The Control of the Ministers

'Bring into the way of truth all such as have erred, and are deceived.'

PARLIAMENTARY CONTROL AND MINISTERIAL RESPONSIBILITY

The Standing Orders make no provision for considering any topic labelled 'personnel', and yet the question of personnel, of who will be entrusted with Government office and political office, is one of the most important issues in Parliament and is always on the minds of the Members. It is a subject on which there is much conversation and gossip, and the goal of high office is tempting to many Members. Although Parliament does not consider personnel as such, the topic penetrates most debates and there is a close relationship between public policy, Ministers, and Private Members.

Parliament's interest in the composition of the Ministry is yet another example where Parliament has extended its control over Government, and this interest is now expressed in the doctrine of ministerial responsibility, with its corollary that the Government must command the support of Parliament. In an earlier period, however, the relationship between the Ministers and Parliament was less explicit, and Parliament attempted to use techniques of control appropriate to its status as a predominantly legal body. In modern terminology, it was at once a grand jury and a court—as a grand jury it could initiate proceedings if the law was improperly carried out, and as a court, it could hear cases on appeal and itself try cases concerning high crimes and misdemeanours. These functions required certain legal powers, certain control over personnel, to secure compliance with its orders.

The Control of the Ministers

The tangled skein of legal relationships that once existed between the King, the King's Ministers, and Parliament may be illustrated by an incident that occurred during the reign of Edward III (1327–1377) when Parliament attempted to clarify its position by restricting the power exercised by the King over his Ministers. Edward III demanded that his Chancellor (John Stratford, Archbishop of Canterbury) be arrested and brought to trial on charges of malversion, but Parliament thought that such a proposal violated its own prerogatives. A committee of twelve Lords reported that 'on no account should Peers, whether Ministers or not, be brought to trial . . . except in full Parliament, and before their Peers.' In substance, Parliament claimed that Ministers who were also Peers could not be punished directly by the King but only by Parliament, acting as a court, and this claim was upheld.[1]

Parliament also made what would now be considered an unparliamentary proposal in suggesting that the Chancellor and other great officers of state should be appointed by the King in Parliament; that a commission elected by Parliament should be created to audit accounts; and that the King should consult Parliament when ministerial vacancies occurred. After first agreeing to these changes, Edward later revoked his promises, saying that acts prejudicial to his royal prerogative were null.[2]

The techniques developed for controlling personnel embraced some venturesome extremes. These included the Bill of Attainder, for instance, where a man could be declared to be legally dead; and impeachment, as in 1388, when the Lord Chancellor (the Earl of Suffolk) was condemned to be drawn and hanged after trial. Professor McIlwain has commented that impeachment 'illustrates best that oldest characteristic of the Commons' House—the function of presentment. They were there obviously the "Grand Inquest of the Nation".' In one state trial, the powers of the House of Commons in bringing charges were compared with those of a Grand Jury, and it was stated that 'The Commons of England in Parliament are supposed to be a greater and wiser body than a Grand-Jury of any one county.'[3] Traditionally, the Commons would present the charges, or, as one commentator put it, they would act as 'informers, prosecutors, and grand jury men, to inform (and) impeach.' The Lords, 'exercising at once the functions of a

[1] G. Barnett Smith, *History of the English Parliament* (London, 1894, 2d ed.), vol. 1, p. 204.
[2] 1st October 1341; see Smith, ibid., p. 205.
[3] C. H. McIlwain, *The High Court of Parliament* (Cambridge, Mass., 1934), p. 189; reference to 8 State Trials, 286.

high court of justice and of a jury, try and also adjudicate the charge preferred.'[1]

Although certain aspects of Parliament as jury-and-court may still be seen, the use of impeachment as a technique for controlling Ministers has fallen into disuse. In all, Parliament has held some seventy trials for impeachment, a quarter of which were held in the years 1640–42. There have been no impeachment trials since 1806, when the First Lord of the Admiralty, Viscount Melville (Henry Dundas) was acquitted of misappropriating public funds. Although now in disuse, a favourable judgment on impeachment is nevertheless given in *May's Parliamentary Practice*, which comments that 'impeachments might still be regarded as an ultimate safeguard of public liberty.'[2]

Another control over personnel, already mentioned, was the Bill of Attainder, a procedure used for more than 150 years but obsolete since the reign of James I. In this extraordinary procedure, Parliament would enact legislation applying a judicial decision to a single individual; it was a unique combination of law making and court sentence, referred to by Erskine May as 'the highest form of parliamentary judicature.'[3] The concept of attainder, borrowed from the vocabulary of law, specified the rights of a criminal after a sentence of death had been pronounced, and according to Blackstone such a person 'was regarded as being out of the pale and protection of the law. He was not allowed to be witness in any case. Nay, more, there were forfeiture of his real and personal estates and the "corruption of his blood".'[4] In other words, by passing such a judgment, Parliament in effect declared a man to have no more rights than those of a criminal sentenced to death.

Several historic Bills of Attainder were enacted by Parliament during troubled periods of its history. After Henry VI had been deposed in 1461 and the throne acquired by the Yorkists, Bills of Attainder were passed against Henry, Queen Margaret, and several of their partisans. In another famous case occurring in 1641, the Earl of Strafford was accused of various misdeeds in his administration of Ireland. It was first proposed that Strafford be impeached, but an impeachment trial was slow and difficult and Parliament wanted no delay. It adopted the suggestion of John Pym that the proceedings against Strafford should take the form of a Bill of Attainder. The vote in the Commons

---

[1] Ibid., p. 192; quoted from Prynne, *Plea for the Lords*, pp. 309–310.
[2] *May's Treatise on the Law, Privileges, Proceedings and Usage of Parliament*, Fellowes and Cocks, eds., 16th ed., (London, 1957), p. 40.
[3] Ibid., p. 41.
[4] From *Commentaries*, vol. 4, ch. 29.

The Control of the Ministers

was 204–59; in the Lords, 26–19; and Strafford was executed 12th May 1641.[1]

Parliament's specific interest in personnel is now centred almost exclusively on the Ministers of the Crown, a concentration stemming from the doctrine that individual Ministers are ubiquitously responsible for almost everything that is done in the name of Government. Even the actions of non-Ministers are discussed within the context of ministerial responsibility. Not only is the Government as a whole held responsible for policy but each Minister of the Government is responsible within the orbit of his jurisdiction. The division of function is further clarified by a distinction in terms. The permanent officials are subsidiary to the Ministers and remain aloof from partisan controversy; they do not comment publicly on political issues and in turn are largely immune from public criticism. The Minister shields the Civil Servant and himself absorbs the political blows as he defends his department in public and fights its battles. The bureaucracy is in theory subordinate to the political realm: its actions have been regularized, its non-partisan role accepted. Under this theory the Ministers, and only the Ministers, are directly responsible in the sense that they make the final explanation to Parliament.

Granted that a Minister is said to be 'responsible', what meaning has this for Parliament? Responsibility is sometimes used as a synonym for 'duty', and one can say that the job falling within a Minister's jurisdiction is 'his responsibility'. It may follow from this that the matter is solely the concern of the Minister, that no one is entitled to give him instructions or to question him about his actions. In the broader sense, however, the Minister is not the sole judge of how he carries out his job. The Minister is accountable to Parliament for his actions in the sense that he must be prepared to explain and defend them, and although Members may make a judgment on his actions and attempt to influence his attitude, he alone decides whether to change the policy.

What must Members do to become Ministers? Primarily, they must secure the confidence of their colleagues, on both sides of the aisle, satisfying them that they can think clearly and can talk convincingly; that they have enough integrity to withstand pressures; and that they have the force of personality to make an imprint on policy. It might also be hoped that they will be testy enough, or be capable of producing enough indignation, to hand in their resignation if they disagree seriously with the Government on questions of basic policy. Although Ministers

[1] Smith, op. cit., vol. 1, pp. 401, ff.

are appointed by their party leader and they must defer to the actions and wishes of their party, it does not follow that a previous assertion of independence is a necessary bar to political advancement; the careers of Churchill, Bevan, Cripps, Thorneycroft, and Macmillan, for instance, show that the rebels of one period may someday sit in the seats of power.

They may be independent, but not quixotic; Members with pleasant phobias may be amusing and tolerated and even respected but they do not become Ministers. It would not be correct to say that experience in Parliament actually prepares a Member to run a department, for success in that realm may depend on additional factors. Indeed, Parliament is much concerned with the question of the Minister's competence, and it is constantly probing and talking and gossiping and raising questions in an effort to make certain that the Minister is actually in control of his department. However, it may also be added that parliamentary experience helps to equip the Minister with the skills necessary for advocating issues and securing their acceptance, and it should also give him some understanding of and sensitivity to the ramifications of political issues.

During the two phases of deliberation, those witnessed by the public and those which take place off-the-record, there is a continuous process wherein the views of Government and of Members are exchanged and an agreement reached. Parliament retains the right to override the decision of a Minister, as it might do by passing unwanted legislation or refusing to appropriate money, but these powers are not used and in practice the normal course of changing policy is by attempting to influence the Minister to change his mind; and the attempt may be carried to the extent of forcing, or threatening to force, his resignation. Ministers may be dropped occasionally, or their assignment shifted, but in recent years no Government has resigned because it failed to receive a vote of confidence. There is a belief shared by many Members of Parliament that the Government may be more impartial and even more representative of all interests and sections than is Parliament itself, and although certain points of view may be strongly advocated in Parliament, there is a reluctance to defend these particular interests to the extent of overriding the Government. On the whole the bureaucracy is not mistrusted; the Government does not seek assistance from Parliament in establishing supremacy over the departments; and parliamentary initiative in developing new forms of control is not encouraged.

Whatever the internal relations between a Minister and his department may be, the concept of ministerial responsibility would not be possible without the existence of a reliable and efficient Civil Service.

The Control of the Ministers

The pyramid of authority gives the Government a considerable amount of power, and the question often arises in Parliament whether the non-professional Ministers, the politicians drawn from Parliament, are in command of their departments and defend the prerogatives of Parliament or whether they are the creatures of the bureaucracy they are supposed to direct. Parliament is constantly probing in an attempt to find the answer to this question. Members who have themselves been Ministers may be able to ask searching questions and take a leading part in debate, and if Governments are turned out with some degree of frequency there is continuity of experience on both sides of the aisle. Also, former Ministers may be able to retain contacts within the bureaucracy which will provide them with useful information.

There are two aspects of the Minister's position, one relating to the department and the policy he is responsible for carrying out, the other relating to Parliament where he must explain and defend his policy. He must keep both in balance. In attempting to fulfil the expectations of Parliament, it is perhaps less important that a Minister knows all about a department than that he knows how to get along with Parliament.

The word responsibility often has a subjective meaning, and the controversy within Parliament is concerned with applying the abstract concept to a concrete case and making a judgment on the question whether the Minister has behaved in a responsible fashion. The expectations of Parliament may vary with Ministers and with Members, and personalities may count for a good deal in securing the general approbation of Parliament. However, if a Minister falters, or some Members think he has, there is no agreed set of conditions under which he should resign. Responsibility, it is clear, is not a precise term for describing the total relationship between Government and Parliament, and it leaves a good deal unsaid.

It is expected that Ministers will treat Parliament with deference and consideration, although Parliament in turn may subject the Ministers to severe tests, even provoking them to anger. If a Minister appears to dodge an issue or to give an impatient or temporizing answer, he may be given a scornful hearing. The attack will be pressed hard and he may be admonished to resign. The Minister's own side may be against him; Mr. R. Douglas Brown has written of the reaction of the House of Commons when Sir Thomas Dugdale, the Minister of Agriculture and Fisheries, made his speech of resignation during the debate over Crichel Down. 'Until this point he was heard in silence. But his next words were greeted by a wave of sound from the Conservative benches which can only be described as a low and menacing growl. . . . He ignored the noise behind him and pressed on determinedly. . . .'[1]

What particular advantages, one may ask, accrue to Parliament by reason of the fact that the Ministers of the Government are recruited from its ranks? One answer, I believe, lies in the subtle trait of confidence, which is not completely measured by performance in debate, much less by formal votes of confidence. One of the constant, informal processes carried on in Parliament is that of evaluating the competence of Members and of Ministers, of testing them out, observing them at close quarters, and reaching a conclusion about their ability to hold high office. Confidence is an essential corollary to the considerable power given to the leaders; once they have been selected, their status recognized, their role defined and authority bequeathed, they have almost unlimited power to make the final decisions. Authority is concentrated in the hands of a relatively few Members, and other Members refrain from action which might duplicate or override the leaders' activities. The leaders may be challenged but not the concept of leadership, and Members are assisted in forming a judgment on the leaders by virtue of their constant association in Parliament.

The confidence and trust acquired from personal knowledge and association is perhaps the most important aspect of parliamentary control over personnel. In selecting Ministers, or even Prime Ministers, the unexpressed opinion of parliamentary colleagues of both parties is always a factor. More than that, the idea is ingrained in the minds of Members that Ministers owe Parliament a direct and continuous accountability of their actions. Their first loyalty must be to Parliament, and Parliament, in its own fashion, reveals its confidence in a Minister.

Although the direct personal contact with Ministers is one of the most effective controls exercised by Parliament over the Government, yet at the same time this control tends to make other forms of control less effective. By upholding the leader, by defending the doctrine of ministerial responsibility, Parliament in effect forfeits its chance to take independent action. Dissatisfaction within Parliament may lead to a change in personnel or in policy, but the decision to make these modifications is taken by the Government and not by Parliament. The Government is often prepared to modify its position to meet the wishes of Parliament, yet the Government alone decides whether to accept the criticism, to reveal certain types of information requested, or to conduct an inquiry.

[1] R. Douglas Brown, *The Battle of Crichel Down* (London, 1955), p. 123.

The Control of the Ministers

The leadership principle operates democratically in Parliament because the leaders are constantly being scrutinized, and there is an implicit understanding that the leaders will be changed if they do not perform satisfactorily. If it were not for these safeguards, the authority given the Ministers might otherwise lead to a form of autocratic rule.

THE SUSTAINED ATTACK ON THE SECRETARY OF STATE FOR THE COLONIES

Now let us consider a particular case where a Minister was under attack because of his policies. This incident illustrates several aspects of parliamentary life. It shows how controversial events in the outside world are brought to the attention of Parliament and are transformed into compelling political issues. It also shows how Parliament attempts to hold the Government responsible for whatever happens under its aegis, how the Opposition is able to carry on a sustained attack, week after week, snapping at the Minister until the issue is somehow resolved or dropped. At the end of it all, the focus may then shift to some other Minister, whose actions have caused comment, and the process begins all over again.

The incident concerns the attempt made by the Labour Opposition in 1959 to force the resignation of Mr. Lennox-Boyd, the Secretary of State for the Colonies. During this period, certain events occurred in Kenya (the Hola Camp tragedy) and in Nyasaland (the Emergency, followed by the Devlin Commission and its report) which provided the Opposition with the occasion for carrying on a sustained attack over several months. For our purpose, the attack may be said to have started in February 1959, and as one tempestuous event in Africa was followed by another, the attack was carried on intermittently until Parliament adjourned towards the end of July. In the immediate parliamentary contest, the Opposition failed to dislodge Mr. Lennox-Boyd, but the issues of the debate were projected into the General Election, and the impact of this strenuous contest was felt in subsequent debates on Africa.

The prolonged debate concerned a subject not immediately at hand and in which the issues or even the facts were not always clear. It reflected the events, or the interpretation of the events, then taking place in Africa, and some of the pronouncements may have distorted the picture one might receive from a closer perspective. We are concerned primarily, then, with the impact on Parliament of events taking place in

East and Central Africa and of the political framework within which the debate was conducted.

The two African events that aroused the sensibilities of Parliament were the deaths at Hola Detention Camp in Kenya and the Declaration of an Emergency in Nyasaland, both, as it happens, falling on 3rd March 1959. The events were otherwise unrelated, except in the broader mosaic of colonial policy, but they became enmeshed in the same parliamentary controversy and in the final week of the session they formed the basis of a two-pronged attack on the Colonial Secretary.

One of the reasons the debates on Hola and Nyasaland were politically contentious can perhaps be credited to the dynamic qualities of the two main adversaries who dominated the deliberations. Each wanted to maintain the confidence of his own party, to secure the confidence of Parliament and the country, and to influence the larger issues at stake. Mr. Callaghan hoped to weaken the position of Mr. Lennox-Boyd and, if fate were kind, to succeed him in office following the next General Election. Mr. Lennox-Boyd wanted to defend his policy.

In his parliamentary appearances, Mr. Lennox-Boyd makes an impressive appearance; he is tall and well tailored, with a commanding presence and buoyant, good-natured enthusiasm. He speaks easily and convincingly before small informal groups, but his prepared speeches are often rushed through at too much of a gallop, and he fails to give proper emphasis to the smaller points. At this period he had been Colonial Secretary for five years, and he was known to be conscientious, hard working, and dedicated to his job. He was respected by many African leaders, and he also retained the support and goodwill of many members of the Labour Party. Mr. Callaghan was one of the few Labour Members who seemed not to like the Colonial Secretary personally.

It is perhaps not an exaggeration to say that Mr. Lennox-Boyd embodies many of the virtues which British people esteem: he has money, social position, and political power; he is personally devout, with talent and charm and manners, and withal a good mixer and easy conversationalist. He was born in 1904 and was a scholar at Christ Church, Oxford, where he was also President of the Union. He came to Parliament in 1931 as the Member for mid-Bedfordshire. His wife, the former Lady Patricia Guinness, is the daughter of the Earl of Iveagh, Chairman of Arthur Guinness, Son and Co.

Mr. Callaghan also makes an impressive physical appearance; he is tall, agile, and muscular, with black hair, and although he is not quite handsome, he might easily play the part of the hero in a Western movie.

The Control of the Ministers

He was born in 1912, the son of a Chief Petty Officer of the Royal Navy, and he himself served in the Navy during the war. He was educated at an elementary school and Portsmouth Northern Secondary School and entered the Civil Service as a tax officer at the age of seventeen. Later, he became interested in trade unions and was Assistant Secretary of the Inland Revenue Staff Federation; he was elected Member of Parliament for South Cardiff in 1945. Mr. Callaghan is less of an expert in colonial affairs than some other Members of his party (two of whom have been Colonial Secretaries), but he was elected by his colleagues to sit on the Front Bench as a member of Labour's Shadow Cabinet, and he is a debater who can deliver a stinging punch in a partisan debate. He is Sandburg's 'tall, bold slugger', a tough, emotional, and sometimes intolerant debater who gives the enemy no quarter. He is steadfast and firm in his likes and dislikes.

THE HOLA CAMP DISASTER

The Kenya Government had achieved considerable success in rehabilitating Mau Mau prisoners and some 70,000 detainees had renounced their Mau Mau oath and returned to lead a peaceful life. As part of the rehabilitation programme, a detention camp had been constructed at Hola, on the Tana River, and the detainees at the camp were encouraged to denounce Mau Mauism and work their way back to freedom. They were permitted to work on the irrigation scheme, for which they were paid, and they could proceed from there to the Open Camp, where they had liberty of movement, and finally to a settlement, where they were now free men with land of their own. The closed camp section housed the hard core irreconcilables who were rejected by their own communities and who refused, because of their Mau Mau oaths, to co-operate with the Government. Discipline in this section was not good, and it deteriorated further when additional hard core Mau Mau were imported from other camps.

Mr. J. B. T. Cowan, the Senior Superintendent of Prisons, had developed a scheme for handling recalcitrants at another camp, but the scheme was applied at the Hola camp with tragic results. The plan attempted to secure the co-operation of the detainees by breaking the force of the Mau Mau oath. At Hola, the detainees were to be 'diluted' into smaller groups and, after instruction, taken to the irrigation scheme. If the prisoner refused to work, two warders were to hold his hand and physically make him go through the motions, as for example, pulling weeds. Having performed this token work, the detainee would consider that his Mau Mau oath was broken, and he might now become co-operative and soon gain his freedom. It had happened elsewhere; and former Mau Mau adherents were now trying to persuade their former colleagues to give up their old cause and renounce the oath.

The nuances of the Cowan plan were lost in its execution at Hola. Mr. Cowan was not himself on the Hola staff, and no officer with experience in administering the Cowan plan was present to supervise its operations. It later developed that there was misunderstanding on how the plan was to be implemented; that the Hola Commander did not actually have a copy of the plan; and that requests for further assistance were rejected or ignored. On the dreadful day, the Mau Mau detainees were not diluted into small groups (according to the plan); they were provided with tools (which the plan did not envisage); and they were twice beaten, first, when they attempted to run away and later, illegally, when they refused to work. The beating occurred during a period when European supervision was temporarily absent, and it is assumed that the anti-Mau Mau Kikuyu warders, taking advantage of the situation, were revengeful and brutal. In all eleven Mau Mau detainees died, and according to the Attorney General of Kenya, the deaths resulted from the use of force, the greater part of which was illegal.[1]

When word of the trouble reached Nairobi,[2] officials visited the Hola Camp at once, and on the basis of their findings an official Government communiqué was released to the press. This communiqué, based on incomplete and perhaps misleading information, gave the wrong impression of what had happened at Hola and was itself the subject of debate. After announcing that an inquest would be held, the communiqué went on to explain that the deaths occurred after the detainees 'had drunk water from a water-cart which was used by all members of the working party and by their guards.' At the inquest, however, there was no evidence that the drinking water was the cause of death in any of the cases.

The brief synopsis of the case shows that the facts were complicated and the evidence not readily available. However, the issue came before Parliament for discussion, and Parliament had to develop a consensus on who, exactly, was responsible for this disaster: the warders at Hola, the camp officials, the officials in the Kenya prison administration, the

[1] H. C. Deb., 4th June 1959, col. 348.
[2] Kenya News Press Office Handout No. 142, 4th March 1959; quoted in Cmnd. 778 (1959), p. 18.

The Control of the Ministers

Ministers in the Kenya Government (who in this case were also Civil Servants), the Governor of Kenya, the Colonial Secretary, or the Government Front Bench.

There had been previous complaints in Parliament concerning the detention camps, and in late February 1959, Mr. Arthur Creech Jones had proposed that the Government create an independent inquiry into their administration.[1] This suggestion came from an influential source. Mr. Creech Jones had been an imaginative and successful Secretary for the Colonies in the Labour Government for four years and was respected on both sides of the aisle. In a debate later in the year, a Conservative Member paid Mr. Creech Jones the compliment of saying that if he had remained Colonial Secretary, his knowledge and courage would have given a lead 'which might have altered the history of Central Africa.'[2] Mr. Creech Jones is a modest and unassuming man, kindly and gentle in manner, soft spoken in debate, and consistently well informed on African problems. Unfortunately for him and for British colonial policy, he lost his seat in the 1950 election and was out of Parliament for four years. Now he was a back-bench Member, no longer the spokesman for the Party in colonial affairs, and Mr. Callaghan sat on the Front Bench.

The Government did not accept the Creech Jones proposal, which it termed 'a Motion of Censure on the policy of the Kenya Government.'[3] However, three months later, the Government announced that a Commission would be appointed to consider the future administration of the remaining camps in Kenya and that it would be headed by Mr. R. D. Fairn, the Director of Prison Administration in Great Britain. Opposition Members thought that events in Kenya would have taken a different course had a commission been created earlier, and now that the Government had acted, Mr. Kenneth Robinson (Lab.) attempted to tighten the screws. Did not Mr. Lennox-Boyd agree, he asked, 'that the eleven Africans might be alive today, if the Government had not rejected the demand of the Opposition for a judicial inquiry into conditions in all the camps?'[4] Mr. Callaghan wanted an apology on behalf of those who, he said, had pressed for an investigation in the face of considerable contumely from the side opposite. Mr. Lennox-Boyd had said that the administration was satisfactory; perhaps he should now consider his own position, and there were shouts of 'Resign'.[5]

[1] H. C. Deb., 24th February 1959, col. 1,019.
[2] Mr. Dodds-Parker, H. C. Deb., 28th July 1959, col. 398.
[3] H. C. Deb., 24th February 1959, col. 1,061.
[4] Ibid., 7th May 1959, col. 565.
[5] Ibid., col. 566.

The Control of the Ministers

The debate in Parliament on the Hola camp was delayed, pending the receipt of further official information from Kenya, and eventually there were reports from the Attorney General of Kenya; from the Resident Magistrate, who conducted the coroner's inquest; and from a special administrative tribunal created to consider disciplinary charges.[1] The Attorney General said that he was satisfied that 'the deaths of the eleven deceased detainees resulted from the use of force and that the greater part of the force used was illegal force,' but there was insufficient-evidence to bring criminal charges. The Mau Mau detainees would not co-operate in the investigations undertaken by the Criminal Investigation Department; they refused to identify warder staff or even the bodies of the dead detainees.

A more detailed account of the events at Hola Camp is contained in the findings of the Hola inquest, conducted by the Senior Resident Magistrate at Mombasa (Mr. W. H. Goudie). The report is an extraordinary document; it is frank and informative and reveals with what judicious tenacity Mr. Goudie developed the story when witnesses would not talk or gave misleading testimony. Mr. Goudie received little co-operation from the witnesses, many of whom were silent, evasive, or misleading, and Mr. Goudie said that he was not able 'to feel that a single witness of the Hola Prison staff, warders, or the detainees, was making any real attempt to tell me the plain unvarnished truth.'[2]

In the meantime, the Kenya Government had created a tribunal (the Conroy Committee, composed of the Solicitor General and two Permanent Secretaries in the Ministries) to consider disciplinary action against camp officials.[3] It proposed that the Superintendent of the Camp, M. G. Sullivan, should retire from the service 'without loss of gratuity'. Charges against the Assistant Superintendent, A. C. Coutts, were not established. The administration of the Prisons Department disclosed 'a serious omission' which had contributed to the disaster, and the Commissioner of Prisons, J. H. Lewis, who was due very shortly to retire in any event, was given permission to retire from the service. No charges were made against any Ministers of the Kenya Government.

The House of Commons debated the Hola Camp affair on 16th June, but the debate was not definitive. Another debate took place on 27th

---

[1] For Magistrate's findings and statement of Attorney-General, see *Documents Relating to the Deaths of Eleven Mau Mau detainees at Hola Camp in Kenya,* Cmnd. 778 (1959); for report of administrative inquiry, see *Further Documents relating to the Deaths of Eleven Mau Mau Detainees at Hola Camp in Kenya.* Cmnd. 816 (1959).
[2] Cmnd. 778 (1959), p. 15.
[3] Cmnd. 816 (1959).

The Control of the Ministers

July, during the final week of the session, and this debate became intertwined with the topic of Nyasaland and the Federation in the concerted attack on Mr. Lennox-Boyd. We will defer consideration of the July debate on the Hola Camp and pick up again the thread of the Nyasaland story.

THE EMERGENCY IN NYASALAND

Parliament was also caught up in the Nyasaland Emergency. Political conditions had been unsettled in Central Africa for some years and markedly so since the creation of the Federation of Rhodesia and Nyasaland in 1953. More recently, Dr. Hastings Banda, a physician-turned-politician, had returned to his homeland after an absence from Nyasaland of over thirty years. There were sporadic outbursts of violence in Nyasaland in January and February 1959, and the Nyasaland Government was further agitated by a conference held by the Nyasaland African Congress at Blantyre on 24th and 25th January, when some very wild talk took place. The question whether plans were made at this time for an organized revolt (the murder plot) or whether there was merely a surfeit of talk, without concrete plans, was a controversial point, much debated in later days. Whatever the nature of the plans, there were a number of subsequent incidents where force was used, and this led to the declaration of a state of emergency in the early hours of 3rd March. Leaders of the Nyasaland African Congress were arrested, including Dr. Hastings Banda.

Parliament again had to consider the issue of responsibility. Were there good reasons for the Governor to declare the emergency, or (as Labour alleged) was he pushed into doing so by Sir Roy Welensky, the Prime Minister of the Federation of Rhodesia and Nyasaland? And Labour constantly raised the question: Was it not a mistake to have created the Federation initially? There was the question, also, of future policy: Now that the emergency had been declared, how could confidence and order again be restored?

Issues relating to Kenya and Nyasaland were familiar enough to Parliament, and in a sense the lines were already formed, with some mercurial Members ready to go into battle at the faintest whiff of smoke from East or Central Africa. Kenya had provided issues enough in the past: white settlement and the White Highlands, the Mau Mau rebellion, self-government, elections, and the franchise. As for Nyasaland, most members of the Parliamentary Labour Party had opposed the creation of the Federation in 1953, and their attitude now was equivocal: they rejected the decision which created the Federation, but they stopped short of advocating its dissolution. The memory of the 1953 debate lingered on, to be discussed time and again. Labour Members wanted to prove that on this issue they had been right and the Conservatives wrong, and now there was another occasion to debate, but not to settle, an old issue once again inflamed like an abused sore.

The current phase of the Nyasaland debate may be said to have begun with a question asked by Mr. Callaghan on 25th February. He wanted to know if the Colonial Secretary would make a statement on the latest troubles in Nyasaland, and Mr. Lennox-Boyd responded by giving a brief account of the disturbances that had taken place. Mr. Callaghan returned to his old theme. Was it not significant, he said, 'that this disturbance should arise in a country which, until the advent of the Federation, probably held a record in Africa for peaceful and harmonious race relations?'[1]

The disturbances in Nyasaland continued, and early in the morning of 3rd March, the Governor of Nyasaland declared a State of Emergency. At this crucial moment, the taut nerves in Parliament (and in the Federation) were strained by yet another exacerbating factor: Mr. John Stonehouse, the voluble Labour Member from Wednesbury, had been touring the Federation, making speeches and, in his double role as reporter, obtaining interviews. Now, on the morning of 3rd March, Mr. Stonehouse was declared a prohibited immigrant and flown out of the Federation.

Mr. Stonehouse was elected in 1957 at a by-election, and in Parliament he participated frequently in debates on African topics as an aggressive, forceful, but somewhat humourless speaker, with a tendency towards bombast and rhetoric. Some of his parliamentary mannerisms emulated the less honoured traditions of Parliament, such as overwhelming the Speaker with a run of pointless points of order and feigned appeals for guidance. As a new boy he talked a lot, without showing very much deference to his seniors on either side of the aisle. It could not be said that anyone in Parliament was glad to see Stonehouse in trouble, inasmuch as his conduct and his predicament reflected on all Members; nevertheless, for a few Members the occasion may have produced a quiet smile.

Mr. Stonehouse had gone to the Federation under the auspices of several groups, including a newspaper, but he was not there in any

[1] H. C. Deb., 25th February 1959, col. 1,123.

official capacity as a Member of Parliament. On 21st and 22nd February (Saturday and Sunday) he had accepted speaking engagements in Salisbury and Bulawayo as a guest of the Southern Rhodesian African National Congress. In view of the incidents in Nyasaland, the High Commissioner had raised the question whether it would be wise for him to proceed with his plan, but (according to the Stonehouse account) the High Commissioner acquiesced when Mr. Stonehouse assured him that he would stress nonviolence. After leaving Southern Rhodesia, Mr. Stonehouse proceeded to Northern Rhodesia, where the Secretariat had arranged a week's programme for him. He planned to leave from Lusaka for Blantyre, Nyasaland, at 7:00 a.m. on 3rd March.

On Saturday, 28th February, just after midnight, he was disturbed at the Government Rest House by the Chief Immigration Officer of the Federal Government, who told him that he should leave the Federation within twenty-four hours and that, if the warning were not accepted, he would be declared a prohibited immigrant. The warning was given because the Federal authorities said they could not guarantee Stonehouse's personal safety and his proposed visit to Nyasaland might lead to breaches of the peace. Mr. Stonehouse was not deterred by the warning and continued his tour. On Sunday, 1st March, he was the guest of the Provincial Commissioner at Ndola, Northern Rhodesia, and on Monday he flew to Lusaka, where he met the Governor, Sir Arthur Benson. He was informed in Lusaka that arrangements could be made to fly him either to Salisbury or to Dar es Salaam, and the Secretary of State for the Colonies sent a message advising him not to go to Nyasaland. For his part, Mr. Stonehouse said that he could not accept the Federal Prohibition Order, and that he considered it his 'duty as a Member of Parliament to visit Nyasaland'.[1]

In the meantime, Mr. Stonehouse had been attempting to get in touch with his leader, Mr. Gaitskell, and the telephone connections were made at 1:30 Tuesday morning. He was told to return to Westminster (if he could not continue his journey to Nyasaland) for the proposed debate on *l'affaire* Stonehouse, then set for Wednesday. Mr. Stonehouse, who apparently did very little sleeping that night, still thought he should go to Nyasaland. He went to the Lusaka airport early Tuesday morning— the sunrise arrests were then taking place in Nyasaland—and he was approached once again by the Immigration Officer. He was now told that a state of emergency had been declared in Nyasaland and that the plane to Blantyre had been cancelled. Arrangements had been made to

[1] Ibid., 13th March 1959, col. 1,615.

fly Mr. Stonehouse to Dar es Salaam. He was not permitted to see the Governor or make further inquiries, he said, and two immigration officers 'then took me by the arm and pushed me towards the tarmac.' The plane, with Mr. Stonehouse in it, took off about 7.30 a.m. Mr. Stonehouse could not make immediate flight connections to London from Dar es Salaam, so he returned to Parliament somewhat later, after the first buzz of excitement over his arrest had subsided; he made a statement to the House of Commons on 13th March. The case was not referred to the Committee of Privileges.

What with Nyasaland, Welensky, Stonehouse and all on people's minds, the debate in the House of Commons on 3rd March was sharp, bitter, and inconclusive. Mr. Callaghan opened the debate with animation. The Colonial Secretary, he said,

will have plenty of opportunity to convince the British electorate that what we are faced with in Nyasaland is a group of power-drunk, mad African leaders desiring only their own power and willing to murder Europeans in the course of achieving it. If he dares to try that explanation once during the next few months, he will be convicted of the grossest lie.[1]

'Let us calm down,' Mr. Lennox-Boyd admonished.

Labour argued that the Government of Nyasaland had been wheedled into declaring the emergency by the sinister influence of Sir Roy Welensky, who wanted a showdown with the Africans. The British Government, said Mr. Callaghan, had shown 'cowardice in yielding to the Federal Government of Rhodesia and Nyasaland over a state of emergency which was quite unnecessary.' Labour's case against the Government, he went on, 'is simply that they have either allowed themselves to be cajoled by the Federal Government, or agree with them, in the imposition of a state of emergency.'[2]

Mr. Lennox-Boyd said that the Opposition was trying to break up the Federation by whatever means it could. 'It is not their lunatic fringe but the Front Bench itself' who put the worst interpretation on the words of Sir Roy Welensky and 'the best possible interpretation on all the words and actions of those who would not hesitate to plunge their country into chaos and confusion. . . . In this vendetta against the Federation they are quite without scruple.'[3]

[1] H. C. Deb., 3rd March 1959, col. 279.
[2] Ibid., col. 279, 284.
[3] Ibid., col. 289.

The Control of the Ministers

The House of Lords was also concerned about the Emergency in Nyasaland, and on 24th March 1959 it carried on a debate until past midnight. Three Peers from the Federation flew to London especially for the occasion and made their maiden speeches. They were Viscount Malvern (Sir Godfrey Huggins), the former Prime Minister of the Federation, and, earlier, of Southern Rhodesia; Lord Robins, the President of the British South African Company; and the Duke of Montrose, who had farmed in Rhodesia for twenty-eight years.

The Government now decided to appoint a Commission of Inquiry to investigate the causes of the disturbances leading to the Emergency, and the names were announced on 6th April. The chairman was to be Sir Patrick Devlin, a Justice of the High Court, King's Bench, and the other members were Sir J. Ure Primrose, Sir Percy Wyn-Harris, and Mr. L. T. Williams. Some satisfaction was expressed in Parliament that this would be a judicial commission, free from political affiliations and therefore, supposedly, impartial.

The numerous debates on Central Africa sustained the interest of the public in the work of the Devlin Commission. The Commission's Report, as it turned out later, appeared at the very end of the session and became enmeshed in the growing bitterness between the parties, as they headed for the General Election. In the meantime, Parliament continued to debate African issues from time to time, and in May the House of Commons debated the attitude towards Federation held by the Church of Scotland in Nyasaland. The Scots had maintained a special interest in Nyasaland since the days of Dr. Livingstone, and there were areas in Scotland where there was strong opposition to the Federation.

In July, the House of Commons debated the constitutional position of the Federation which was due to be reviewed in 1960. In this debate, the Government announced its intention to create an Advisory Commission to explore the problems that would be raised in revising the Constitution, and as it turned out, this proposal was also contentious. The Advisory Commission was to consist of twenty-six members, some of whom were to be drawn from the Federation itself and of whom five would be Africans. Objection was raised to the size of the Commission, the nature of its membership, and the scope of its authority. Attempts to secure the co-operation of the Labour Party in setting up the Commission had failed, for Labour wanted a smaller Commission, composed of Members of Parliament only, and greater scope to reject the concept of Federation. One can gauge the political heat of the day by some of the colloquies that occurred at that time. Mr. Gaitskell, in attempting to clarify his opposition, denied that he said that Africans who served on the Commission would be stooges. 'What I said was,' he explained the following day, 'that it would serve no useful purpose if persons who were regarded by their fellow Africans as "stooges" were supposed to represent the Africans.' And the Prime Minister answered back: 'This is the well-known parliamentary way of trying to make an insinuation indirectly instead of honestly.'[1] Mr. Callaghan also took up the theme, saying that Africans who served on the Commission 'would be regarded in exactly the same way as the Norwegians regarded Major Quisling during the war.'[2] Now Mr. Lennox-Boyd joined in with a rebuke, saying that Mr. Callaghan had never held high office, 'and it is clear from some of the words he used that he does not expect to do so.'[3]

THE DEVLIN REPORT

At last the Devlin Report was published, successfully circumventing the printer's strike, and many Members were anxious to debate the Report before the end of the session.[4] The debate was set for 28th July. Somehow the Press had received an advance copy, and there were hints in the editions of Sunday, 19th July that parts of the Report were not favourable to the Government.

The Devlin Report is a puzzling document, and like the reputed construction of a camel, appears to have been put together by a committee. It is a mixture of fact and opinion, of facts clearly mobilized and cogently expressed, of opinion often illuminating but sometimes vacuous. Some portions contain mature observations, as if expressed by individuals with knowledge, discernment, and a background of Africa; but there are also portions which are overly simple and even tendentious, sometimes phrased so obtusely that the meaning is obscure. The Report *seems* to support the Government, and yet in a curious, uneasy way, it doesn't quite do so. The issue is not clearly drawn, and the Report contains innuendoes, sly hints, and parenthetical expressions, as if more were known than could be told, more were thought than could be said. The Report is coy when it might have been frank. The Government had a case, it says, but this judgment seems to be given with an upward

[1] H. C. Deb., 22nd July 1959, col. 1,307.
[2] Ibid., col. 1,389.
[3] Ibid., col. 1,393.
[4] Report of the Nyasaland Commission of Inquiry, Cmnd. 814 (1959); also Nyasaland Dispatch by the Governor Relating to the Report of the Nyasaland Commission of Inquiry, Cmnd. 815 (1959).

inflection at the end of the sentence. It raises questions that are left unanswered and plants doubts that are not allayed.

The Commission found that there was nothing to the Opposition's charge that the Emergency was brought about through the connivance of Sir Roy Welensky.[1] To this extent, then, the action of the Government was vindicated in that it had not taken part in a conspiracy to create the Emergency and smash the nationalist political movement. However, the curious phraseology of the Report has the effect of holding back, with one hand, the concessions that are apparently granted with the other. As for the necessity for the Emergency, the Report states: 'On the facts we have found and in the situation that existed on 3rd March, *however it was caused*, the Government had either to act or to abdicate.'[2] (Italics supplied here and subsequently.) On the Government using force in dealing with rioters: 'We are satisfied that each man did what he did *because he honestly felt that he could not discharge his duty in any other way*.'[3] On the police action: 'We think that for many of these actions *there are thought* to be sound administrative reasons. If that is so, *no doubt* you will be furnished with them.'[4] On conditions in the colony: 'Nyasaland is—*no doubt only temporarily*—a police state.'[5]

The Commission laboured small points. The Governor's Message had quoted the following statement, attributed to Dr. Hastings Banda:

You have heard about the riots. I have set Blantyre and Zomba on fire, I hope soon to set the whole of Nyasaland on fire.

The correct statement, the Commission said, was this:

You have heard of the so-called riots. Well things are hot here. I have the whole of Blantyre and Zomba on fire. Very soon, I hope to have the whole of Nyasaland on fire.

'The most important of these differences,' the Commission explained, 'is the omission in the White Paper version of the word "so-called". Without that word the text gives the impression that Dr. Banda approved of rioting; the inclusion of the word shows that he was refusing to treat the disturbances as riots at all.'[6]

Was there a plot? The word plot was not used in the White Paper submitted by the Governor, and the first parliamentary reference seems

[1] Cmnd. 814 (1959), pp. 78–79.   [2] Ibid., p. 74.
[3] Ibid., p. 128.   [4] Ibid., p. 142.
[5] Ibid., p. 1.   [6] Ibid., p. 30.

to be found in a question raised by Mr. James Johnson on 10th March, when he spoke of an 'alleged plot',[1] but later the term came into common use through the newspapers. However, the Commission used the term 'murder plot', although conceding that it was 'not one which is actually used in the White Paper.'[2] The Commission did not find 'anything that can be called a plot nor, except in a very loose sense of the word, a plan,'[3] but the Report lists[4] a series of actions which were developed at the meeting of the African National Congress and refers to 'the *policy* of violence decided upon in January.'[5] As for the attitude of the Congress towards Europeans, the Commission found 'that there was talk of *beating and killing* Europeans, but *not of cold-blooded assassination or massacre*,'[6] a distinction, some Members thought, without an important difference.

THE FINAL CONTEST ON HOLA CAMP AND NYASALAND

The two important debates on Africa took place in the final week of the session: Hola Camp on Monday, 27th July, and the Devlin Report on Tuesday, 28th July. The fact that Parliament would shortly adjourn, with the likelihood that the General Election would follow closely thereafter, gave a sense of urgency and expectancy to the proceedings. The Parliamentary Labour Party planned to take advantage of this opportunity by making a concentrated attack on Mr. Lennox-Boyd. As the date drew closer, suspense mounted, and there was increased speculation that this would be the Day of Judgment for Mr. Lennox-Boyd. Could the Labour Party, or perhaps even back-bench Members on the Government side, force him to resign?

Before considering the Hola Camp debate, it is necessary to make a slight digression and refer to changes in procedural arrangements which, in the end, had a shattering impact on the unity of the Labour Party and even on the outcome of the debate itself. It was agreed between the parties that the Hola camp was to be the first of four topics considered on Monday, but at the beginning of Monday's session Mr. Gaitskell announced a modification of the plans. The debate on the Hola camp, he said, would now be the last of the four subjects selected during this 'back-bencher's day'. 'It is purely out of the consideration of the con-

---

[1] H. C. Deb., 10th March 1959, col. 91.   [2] Cmnd. 814 (1959), p. 74.
[3] Ibid. (1959), p. 84.   [4] Ibid., on pages 50–51.
[5] Ibid., p. 54.   [6] Ibid., 84.

venience of the House that we have made these arrangements,' he said, without telling all he knew.[1]

The decision of the Labour Opposition to rearrange the time of the Hola debate was a strategic device, somewhat vindictive and overly clever, designed to wear out Mr. Lennox-Boyd for the debate on the Devlin Report on Tuesday by keeping him up most of the night on Monday. There were internal divisions on the wisdom of this strategy, and some Members of the Shadow Cabinet thought it plain silly; they were right. The Hola debate, ending after midnight, did not get the publicity it deserved, and it was either played down or passed over by the Press. As for the physical contest, Labour succeeded only in knocking itself out; Mr. Lennox-Boyd, for all his lack of sleep, appeared fresh, energetic, and full of spirit at the Devlin Report debate; and some Labour Members, themselves wearied by the strain or annoyed by the tactics, didn't show up for the division, thereby giving the Conservatives a somewhat larger majority than they would normally have expected.

The Hola debate began at 10:22 p.m., continuing on until 2:48 a.m., and the House adjourned an hour later. Even at these inconvenient hours, the House was well attended, and several impressive speeches were given. There was an awareness of the high stakes of the debate: the more immediate ones of partisan advantage; the vague, unclear, inchoate issue of ministerial responsibility in the Kenya Government, and in the British Government as well; and, in the broadest sense, the good name of British justice. On the Labour side, Mrs. Barbara Castle gave a stern, emotional speech, one of some bitterness and sharp accusations. Mrs. Castle is in many ways an attractive parliamentarian, well groomed, with a distinguishing head of rust-red hair, and she has considerable following among the rank and file of what the faithful are pleased to call the 'Movement'. She was born in 1911; attended St. Hugh's College, Oxford; and entered Parliament in 1945. Her greatest political triumphs have been in reaching high office in the external Labour party, becoming a member of the National Executive in 1950 and Chairman in 1958–59. Her prejudices are well developed, with the blacks very black indeed and her whites (like the soap ads) whiter than white. Her arguments are not always discerning, and are often on a personal level; wicked motives are imputed, and during the Hola Camp debate she made the calumnious charge that 'Members opposite do not believe that an African life is as important as a white man's life.'[2]

[1] H. C. Deb., 27th July 1959, col. 34.
[2] H. C. Deb., 27th July 1959, col. 220.

The Control of the Ministers

When appearing before Labour admirers, Mrs. Castle exudes warmth and personal charm, but when assaulting the enemy, whether in the House of Commons or in party conferences, she tends to be stern and humourless. Bending over slightly, and menacingly wagging a finger at her audience, she calls forth the verdict of Doom on her opponents. One shrinks from such an assault. She is the desperate woman from whom one turns and walks the other way. Her theme on this night was that the Government had been complacent, that 'The right hon. Gentleman the Colonial Secretary stands in the dock and does not deserve to hold office.'[1]

Complacent the Government may have been, but many of its Conservative supporters were anxious about the Hola Camp affair and about the Devlin Report as well. Among these was Mr. Enoch Powell, a poet and Greek scholar, now turned politician. Mr. Powell was a man of strong conviction and determined action. In 1939, at the age of twenty-seven, he had resigned his position as Professor of Greek in the University of Sydney, Australia, and entered the British Army as a private. He entered Parliament in 1950 and became a junior Minister in 1955. However, in 1958 he disagreed with the Government's fiscal policy and resigned as Financial Secretary to the Treasury. Now he was again taking a strong, forthright position. He told the House that the Hola affair was 'a great administrative disaster'. Mr. Lennox-Boyd was 'without a jot or tittle to blame for what happened in Kenya,' but the Ministers in the Kenya Government should be called to account. Representative institutions could not be planted elsewhere if one were to shirk 'the acceptance and the assignment of responsibility', and it was important in Africa, of all places, that the British must not 'fall below our own highest standards'.[2] It was a moving and effective speech, at the end of which Mr. Powell sank back in his place and held his head in his hands. There was no vote on the Hola affair; and the House adjourned at four minutes to four o'clock, Tuesday morning, with plans to go on to debating the Devlin Report later in the day.

The final debate on Nyasaland and the Devlin Report, so publicized and even dreaded, turned out to be an anticlimax, an almost routine affair of set speeches; there were no oratorical pyrotechnics, and Mr. Lennox-Boyd neither resigned nor was driven from office. As the debate ended, the Colonial Secretary was in good humour and victorious, the Opposition divided and disconsolate.

To the surprise of some people, Labour decided to accept the Devlin

[1] Ibid., col. 231.   [2] Ibid., col. 237.

Report, although the Report did not uphold Labour on the reasons it had advanced for the proclamation of the Emergency. The Government, on the other hand, found the Report a bittersweet document, one which it was loath to embrace in its entirety, and it put down a verbose motion in which the House 'took note' of the Report. There were in all some fourteen speeches, divided between the parties, but the speeches appeared to be part of a well-learned exercise, now stale after many performances, and there were few interruptions to enliven the proceedings. The Attorney General, Sir Reginald Manningham-Buller, who opened the case for the Government, defended the policy of merely 'noting' the Report without actually approving it. In appointing a commission, he argued, no Government pledged itself or was bound to accept all of the conclusions, criticisms, or recommendations of the commission.[1]

Mr. Stonehouse was provocative. The Government, he said, thought more in terms of winning the next General Election than about the future of Nyasaland,'[2] and as for Mr. Lennox-Boyd, 'I say that the Colonial Secretary is a cardsharper and a confidence trickster.' Was this parliamentary language? 'It is hard language,' replied Mr. Speaker. 'No one has ever seen the Colonial Secretary perform feats of prestidigitation with cards, and the remark must have been meant in a metaphorical sense. But it is not an expression the use of which raises an hon. Member in the eyes of his fellows.'[3]

Mr. James Johnson, the Labour Member for Rugby, made perhaps the most informed and useful speech of the day. He himself had been to Nyasaland during the Emergency (but without the fanfare of a Stonehouse), and was able to speak with first-hand knowledge of events.

Mr. Aneurin Bevan closed the debate for the Opposition, but he no doubt disappointed those colleagues who expected that his forensics would pull the Government down in ruins. He predicted that 'this Parliament will be known in history as the squalid one,'[4] an amusing reminder of how the word had been used on a prior occasion by Sir Winston Churchill; but as for the Report itself, he seemed to be advising the Government, with wisdom and not rancour, that it had a better case than it would admit. He was benign and fatherly, a parliamentary veteran giving advice to the younger generation. He argued that the case of the Colonial Secretary would not have been gravely weakened by accepting the Report, for paragraph 177 stated that the Government considered

[1] Ibid., 28th July 1959, col. 318. [2] Ibid., col. 396.
[3] Ibid., col. 393. [4] Ibid., col. 429,

the plot to be a possibility rather than a probability.[1] If the situation went on deteriorating, it would make the government of Nyasaland impossible. 'That is a perfectly good reason for taking temporary emergency measures.'[2] In all, it was a kindly speech, and it contained wise words which were meant to be helpful.

In the final speech of the debate, in which Mr. Lennox-Boyd was to have been cast in the role of a Minister fighting for his political life, a small incident occurred which changed the focus of the debate and re-established friendly relations between the Front Benches. Mr. Lennox-Boyd was apologizing for the condition of his throat, which was becoming sore from strain and use, when Mr. Bevan, in a good-natured gesture, tossed a pastille across the dispatch box. The pastille was then handed on to Sir Reginald Manningham-Buller, who examined it with mock forensic thoroughness, then shook his head advising against its use. The spell was now broken, the pressure relieved, the friendship and respect underlying the parliamentary struggle was beginning to show through. However, some Labour Members thought the incident unamusing, for it appeared that the leading participants were turning this crusade for principle into a charade, or the humour of a dumb show.

The final vote was 317–254, giving the Government a majority of 65. A few Labour Members appear to have abstained: they may have been physically exhausted by the Hola Camp debate, or otherwise unhappy at the arrangements; or they may have been dismayed that Mr. Bevan had not scored a knockout, and had not even tried.

In all, Mr. Lennox-Boyd displayed considerable flexibility in the long debate. He gave in to criticism, although appearing not to do so, and as he gave ground he consolidated his support within his own party and within the party opposite as well. The Opposition proposal for investigation of Kenya prisons was rejected as such, but the Government nevertheless appointed a commission of its own shortly afterwards, and in time the Fairn report led to considerable changes in the Kenya prison system. The facts of the Hola Camp disaster were at last disclosed, and in this case the persevering tactics of the Resident Magistrate were most valuable. The principle of responsibility was enforced in the area of direct administration, and some of the officers were disciplined. The applicability of the concept of ministerial responsibility to a colonial legislature, where some Ministers are also pensionable civil servants, was not resolved, although the problem was recognized. The device of appointing a judicial commission to investigate the facts at first hand

[1] Ibid., col. 424.   [2] Ibid., col. 425.

was not entirely successful, and the ambiguous phraseology of the Report created new opportunities for political controversy.

Although the sustained attack of the Labour Party failed in its immediate purpose, it may be relevant to add that Mr. Lennox-Boyd resigned as Secretary of State for the Colonies following the General Election and shortly afterwards was made a Peer, taking the title of Viscount Boyd of Merton.

Parliament seems drawn to some types of issues in African politics like steel to a magnet, and these issues are approached with the zest, the zeal, and some of the vituperation of domestic political controversy. Parliament often skirts around certain contentious domestic issues so that the community will not be torn apart by dissension. However, in debating some types of African issues, there is less evidence that the impact of such debates on the African civil population is taken into account. The entire debate in this instance was inconclusive, but there was hope for the future with the appointment of a Constitutional Commission under the chairmanship of Lord Monckton, and there would be more opportunities at a later date for Parliament to debate the enticing subject of African politics.

CHAPTER IX

Parliamentary Privilege and Bureaucratic Control

The claims of privilege take up no considerable part of the business of Parliament, although controversial issues are still raised from time to time, and it is also of considerable historical interest because of the part it has played in developing an independent Parliament. The extent and application of privilege has not been fully determined, and in 1957–58 in the interesting Strauss case, the House of Commons rejected the thesis that an unpublished letter from a Member to a Minister on an item of public interest was a 'proceeding in Parliament' and therefore privileged.

Historically, Parliament has made claims for its Members and for itself which may be regarded as essential for an independent and autonomous Parliament. The most important of these claims are perhaps the right of Members to be free from arrest and from judicial complaint for words spoken in debate and the right of Parliament to exercise disciplinary powers over Members and non-Members in order to carry out its functions and preserve its autonomy. The privileges claimed by Parliament are very ancient, and they are related to the historic function of Parliament as a court. Its power to enforce its authority, according to Erskine May, 'is a general power of committing for contempt analogous to that possessed by the superior courts', and the power to punish for contempt 'is not restricted to cases in which the privileges enjoyed by the House, in its collective capacity or by its Members as such, have been violated.'[1]

After his election at the beginning of a new Parliament, the new Speaker goes to the House of Lords, submitting himself 'with all humi-

---

[1] *May's Treatise on the Law, Privileges, Proceedings and Usage of Parliament*, Fellowes and Cocks, eds., 16th ed., (London, 1957), p. 89. See also the recent study by Viscount Kilmuir, the Lord Chancellor, *The Law of Parliamentary Privilege* (London, 1959).

lity for Her Majesty's gracious approbation', and lays claim on behalf of the House of Commons to certain traditional privileges. 'It is now my duty,' he says, 'in the name and on behalf of the Commons of this United Kingdom, to lay claim by humble petition to her Majesty to all their ancient and undoubted rights and privileges; especially to freedom of speech in debate; to freedom from arrest; and to free access to Her Majesty whenever occasion shall require; and that the most favourable construction shall be put upon all their proceedings. . . .' The Lord Chancellor, speaking on behalf of the Queen, informs the Speaker 'that Her Majesty doth most readily confirm all the rights and privileges which have ever been granted to or conferred upon the Commons by Her Majesty or any of Her Royal Predecessors.'[1]

One of the consequences of parliamentary privilege is the right to punish offenders. This right gives Parliament a valuable weapon in conducting inquiries in that it can compel witnesses to attend and to produce the required papers. In considering questions of privilege, Parliament acts independently, without Government initiative or reference. Claims for privilege are referred to the Committee of Privileges in the House of Commons and the Committee for Privileges in the House of Lords.

THE STRAUSS CASE

One of the recent cases of privilege concerned the dispute, mentioned above, between Mr. G. R. Strauss, a former Minister of Supply in the Attlee Government, and the London Electricity Board. The case was of special interest to Members not only because it affected the relationship between Members, Ministers, and the Nationalized Industries, but also because it raised the question whether a letter written in confidence to a Minister was privileged. The case was decided by a free vote which went against Strauss.

The facts of the case are technical, concerned as they are with the recondite topic of how the London Electricity Board disposes of surplus scrap metal, but they are of some importance in determining the basis of Mr. Strauss's charges. The issue immediately before the House, however, was restricted to the question whether a letter written by a Member to a Minister is 'a proceeding in Parliament'.

The quarrel between Mr. Strauss and the London Electricity Board was first called to the attention of Parliament in April 1957, when Mr.

---

[1] See, for example, H. L. Deb., 21st October 1959.

Strauss told a somewhat startled House of Commons that he had been threatened with a law suit by the Board because of comments he had made in a private letter to a Minister, Mr. Maudling, the Paymaster General. Mr. Strauss said that he had complained in the letter that the Board was disposing of surplus wire at uneconomic prices. Subsequently he had been invited to lunch by officials of the London Electricity Board, where the matter was discussed, but Mr. Strauss remained convinced that the Board was not following economic procedures in disposing of surplus scrap. He had given no publicity to the charges and had taken the matter up confidentially through the Minister, rather than making the charges on the floor of the House. After the explanation had been made, the L.E.B. asked Mr. Strauss to withdraw the charges, but this was not done, and the threatened law suit followed. Mr. Strauss told the House of Commons that the actions of the Board were calculated to impede him in the performance of his parliamentary duties, and there was no dissent when the matter was referred to the Committee of Privileges for further consideration.

It may be convenient to consider the dispute in three stages, taking up first the quarrel between Mr. Strauss and the London Electricity Board, then the action of the Committee of Privileges, and finally the debate in the House of Commons. The exchange of letters between Mr. Strauss and the London Electricity Board, printed in the Report from the Committee of Privileges, reveals the rising tension between the participants.[1] In his initial letter, Mr. Strauss said that the relations between the National Association of Non-Ferrous Scrap Metal Merchants and the London Electricity Board were unsatisfactory, the point at issue being the method by which the Board disposed of its surplus scrap. There was a degree of personal interest involved, and Mr. Strauss said that he himself had an indirect personal financial interest in a subsidiary firm of nonferrous metal merchants. The Strauss letter appears to be a sincere effort to secure an explanation of why the London Board followed procedures in selling scrap which differed from those followed in other regions and to indicate the extent of dissatisfaction in the trade with these procedures. However, the letter contained two passages which some people found offensive and which the London Electricity Board believed to be libellous; in one passage Mr. Strauss used the phrase 'scandal', and in the other 'strong suspicion'. 'This subsidiary,' Mr. Strauss wrote, 'together with everyone else in the in-

---

[1] See Fifth Report from the Committee of Privileges, 'Complaint of Certain Actions of the London Electricity Board,' 30th October 1957, H. C. 305.

dustry, considers the behaviour of the London Electricity Board a scandal which should be instantly remedied. It is considered a scandal in the sense that the particular industrial practice complained of must lose the Board, and of course the public, substantial sums.' He also wrote that 'None of the other electricity boards act in this way. Inevitably strong suspicion has been engendered throughout the trade by the behaviour of the Board.'[1]

The Board sold scrap metal by inviting tenders for the scrap metal expected to accumulate over the ensuing twelve months. However, the amount of metal in scrap varied widely, and, according to Mr. Strauss, many dealers were reluctant to make bids when there was uncertainty about the content. As a result of the procedures followed, the bidding was not fully competitive, and the same few firms were believed to have held the contract for a considerable number of years. In other areas, the electricity boards would invite tenders after large parcels of stock had accumulated, and they were subject to individual inspection and tenure. The London Board claimed that there was not sufficient storage space in London to permit this type of accumulation and inspection before bidding.

Other letters followed. On the twenty-eighth of February, the Board defended its procedure and asked Mr. Strauss for the 'unqualified withdrawal' of 'your unsubstantiated statements'. Strauss answered on the fourth of March, enclosing a list of comments on the Board's defence of its procedure, and the comments, it would appear, were pertinent, clearly stated, and deserved the courteous attention of the Board. But Mr. Strauss did not withdraw from his position; rather, he said that 'the explanations given me in support of the present procedure of the Board have confirmed me in the views I originally expressed'.[2]

The attitude of the London Electricity Board now began to calcify. In reply, the Chairman wrote that Mr. Strauss's comments 'seem to me to be concerned wholly with the commercial merits of the method of disposal', whereas the Chairman wanted to take up the 'serious and defamatory accusations against my Board and its officials'. The Chairman was sorry and surprised 'that after the explanations given to you, and your admission to me that you have no evidence in support of the allegations you had made, you are not prepared to withdraw these accusations'. And then came the threat: 'You will appreciate that if you maintain this attitude, we shall be left with no alternative but to proceed

[1] Ibid., pp. viii–ix.   [2] Ibid., pp. xi–xii.

with such other steps as we may be advised are open to us to clear the names of the Board and of its officers.'[1]

Now the lawyers enter the controversy. The solicitor for the London Electricity Board wrote to Mr. Strauss on 27th March, saying among other things that 'If . . . you are not prepared to withdraw and to apologize, we have categoric instructions to institute proceedings for libel against you. . . .'[2] Mr. Strauss's lawyer answered. The practice complained of 'was in no way attributable to any improper conduct', he said, and he claimed that the letter to the Minister was written 'on an occasion of qualified privilege'.[3] But this did not satisfy the Board, whose solicitor wrote on 4th April:

We observe that your client, though he has refused two previous invitations to do so, appears now to be withdrawing the imputation of dishonesty, but without expressing one word of regret for having made it. In this respect, as in others, your letter is wholly unsatisfactory and we are instituting proceedings which we expect to serve upon you during the course of next week.[4]

One may be intrigued to know what rumours and speculations permeated the scrap metal trade at the time Mr. Strauss wrote his insinuating letters. To learn about this background, however, one must anticipate the developments of the story as it was unfolded in Parliament. An inquiry into the methods followed by the London Electricity Board was authorized 28th July 1958, after Parliament had acted on the question of privilege. The report of the inquiry was presented in December of that year.[5] Regarding the suspicions existing in the trade concerning the actions of the London Electricity Board, the tribunal had this to say:

1. The only accusation which was capable of inquiry was that a named member of the Board's staff, who is employed in the purchasing department under the Purchasing Officer and whose duties are, *inter alia,* connected with scrap cable, had purchased a motor-car from a company of scrap metal merchants for £200 although the car was said to be worth £400 at the time.[6]

2. Some five years ago a scrap metal merchant had sent £50 in notes

---

[1] Ibid., p. xiv.   [2] Ibid., pp. xiv–xv.   [3] Ibid., p. xv.   [4] Ibid., p. xvi.
[5] 'Report of an Inquiry into the Methods Adopted by the London Electricity Board for the Disposal of Scrap Cable,' December 1958, Cmnd. 605.
[6] Ibid., p. 18.

through the post to the home address of the officer of the Board's purchasing staff. . . . The officer reported the matter to his superior officer. . . . The merchant was requested to attend at the offices of the Board when the £50 was returned to him and he was informed that he would be prohibited from tendering to the Board for scrap metal for two years.[1]

3. At Christmas each year officers of the purchasing department 'are accustomed to receive presents of bottles of wine or spirits and occasionally boxes of cigars from scrap metal merchants who have successfully tendered for scrap cable. . . . I was informed by the present Chairman of the Board . . . that the practice was approved provided, as I am told is the case, the gifts were shared among the staff. I was also told that gifts of a similar nature were sometimes tendered to members of the Board's staff at Christmas time by scrap metal merchants who had tendered unsuccessfully, and that such gifts were returned to the merchants concerned. . . . The practice is, for obvious reasons, undesirable.[2]

THE COMMITTEE OF PRIVILEGES

We now shift our attention to the Committee of Privileges, an entirely different world where the issue no longer pertained to the gossip or the procedures relating to the sale of scrap but to the abstract question whether a letter written to a Minister was in fact a proceeding in parliament. In terms of law, the pertinent references were found in Article 9 of the Bill of Rights of 1689 which declared that 'the freedom of speech and debates or proceedings in Parliament ought not to be impeached or questioned in any court or place out of Parliament.' In 1939 a Select Committee gave a broad interpretation to the phrase, 'proceedings in Parliament', although not specifically including a letter from a Member to a Minister. According to the Committee, proceedings in Parliament included 'both the asking of a question, and the giving written notice of such a question, and includes everything said or done by a Member in the exercise of his function as a Member in a committee of either House, as well as everything said or done in either House and in the transaction of parliamentary business.'[3] When the Committee of Privileges considered the Strauss case, it was argued by Sir Edward Fellowes, the

---

[1] Ibid., p. 19.
[2] Ibid., pp. 19–20.
[3] Quoted in Report from the Committee of Privileges, op. cit., p. xxi.

Clerk of the House, that the phrase, 'proceedings in Parliament', should also cover correspondence with Ministers. 'Just as Questions developed a procedure of their own in the course of the last century because of the lack of time for Motions', he said, 'so letters to Ministers or their equivalents are now developing into a parliamentary procedure because of the overcrowded Question paper.'[1]

The Committee of Privileges concluded that in writing to the Paymaster General, Mr. Strauss was engaged in a 'proceeding of Parliament' within the meaning of the Bill of Rights, that in threatening to sue Mr. Strauss for libel the London Electricity Board and their Solicitors 'acted in breach of the Privilege of Parliament'.[2] The vote was 7 to 1, the Attorney General casting the negative vote. The Committee also found that there were special circumstances in this case: it was the first of its kind, and bearing in mind that no proceedings had been taken, no further action was recommended.

THE DEBATE

The debate in the House of Commons on the Strauss case extended through one day's session, ending in a free vote in which the Committee's recommendations were rejected. The House adopted in lieu thereof a motion proposed by Mr. Herbert Morrison stating that the House did not consider Mr. Strauss's letter of 8th February 1957 to be a proceeding in Parliament and that the letters of the Chairman of the London Electricity Board and the Board's Solicitors 'constituted no breach of Privilege'. It was a remarkable debate and it produced some intriguing political combinations: Mr. Butler and Mr. Strauss were on one side of the issue, for example, and the Attorney General (Sir Reginald Manningham-Buller) and Mr. Morrison on the other side. Speeches seemed to sway attitudes, first one way, then the other, and back again, and the outcome of the debate was uncertain until the vote was announced.

Mr. Butler opened the debate, presenting the case for the Committee of Privileges cogently and clearly. Although he himself supported the Committee, he did not attempt to persuade others to accept his view, and he said that the House would have 'to weigh up these considerations

[1] Ibid., p. 4.
[2] Ibid., p. xxviii. Subsequently the Committee referred to the Judicial Committee of the Privy Council the question whether the House would be acting contrary to the Parliamentary Privilege Act of 1770 if it treated the issue of a writ against a Member of Parliament as a breach of its privileges; the answer was no. The decision does not affect the above findings. See Order in Council, May 1958, Cmnd. 431.

in deciding the issue. . . . Whether it would be wiser to support the Committee of Privileges . . . by suggesting an interpretation of parliamentary Privilege which covers a letter from a Member to a Minister or whether it would be better to leave things as they are and rely on the protection which will, in the absence of malice, be afforded to a Member under the ordinary law of the land, by reason of the application of qualified privilege.'[1]

Mr. Strauss was a more contentious debater, and indeed he might be considered to have been one of the unarticulated issues of the case. Mr. Strauss, the son of a former Conservative M.P., was born in 1901 and was elected to Parliament in 1929; he was defeated in 1931 but was returned at a by-election in 1934 and has served continuously since then. He was also a member of the London County Council, 1925–46. Mr. Strauss served as parliamentary private secretary to Mr. Herbert Morrison as well as to Sir Stafford Cripps and was Minister of Supply, 1947–51. He is a Privy Councillor. As one of the wealthier Members of the Labour Party and active in the commercial world, Mr. Strauss is somewhat of a Labour showpiece. He talks with the assurance of a man who is accustomed to having his own way, and he gives one the impression that he would be a resourceful opponent, either in business or in politics.

Mr. Strauss was persuasive when he first raised the question of privilege in the House of Commons, and Members who heard his complaint were shocked at the audacity of a nationalized industry threatening to sue a Member because of a letter written in confidence to a Minister. In the final debate, however, Mr. Strauss was less persuasive. Some Members thought that Mr. Strauss had written an impetuous and impolite letter, using words that might offend, and it was possible to identify the issue of privilege with Mr. Strauss himself; to make a judgment on the incident rather than on the issue. Moreover, Mr. Strauss was unrepentant. He defended the language he had used in the letter, which he said 'expressed the views which I held then and which I hold today', and he argued that a Member of Parliament must be free to write to a Minister on a matter of public concern 'in such terms as seem to him appropriate'.[2] He had used the word scandal in the broad sense of the term, that which, according to Webster, 'causes censure for being wrong or flagrant'. It was 'a provable fact' that 'strong suspicions' existed in the scrap metal trade concerning the behaviour of the Board, and he hoped the Minister would inquire into the matter.

[1] H. C. Deb., 8th July 1958, col. 219, 221.   [2] Ibid., col. 238.

Mr. Strauss was interrupted in his statement by Mrs. Freda Corbet, the chief Whip of the Labour group in the London County Council, who for twelve years had been associated with Mr. Strauss on the Council. She asked her questions scornfully and sharply, as if in rebuke: 'What was the insinuation? Suspicious of what? That is the important point.'[1] But Mr. Strauss did not give a full reply. He was prepared to go into the letter further with the Minister, 'but I shall not go into those details today.' There were cries of 'Why not?' The answer did not satisfy the questioners, and one sensed that at this point opinion began to turn against Strauss.

Mr. Strauss also argued that it was necessary for the House of Commons to exercise some control over nationalized industries, but the value of this point was lessened by his conclusion that if a letter to a Minister regarding a nationalized industry is to be of any value, 'it must be full, forthright, and contain all the information which the Member has in his possession, however libellous it may be.'[2]

The claim that a letter written to a Minister was privileged was attacked from different points of view by Mr. Morrison and Sir Reginald Manningham-Buller. Mr. Morrison was the wise and kindly politician who believed that relations between people in public life should be tempered by moderation. Sir Reginald Manningham-Buller was the cool, high-minded, and resolute lawyer who relied on the law and the courts to protect an injured party. Mr. Morrison had known Mr. Strauss for many years. Their careers in the London County Council covered practically the same span (Mr. Morrison, 1922–45; Mr. Strauss, 1925–46), and when Mr. Morrison was Minister of Transport in 1929–31, Mr. Strauss was his Parliamentary Private Secretary. Now, however, they were on the opposite sides of the issue. Mr. Morrison, who could be called a House of Commons man, was attempting to protect the traditions of the House. He believed that Mr. Strauss had, in effect, been acting as a representative of a trade association in negotiating with the London Electricity Board, and in the opinion of some people, he said, the National Association of Non-Ferrous Scrap Metal Merchants was 'something in the nature of a ring'.[3] Mr. Morrison could foresee the possibility of abuse if the Privilege of Parliament were extended to cover this type of activity. Moreover, the letter was indiscreetly phrased; Mr. Strauss 'could have put his case without employing language of that

---

[1] Ibid., 8th July 1958, col. 239.
[2] Ibid., 243.
[3] Ibid., 8th July 1958, col. 223.

sort'. If the House adopted the Report, Mr. Morrison said, 'we are saying that this language from a Member to a Minister is legitimate in all circumstances, that it can be used and that it will bring parliamentary Privilege to protect it . . . I think that is wrong.'[1]

The argument advanced by Sir Reginald Manningham-Buller, the Attorney General, was of a different sort. He contended that, for the law of libel, the courts already regarded as privileged any letter written in good faith by a Member to a Minister on a subject of common interest. If it were now held that such a letter was privileged, the only result would be to deny an injured party the protection of the law. If the House adopted the Report, it would be expressing the view 'that the inalienable right . . . of Her Majesty's subjects to have recourse to the courts for the remedy of their wrongs should be restricted.'[2] If that was the view of the House (and it was not his), it should embody its proposal in legislation, rather than attempting to give 'a wholly unreal meaning' to the phrase 'proceedings in Parliament'.[3] Sir Reginald made an impressive argument; he brought the debate back to a consideration of constitutional principles and he gave a plausible argument to those who did not want to extend the privileges of Parliament to letters which were injudiciously phrased. Sir Reginald was also able to gain support for his views, for whereas in the Committee he had been a minority of one, he was now supported by the majority of the House. The Report was rejected by a vote of 218–213: Against Report and against Strauss (Manningham-Buller and Morrison), 218 (204 Conservative, 13 Labour, 1 Liberal); For Report and for Strauss (Butler and Gaitskell), 213 (28 Conservative, 182 Labour, 3 Liberal).

The debate was over, and the House of Commons decided that Privilege should not be extended to cover letters from Members to Ministers. However justified this view may be, one is nevertheless amazed at the audacity of the London Electricity Board in threatening to bring a libel suit against a Member because of a letter written in confidence to a Minister. (The suit was not pursued after the action taken by Parliament.) The threat may not have violated parliamentary Privilege, but it was nevertheless the kind of action which seemed to challenge the right of Members to secure relevant information. Even if Mr. Strauss had been sweetly polite, there is no indication that his legitimate inquiry would not have been similarly brushed aside. The main question, really,

[1] Ibid., col. 224.
[2] Ibid., col. 265.
[3] Ibid., 8th July 1958, col. 265.

was how Parliament could get a full explanation of the controversy which agitated the scrap metal industry. By all counts, this was a legitimate type of inquiry, one in which Members are constantly engaged. In the case of the London Electricity Board, however, the acquisition by Parliament of relevant information was made extremely difficult. One surely must conclude that the inquiry which was finally made should have been authorized at a much earlier date, and that if the Board had been less arrogant and more helpful, the embarrassing episode need not have arisen.

CHAPTER X

Party Unity and Division

'From all sedition, privy conspiracy, and rebellion . . . Good Lord, deliver us.'

THE PROBLEM

In the final stage of the proceedings, after the debate is over, the great decision is made on whether to accept the proposal. The results of a division in Parliament are normally predictable, and no one is surprised when the Government wins. The size of the majority may vary slightly, but the results are seldom in doubt; in one division after another, year after year, the serene position of the Government (whichever party is in power) is rarely challenged. The predictability of the results of a division creates some ambiguities, and the aspect of parliamentary life which is frequently criticized is the power of the parties to submerge individual differences and present a united front at a division. Some people, disturbed by this exhibition of party strength, make the charge that the relationship between deliberation and decision is often tenuous, that for the sake of party unity Members are compelled to vote for what, in all conscience, they may not support. However, the strong party system has often been defended and rationalized as an essential part of parliamentary government and the power of a united party is now a conspicuous reality. Nevertheless, massed party voting to the extent that it is now practised is a relatively new development, and the trend might be reversed, say, if the parties were less competitive and one of them achieved a position of overwhelming dominance.

Even with the persistent regularity of results, the process of dividing the House is a subtle form of political conflict, and its implications are not all on the surface. A division performs several functions, the obvious one being that of recording a decision on the issue before the House. It also tests political support within the parties and stimulates conflict between the parties.

The entire parliamentary process may be considered as an attempt to develop opinion within Parliament, considered as a corporate body, and eventually to secure its consent. In considering many items of business, the consent of Parliament is implicit, rather than explicit; on the few items in which a vote is actually taken, the division may be considered to be a mechanistic device for determining and re-establishing the corporate whole. The concept of corporativeness helps to explain what Parliament does, or attempts to do. Unity is promoted and often assumed, and the united whole is considered to be greater than any of its parts. When there is a question whether unity exists in fact, whether there is a corporate opinion, the division determines which party is predominant and unity is again recreated. One may note here the slightly different voting procedure followed in the Elizabethan Parliaments. Professor Neale has commented that 'on a division the Ayes went out of the House into the lobby, while the Noes, because they were against a novelty, had the privilege of sitting still.' If the Noes were the innovators, they went into the lobby and the Ayes retained their seats. There was also an ancient order that 'when a division resulted in the passing of a Bill, the whole House, as well opponents as supporters, must go out with the Bill and fetch it again, presenting it to the Speaker and saying they affirm it.' 'The practice', according to Professor Neale, 'clearly had its origin in the twin medieval ideas that law-making involved the consent of the whole community and that members were attorneys for their constituencies.'[1]

One can cite other examples where the emphasis is placed on developing and preserving the unity of the corporate body. The British Cabinet, for instance, attempts to arrive at decisions by a general consensus. Any test of strength through a show of hands is abjured, and enthusiasm or apathy may be considered as important as strength of numbers in making the decision. Similarly, many decisions in the House of Lords are made by a general consensus rather than by a formal vote. An attempt is made to preserve the corporativeness of the whole body, for unlike the House of Commons unity cannot be recreated after an appeal to the electorate.

As a general statement, then, it can be said that Parliament is constantly expressing its views and giving its consent, without the necessity

[1] J. E. Neale, *The Elizabethan House of Commons* (London, 1949), pp. 397–398

for a formal division. Adjustments in points of view are made through the various procedures. In some legislatures, the casting of a vote may be an integral part of the process of developing agreement; proposals are voted up or down, sentiment is tested, there are public assessments of strength, and the final instrument develops as the product of a series of agreements. This is less true in Parliament, where the necessary adjustments are often made circumspectly by the Government. It will agree to modify its position, here and there, in order to maintain support and secure the broadest area of agreement, and the process of reaching a final consensus will be less obvious to the public.

Discontent is not necessarily expressed in a division. Both the Government and the Opposition have a network of communications by which the attitudes of the Members can be ascertained and evaluated, and appropriate modification in policy may be made as a result. The Government need not be compared with a heavy steamroller that crushes all dissent; a more apt comparison might be to a sensitized nervous system which reacts to various stimuli—in this case to the criticisms in Parliament—and constantly modifies its position accordingly. If the Government were completely inflexible, permitting no modification in its proposals, it might be faced with a rebellion on the part of the Private Members on the back benches. It has been mentioned that there is a propensity in British politics to anticipate the effective decision; the conflict comes at an earlier stage and the final procedure is often ceremonial in character. To a degree this is true of the division.

In summary, then, it can be said that the final division is not only an act in which consent is given but it is also a test of confidence in the overall decisions made by Government. Intrinsically, the divisions in the House of Commons become associated with the question of political support, and the issue becomes, in effect—Do you now agree with the proposal, after it has been discussed, amendments accepted, promises given, and hints dropped? The major divisions in which the Members align themselves do not necessarily reflect accurately the degree to which a particular proposal is acceptable. The process has by now achieved a somewhat broader meaning, perhaps only indirectly connected with the issue at hand; and the division may stimulate the partisan spirit in preparation for the upcoming election. A division, in other words, may have ramifications which go beyond the immediate subject at issue and affect also the political competition within the chamber itself as well as in society at large. Important political stakes may rest on little issues.

DIVISIONS: FACTS AND FIGURES

Before carrying these theories any further, it will help to examine factually the nature of parliamentary divisions. The request for a division is normally made by the Government or by the Opposition Front Bench, although Private Members may also request a division, and a division is mandatory if requested by forty Members. The Speaker may permit divisions if fewer than that number make the request, but he may not be inclined to do so a second time if there is not substantial support for the proposal. The Speaker also has some discretion in selecting the Amendments on which there will be a division. When the Street Offences Bill was being considered, for instance, the Speaker followed precedent in selecting the broadest Amendment, in this case a proposal that the Bill be read a second time 'upon this day six months', which is a parliamentary device for rejecting the Bill. However, the House was now unable to consider a more popular but narrower amendment, tabled by some sixty-five Members and supported by many women's organizations, which proposed various changes in the Bill and avoided using the term 'common prostitute'. The Speaker's choice of Amendments, according to Mrs. Slater (Lab.), put those who signed the Amendment 'in very great difficulty because we do not want to vote against the whole Bill, but to express a point of view.'[1]

The divisions are not all of a kind, as we shall see, but the politically important divisions are those which in some way challenge the Government, and on these occasions the party lines usually hold fast. On free votes, particularly those concerned with Private Bills and Private Members' Bills, there may be some cross-voting. The rigid pattern of party voting is to some extent balanced by the freedom permitted in debate, and it could be argued that dissent is expressed in other ways than in voting against the party. In the debate on unemployment in 1958, Mrs. Patricia McLaughlin, a Conservative Member from Belfast, held up before the House a red glove which she described as 'the red hand of Ulster'. The problem of unemployment in Ulster must be solved, she said, and throwing down the glove as a challenge to the Government, she asked: 'Can you, will you, solve our unemployment problem?' Mr. Sydney Silverman, a Labour Member, taunted her: 'If the hon. Lady

[1] H. C. Deb., 29th January 1959, col. 1,268.

means what she said in her speech, then her duty to herself and to her constituents is to come into the Lobby with us at the end of the day and back her opinion with her vote.'[1] But Mrs. McLaughlin voted with the Government.

Some degree of preparation is required for a division: tellers must be supplied for the two lobbies; Members have to be informed and in some cases persuaded; and in all of this activity the Whips play an important role. The requisite number of Members do not suddenly appear at the right time to cast their votes. They have to be mobilized, and the mobilization of Members for a division is no haphazard affair, lightly undertaken. As the hour of 9:57 p.m. approaches, when many end-of-the-day divisions occur, socializing Members make their apologies to their hostesses and take their leave; taxis and cars begin to converge on Westminster; division bells ring through the Palace, in neighbourhood restaurants, and even in some private homes. Members have considerable freedom in many aspects of parliamentary life; they need not attend every session and can make up their own minds about participating in debate, but on important issues they are expected to be present to vote with the party. This is an obligation which they are expected to fulfil, however inconvenient it may be or however awkward the hour.

The mobilization of support in the physical sense, of knowing where absent Members may be located and of making certain that they are present and voting, requires constant diligence on the part of the party Whips. The anticipation of divisions also requires careful controls over the parliamentary programme, in order that Members can have some freedom in attendance, so long as they are present at the crucial time. The Whips' offices are strategically located at the entrance to the debating chamber, and it is considered obligatory for a Member to leave the building through that corridor, giving the Whips a sporting chance to impress his services. The effect of absent Members can be offset by pairing, where Members from the different parties cancel the effect of their joint absences by agreeing not to vote, but on important votes the Whips disapprove of pairing and prefer to mobilize the maximum number of Members for an impressive show of partisan unity. During the bitter days of the 1950–51 Parliament, when Labour had a slender majority of six Members, the use of pairs was greatly curtailed. The Conservatives forced the party fight through divisions, compelling Labour Members, and Ministers, to attend in full force.

[1] Ibid., 17th December 1958, col. 1,241–42.

Party Unity and Division

When the division bells are rung and the lobbies are cleared, there is an air of excitement in the chamber, even though the results can often be anticipated. The division itself requires some physical effort on the part of Members: they must walk about, leave their seats to be jostled together with their colleagues in a narrow lobby, and then return. Mr. Morrison has written that he found 'moving through the Division Lobbies' to be 'a useful and pleasant social occasion'.[1] There is no simple method of recording one's opinions, such as answering one's name or pushing a button. After the proper formalities have been observed, Members assemble in the Aye or the No lobby, as the case may be; their names are checked off on leaving, and they are counted; the tally is then presented by the tellers to the Speaker, who formally announces the result. Ordinarily, decorum prevails when a division takes place, although a former Member has recorded that when the Act nationalizing the mines was passed, 'Miner M.P.'s and others marched through the "Aye" lobby singing songs of victory.'[2]

The number of divisions per session varies, depending in part on the number of controversial issues before the House and the strategy of the Opposition in using divisions as a tactical weapon. There were 177 in the 1958–59 session. Similarly, the number of Members participating in divisions also varies. There was never a full turnout of membership in the 1958–59 session; the highest attendance of the session was recorded in the first division, on the approval of the Queen's Speech, when 579 Members participated (vote: 255–324); assuming full membership, there were fifty absentees on this occasion. In the twenty-nine divisions on the Finance Bill later in the session, the number participating ranged from 237 to 460; the number of absentees (again assuming full membership) ranged from 170 to 393. When the Government is not interested in the outcome of an issue (and the Whips are not applied), the number of participating Members may fall below one hundred.

On measures supported by the Government, the margin of victory remains fairly uniform, although there are minor fluctuations in the totals. The following table shows the number of Members participating in the Finance Bill and the size of the Government majorities in each case:

[1] Herbert Morrison, *Government and Parliament* (London, 1954), p. 215.
[2] Raymond Blackburn, *I am an Alcoholic* (London, 1959), pp. 64–65.

DIVISIONS ON FINANCE BILL, 1958–59

Members Voting	Govt. Majority	Members Voting	Govt. Majority
460	42	388	38
452	46	384	36
450	44	383	43
438	46	377	39
435	39	374	40
434	46	358	34
422	32	357	41
415	29	338	50
411	43	321	45
411	23	320	42
407	39	307	51
401	37	306	52
393	37	239	223
389	35	237	55
389	33		

It will be observed that the size of the Government majority is not correlated with the number of Members who voted. The fact that the margin of victory remains fairly constant is partly the result of pairing, which equalizes the effect of absence. There are, however, some fluctuations in the majorities; in the Finance Bill (with one exception) they ranged from twenty-three to fifty-five and in the divisions for the entire session in which the parties were polarized, they ranged from twenty to seventy. The explanation for the range of the majorities lies in part in the abstentions and absences that occur but it is not possible for an outsider to differentiate between those Members who abstain, as a matter of principle, and those who are merely absent because it is inconvenient to be present and they have no pair. The morning following the divisions, the Whips may check the published lists to see who was unaccountably absent, but on an important division the Government Whips would know in advance who would be present and who absent.

Abstentions may occur with the knowledge and consent of the Whips, but cross-party voting is rare and is officially discouraged. Unless an issue is made of the event at the time, and the press informed, irregularities in party voting may pass unnoticed by the public. It should be added that some of the variations in the size of the majorities may be affected by the irregular pattern of the Liberal vote; the six Members do not vote consistently with the Government, or against it, and sometimes they split their vote. Considering the evidence, then, one may conclude that, normally, the variations in the size of the Government majorities have no necessary political significance.

Votes on policy measures may take a number of forms, varying from specific approval of policy to a deceptively simple motion to adjourn. The policy divisions may be important politically, however, inasmuch as they are a public indication of the measure of support given the Government. Following the Queen's speech at the opening of Parliament, some two weeks are spent in debating the policy of the Government announced in the speech (this is the so-called debate on the Address), and votes on amendments to the Address provide an opportunity for indicating confidence in the Government at the very beginning of a session. In January 1924 the Baldwin Government was defeated on the Address, and was followed by the first Labour Government.

The manner in which motions are phrased may make some difference in the outcome, and an instance of this occurred in March 1959, when the House of Commons was asked to approve the Anglo-Egyptian Financial Agreement. This was a sensitive issue for the Conservatives, for it was yet another aspect of the Suez affair on which defections had taken place previously. The financial agreement with Egypt was less favourable than many had hoped, and there was now another possibility that some Conservative Members would fail to support the Government. The Government put down a simple motion, asking merely that the House approve the Agreement. If the Opposition had followed a similar procedure, offering a motion which simply opposed the Agreement, they might have gained support, or at least persuaded some Conservatives to abstain. However, the Opposition put down a motion which not only criticized the agreement and the 'heavy losses' that would have to be accepted, but it also deplored the actions of the Government in 1956. The Suez affair, it said, 'is now generally admitted to have been a disastrous act of folly almost without parallel in our history'.[1] No Suez Rebel would swallow that bait!

Although the predominant pattern of voting in the House of Commons is that of one party massed against another, with the few Liberals overwhelmed by their giant competitors, a heterodox type of alignment appears from time to time. A division on the Finance Bill in 1959, for instance, resulted in a vote of 231–8 (231 Conservatives against 4 Liberals

[1] H. C. Deb., 16th March 1959, col. 43.

and 4 Labour). The explanation for this peculiar alignment is found in the fact that the motion (an amendment on the so-called Schedule A property tax) was proposed by a Liberal Member; many Labour Members supported Schedule A and thus opposed the amendment, but they abstained rather than voting to support the Government, and the Liberals were divided.

On a division concerning the Street Offences Bill, the vote was 235–88, giving the Government the abnormally large majority of 147. The explanation here is that the Government applied its Whips whereas Labour permitted a free vote; the Bill was supported by 221 Conservatives and 14 Labour Members (total, 235) and it was opposed by 84 Labour Members and 4 Liberals (88). It is apparent that many Labour Members abstained.

The voting pattern is also different when Private Members' Bills are considered. In a division on the so-called Landlord and Tenant Bill, the vote was 60 (52 Labour, 8 Conservatives) to 7 (all Conservatives). This was not a Government measure in the usual sense of the term; nevertheless, a Minister told the House that 'We regard the Bill as a worthwhile measure and we hope that the House will give it a Second Reading.'[1] In a division on a Private Members' Bill relating to the publication of wills, the vote was 30 (28 Conservatives, 2 Labour) to 26 (20 Labour, 5 Conservatives, 1 Liberal). The Government took no stand on this occasion, and the Solicitor General said that the position he was taking 'was one of completely cold neutrality'.[2] It is evident from these two Bills that cross-voting may develop if the Whips are not on, in which event other groups will attempt to persuade the Members to follow their own party line. Still another pattern developed when the House divided on a Private Bill concerning the powers of the London County Council. On this division, taking place at 1:25 a.m. on the morning of 7th July, the vote was 45–0. The Bill was supported by Conservative Members only, no Labour Members or Liberal Members voted.

The pattern of Liberal voting does not follow that of either major party: the Liberal *bloc* may support first one side, then the other, and there is also considerable free voting. One newspaper story (whose figures were not checked) has stated that between 1952 and 1959 there was Liberal cross-voting on nearly fifty occasions; the six Members were divided on issues of national health, taxation, transport, denationalization, defence, television, rating and valuation, restrictive trade prac-

[1] Ibid., 2nd December 1958, col. 695.
[2] Ibid., col. 790.

of a form of Gresham's law (that bad money drives out good); the mass-party vote on one side of the aisle tends to beget mass-party voting on the other side of the aisle. The party opposite cannot afford to let down its guard, or to show that it is less united.

The attitude of the Conservative Party towards party voting is slightly different, although the results may be similar. Under the leadership principle, the Leader takes into account the various attitudes of the party and indicates the direction, but neither he nor the party binds the membership. Voting is a matter of conscience and individual decision. One may be persuaded but he is not compelled. Moreover, the party is relatively tolerant of dissenters, and within the party itself there are various strands of opinion.

There is no agreed legislative principle on the extent to which the individual should be a free atom in voting. Party membership places a Member under some obligation to his colleagues, and in a political organization that is constantly striving to maintain a majority, an increased value is placed on the marginal utility of dissent. The man who holds the balance may have more potential power than the weight of his single vote would suggest.

It was mentioned earlier that Parliament is composed of amateur Members, a large portion of whom do not attend all sessions constantly, and this factor also has a bearing on divisions. If parties did not exercise control, divisions would be less likely to express the opinion of the party membership and the decisions would be made by the transient majorities of whoever happened to be present. Even under present controls, it is sometimes difficult to maintain a respectable party showing at meetings of standing committees, and if divisions were held on such occasions, the decision would not necessarily express the opinion of the committee. An argument is also made that Members are rarely interested in free voting, and there is some evidence to support this point of view. The opportunities for casting free votes when Private Members' Bills or Private Bills are being considered are not widely popular, and by no means all Members are interested in promoting private legislation or participating in its consideration. The period of greatest excitement and participation occurs when the major party divisions are held.

Moreover, there seems to be little demand for free voting outside Parliament, and the local constituency parties are normally strong defenders of party solidarity. The parliamentary division demonstrates to the local party that Members are constantly fighting the partisan battle, and the issue on which a division is held points the direction to be taken by the local parties. Many constituency organizations have shown that they want their Member to be the paragon of party fidelity. In fighting an election, the various shades of opinion, the doubts and anxieties and indecisions, are distorted into issues of black or white, and the constituency parties prefer to support Members who do not require complex explanations to be made of their voting. Quixotic behaviour is not encouraged. The electorate, also, would expect a Member to vote with his party and would be surprised if he didn't; it might be pleased as well, according to individual convictions or interests.

One may conclude that the local constituency parties are often the effective sanction for the more gentle admonitions of the Whips. When Members fall out with their party in Parliament, they return post-haste to their constituency to explain, to make things right, and hopefully to be supported and forgiven. The local organization may go to the extreme of failing to readopt its Member; and local dissatisfaction may affect the raising of party funds and the enthusiasm of party workers. The Members are far more than agents for their constituency party, but on questions of party loyalty in the division lobbies, they antagonize the local party at their own risk. Without the guidance or the support of the party, Members may find that they have taken an unpopular line which must constantly be defended. Indeed, if a Member becomes too independent, without the political strength to carry it off, his political career may be prematurely ended.

It is probably true also that Government departments favour party voting in Parliament and that officials encourage the Ministers to give a strong lead to Parliament on what to accept and what to reject. Mr. Herbert Morrison has written to this effect: 'An act of Parliament', he says, 'has to stand up as a coherent whole, or administrative and possible legal trouble may follow.' If Members were left to decide whether there should be a free vote, 'parliamentary difficulty and confusion of an awkward character' might arise. 'What may appear to be an issue of detail to back-benchers may not be so much a matter of detail or may at any rate involve serious repercussions which Ministers can see but which back-benchers cannot so readily understand.' He cites as an example of ministerial wisdom the 1944 vote on equal pay for men and women teachers; in this famous case, the House of Commons first approved equal pay, but after the intervention of Mr. Churchill, it reversed its vote. 'The Coalition Government', explains Mr. Morrison, 'took the view that this was certainly a matter where there would have been considerable repercussions in the Civil Service, the local government services, and, quite possibly, in private industry; and if the principle was to be established in legislation it should not be for one calling only but after comprehensive consideration.'[1]

If the minority party does not accept the results of a division, it may be in a position to reverse the decision when it reaches power, or to threaten the tranquil administration of the policy; and to this extent the decision made by a partisan majority may be more precarious than one representing the agreed opinion of most Members, reached by a continued process of compromise and adjustment. The nationalization of steel is a case in point; Labour has promised to renationalize steel, if they gain power, and the Conservatives, if they lose power and then regain it, to redenationalize it. Another case is the Central African Federation, for the Labour Party seems not to have accepted fully the decision on federation made by Parliament in 1953, and the attitude of the Party then and subsequently may have helped to influence the attitude of Nyasaland Africans against Federation. Moreover, with the parties organized on a hierarchical principle, it may be possible for leaders to make statements on policy which, in effect, will commit a future Government in which they serve and determine the result of a division some period of time before the event actually occurs. The effective decision might be made, say, in a speech before a party conference or even in response to a question at a press conference.

INDIVIDUAL DELINQUENCIES

What happens to a Member when he disagrees with his party and refuses to join his colleagues in the division lobby? There is no single answer. In some cases the act of defiance may end his career, but if neither the party nor the Member is bellicose and makes an issue of the insurgency, the incident may be passed over smoothly and eventually forgotten. However, it is also possible that a Member may develop new stature through his independence and, like Churchill and Eden and Macmillan, eventually become Leader of the party. If there is a split between the Member and the party, an attempt will be made to heal the breach or, failing this, to establish a new type of relationship. The Member may take the initiative by 'resigning the Whip', as it is called, which places him beyond the borders of party regularity, and he no longer receives official party communications. He is on the outside, but remembered, and he may be able to return to the party without loss of

[1] Morrison, op. cit., pp. 163–164.

Party Unity and Division

face. In the meantime, the dissenting Member may retain some token of party identity, perhaps calling himself, say, an Independent Conservative.

The posture of independence may be temporary, like a ballerina standing on her points. If a Whip is refused or withdrawn—that is, if official communications are severed and party authority is not invoked or not recognized—the act of insurgency will be followed by attempts to effect a reconciliation. Letters will be exchanged between Members and party Leaders, and some of the letters may find their way into the press; the Whips will hold searching conferences in an attempt to work out some conciliating agreement; and as the election draws nearer, when every candidate will wish for a party home, the Member and party may once again hope to be united. By this time public interest in the recalcitrant Member may have faded and the reunion pass relatively unnoticed. However, a careful reader of Vacher's *Parliamentary Companion* will note the slight emendation in the party symbol next to the Member's name, which can be interpreted to mean that the Member has discreetly, coyly, quietly, tiptoed his way back to party respectability.

In the Conservative Party a Member may resign the Whip on his own volition, but it is normally possible for the Member to abstain from voting without breaking with his party. The Whip is rarely withdrawn from a Member, and then by action of the Leader, but it appears not to be withdrawn for independence in voting. There are many instances of Conservative insurgency, perhaps the most notorious in recent years being the division on 8th May 1940, when over forty Conservative Members voted against the Chamberlain Government and others abstained. The Government resigned, to be followed by one formed by Winston Churchill.

More recently, the Government policy towards the Suez Canal and the Middle East has created internal party divisions within the Conservative Party. There have been two significant fissures: one dissident group opposed the original plan to evacuate the Suez Canal area in 1954, and it later opposed the Suez settlement; the second group opposed the Suez intervention in 1956.[1]

Item: July 1954. Twenty-eight Conservative Members opposed the removal of the British base in the Canal Zone. Major Legge-Bourke resigned the Whip.

[1] See Leon D. Epstein, 'Partisan Foreign Policy: Britain in the Suez Crisis,' *World Politics*, January 1960, p. 201 ff.

Party Unity and Division

Item: 8th November 1956. Eight Conservative Members, opposed to the Suez intervention, abstained on a vote of confidence.

Item: 5th December 1956. Fifteen Conservative Members who opposed the withdrawal of troops from Suez abstained on a vote of confidence.

Item: 1st and 8th November 1956. One Labour Member (Stanley Evans) abstained from voting and resigned his seat at the request of his Constituency organization at Wednesbury.

Item: 13th May 1957. Fourteen Conservative Members, opposed to the re-entry of British ships in the Suez Canal, abstained in the division, and eight of this number resigned the Whip.

In the Suez controversy, the name of Nigel Nicolson is prominent; his opposition to military intervention in Suez led to a break with his Constituency organization at East Bournemouth, which failed to readopt him. In discussing his experiences in Parliament at the time of Suez, Nicolson said:

Thus I reached my personal decision. I only knew for certain of a few other Conservatives in Parliament who felt in varying degrees as I did, although I have since heard of several more. We were still unorganized. Few of us knew of Anthony Nutting's or Sir Edward Boyle's impending resignations from the Government until they occurred, and neither of them attended our haphazard meetings. We met not more than twice as a group between the ultimatum and the cease-fire. We had never combined before and never combined afterwards. We let the Whips know of our attitude, but it remained in doubt until the last minute how many of us would actually abstain in the crucial vote of confidence on 8th November. In the event, eight of us did so. They were Sir Robert Boothby, Anthony Nutting, Sir Edward Boyle, J. J. Astor, Sir Frank Medlicott, Colonel Banks, William Yates, and myself. From none of us was the Whip withdrawn. But within a month, one had resigned his seat in Parliament, one had become an Independent Member, one had previously announced his intention not to stand again, two had been ostracized by their constituency associations, and two were in deep disgrace with theirs. Only Sir Robert Boothby emerged relatively unscathed.[1]

The reprisals mentioned by Mr. Nicolson were taken by the Constituency associations. The attitude of the Government was more tol-

[1] Nigel Nicolson, *People and Parliament* (London, 1958), pp. 133–134.

erant. Sir Robert Boothby was made a Life Peer in 1958; Sir Edward Boyle came back into the Government as Parliamentary Secretary to the Ministry of Education; and a Government Minister remarked that the Bournemouth Constituency association had treated Nigel Nicolson in an uncivilized manner.

The subsequent parliamentary and electoral status of some of the more conspicuous members of the two factions is given below.

The Anti-Suez Group

J. J. Astor (Plymouth, Sutton) did not stand for election, 1959.

Col. Cyril Banks (Pudsey) remained an Independent; did not stand for election, 1959.

Sir Robert Boothby (Aberdeenshire, East) was made Life Peer, 1958.

Sir Edward Boyle (Birmingham, Handsworth) was brought back in the Government as Parliamentary Secretary to Minister of Education; was re-elected, 1959.

Sir Frank Medlicott (Norfolk, Central) became an Independent; was not readopted by his Constituency Organization; and did not stand for election, 1959.

Anthony Nutting (Melton) resigned seat, 1956; did not stand for election, 1959, but spoke for Conservative Party.

Nigel Nicolson (Bournemouth East and Christchurch) was not readopted by Constituency Organization and did not stand for election, 1959.

William Yates (The Wrekin), re-elected, 1959.

In all, two of this group were re-elected to the new Parliament in 1959, and one was made a Life Peer.

The Suez Group

John Biggs-Davison (Chigwell), re-elected, 1959, as a Conservative.

Anthony Fell (Yarmouth), re-elected, 1959, as a Conservative.

Viscount Hinchingbrooke (Dorset, South), re-elected, 1959, as a Conservative.

Patrick Maitland (Lanark), defeated, 1959, as a Conservative.

Angus Maude (Ealing, South) resigned seat, 1958, when he became editor of *Sydney Morning Herald*.

Sir Victor Raikes (Liverpool, Garston) resigned seat, settled in Southern Rhodesia, and did not contest 1959 election.*

Lawrence Turner (Oxford) remained an Independent; did not contest 1959 election.*

Party Unity and Division

Captain Charles Waterhouse (Leicester, South-East), who was often called the leader of the Suez Group, resigned his seat in 1957 and did not contest the 1959 election.*

Paul Williams (Sunderland, South), re-elected, 1959, as a Conservative.

*There is a presumption that these Members did not intend to stand in the next General Election; hence, perhaps, their greater independence. For a detailed analysis of this controversy, see the article by Leon D. Epstein, 'British M.P.'s and Their Local Parties: The Suez Cases', *American Political Science Review*, June 1960.

In all, four Members of this group were re-elected in 1959; one was defeated; four did not stand.

Another example of a Conservative Member's resigning the Whip is that of Sir David Robertson, who in 1959 took this step to express his disapproval of Government policy in the Scottish Highlands. He had been disappointed in the amount of assistance the Government had extended in bringing new industry to depressed Scottish towns, and he was annoyed that a Private Member's Bill, proposing a North of Scotland Development Corporation, had been 'talked out'. The suggestion that the best hope for northern Scotland lay in tourism, was, he said, 'the most pitiful I have ever heard from a Minister in this House.' Sir David also implied that Ministers did not have control over the departments. 'Ministers come and go like leaves in the autumn. The higher Civil Service want complacent individuals—men from Eton and Harrow who have been kicked around as fags.'[1]

This was a case of a Private Member attempting to bring pressure on the Government. The procedure was somewhat unorthodox and not without risk, but Sir David was encouraged to make the gesture because of his own considerable personal popularity. In 1959 he was re-elected for Caithness and Sutherland as an Independent, increasing his majority from 56 per cent to 65 per cent of the vote. We may conclude from the experience of Sir David Robertson and from that of some of the Suez insurgents that a Member may be in a stronger position to assert his independence if he is well known locally and has created a loyal personal following. If the insurgent Member is not nominally a resident of the area, the relationship with the constituency organization may be one of political convenience, and the Member may have no reserve strength in a contest with the local party. The possibility exists that a Member can be adopted by another constituency, more tolerant of insurgency, but this course is speculative at best.

[1] *The Times*, 6th February 1959.

236

Party Unity and Division

In the Labour Party, Members do not customarily resign the Whip, although the Whip may be withdrawn by the party, and it is also possible for the Member to be expelled. Defection in the Labour Party may be a serious affair in that it is an attack on the principle of collective decisions, and there are provisions within the party for punishing the offending Member. The central organization as well as the local organization may take disciplinary action. There have been many opportunities for applying these procedures inasmuch as there has been considerable dissent in the Parliamentary Labour Party, relating both to policy and to personalities, and the ideological disputes have been intertwined with a continual struggle for influence within the party. According to Richards, there were thirteen major rebellions in the Parliamentary Labour Party between 1945 and 1955, and more than 200 Members were concerned in one or more of the incidents.[1] Mr. Herbert Morrison has described the discipline inflicted on some of the dissenters. 'In the latter stages of the 1945–50 Parliament', he has written, 'the National Executive itself initiated action against certain Labour M.P.'s by expelling them from the party on policy grounds. So, as they were no longer members of the Labour Party, it was necessary to withdraw the parliamentary Whip from them. They all stood independently at the General Election of 1950, but they were all defeated by official Labour candidates'.[2]

Item: In November 1954 the Parliamentary Labour Party decided to abstain from voting on the ratification of the London and Paris agreements: six Members defied the policy, five Members voting against the agreements and one Member voting for them. The Whip was withdrawn, but returned before the 1955 elections.

Item: Mr. Aneurin Bevan has had many disputes with his party and his party leaders. In March 1955 he challenged the party leader, Mr. Attlee, on the attitude of the party towards the use of thermo-nuclear weapons, following which sixty-two Labour Members abstained from voting for the official Opposition amendment on defence. Subsequently, by a vote of 141–112 the Parliamentary Labour Party voted to withdraw the Whip from Mr. Bevan. The National Executive of the Labour Party decided not to expel Mr. Bevan, and the Whip was restored before the General Election.[3]

[1] Peter G. Richards, *Honourable Members, A Study of the British Backbencher* (London, 1959), p. 148.
[2] Morrison, op. cit., pp. 114–115.
[3] Richards, op. cit., pp. 149–150.

Party Unity and Division

The Divisions in the House of Lords take up no considerable amount of time, and, as mentioned earlier, an attempt is made by the Lords to reach agreement by common assent and not to press for continued divisions. One can see in the attitude towards divisions the changing role of the House of Lords, where the emphasis is placed on the expression of opinion or on revising legislation, not on approving legislation as such. Of the twenty-six divisions in the 1958–59 session, only one was concerned with the passage of a Bill (that relating to Street Offences). It is the prevailing custom for the House of Lords to accept the substance of Bills but in some cases to offer revisory amendments. In the same session there were some seventeen divisions on amendments applicable to ten different Bills.

When the House of Lords discusses policy questions, the usual procedure is to withdraw the motion at the close of the debate, with no division taking place. Sometimes, however, there is a vote, and in the 1958–59 session there were divisions on motions relating to the following eight topics:

> Egypt: Distress of Expelled British Nations
> Officers' Retired Pay and Widows' Pensions
> Seats for Hereditary Peeresses
> Princess Louise Hospital for Children
> Problem of Unemployment
> Strength of the Royal Navy
> Nyasaland: Devlin Report
> Hola Camp Disaster

The popular image of a flood of Lords (the so-called backwoodsmen) descending into the gilded chamber to vote against progress has little factual basis. In 1956, it is true, 333 Lords voted on the Capital Punishment Bill, but in a normal session there is no extraordinary turnout on any issue. (The Silverman Bill on Capital Punishment was rejected in July 1956 by a vote of 238–95; a compromise Bill became law in March 1957.) The division in 1958 which brought out the largest number of Peers was on an amendment to the Legitimacy Bill, and in this case the 'liberal' side won, 83–64. The number of Peers participating in divisions ranged from 36 to 147, with the median in the range of 70.

Partisan voting is modified in the House of Lords, but it is not without meaning; strict party voting is more pronounced among Labour Peers than among Conservative Peers. The Conservative label often rests lightly, and many Peers may consider themselves Conservative in the sense that they are anti-socialist but who are independent in expression and feel free to oppose the Government. It is not unusual to find Conservatives pitted against Conservatives; Bishops against Bishops; and Judges against Judges. It is more unusual, however, to find a pronounced division in the ranks of the Labour Peers. In a division on an amendment to the Legitimacy Bill, the Archbishop of Canterbury and the Bishop of Chichester were 'Content', the Bishop of Exeter was 'Not-Content'. Lord Denning, a Law Lord was 'Content', Lord God-dard, the former Lord Chief Justice of England, was 'Not-Content'. Lord Goddard had come down 'to your Lordships' House somewhat doubtful about which way he should vote,' he said, 'and the more I listened to this debate the more I came to the conclusion that it is a great pity that this subject should have been raised at all.'[1]

[1] H. L. Deb., 21st July 1959, col. 351.

CHAPTER XI

Conclusions: 'A Happy Issue out of all their Afflictions'

I t was mentioned in the first chapter that parliamentary institutions cannot be taken for granted, that they are challenged externally by dictators who would use force to solve political problems; and in a more subtle way they are challenged on the home front by the great bureaucracies, with their special areas of competence, which may view with some impatience the exercise of external political control. Yet it is the achievement of parliamentary government that it has developed a type of political system which provides order and freedom over a broad territory, which combines government direction with political accountability, and this singular political achievement should not be lightly regarded.

One constantly hears criticisms of Parliament: that it is overworked and underpaid; that the Government makes all important decisions; that the parties stifle initiative; that Parliament can't cope with details; that Members are too prone to claim parliamentary privileges; that Private Members have too little power. Some of the criticism is not persuasive, based as it is either on incomplete observation or on a faulty theory of what particular functions Parliament, as an arena of political conflict, should rightly perform. But some, indeed, is relevant. However, such criticism is in a minor key and it does not challenge the essential part played by Parliament in the political system. One should also note that Parliament itself is not insensitive to the criticisms and to its own shortcomings, to the difficulties it faces in doing everything that should be done, or that people want done, within the amount of time available. It is constantly reviewing its procedures and its organization, attempting to adjust its internal structure to the continually challenging demands.

In this concluding chapter, I would like to make some general ob-

Conclusions: 'A Happy Issue out of all their Afflictions'

servations on Parliament, without pretending to anything so presumptuous as an 'evaluation'. I will consider first that elusive subject, here called the Spirit of Parliament, followed by comments on political stability and parliamentary controls, and, in the final section, the transference of parliamentary institutions.

THE SPIRIT OF PARLIAMENT

The above phrase has some shortcomings as a concept with precise meaning but it is used here to cover certain characteristics of Parliament which are not readily definable and which are not necessarily encompassed in any description of the procedures as such. One finds in the proceedings of Parliament a sense of order and purpose and achievement, a respect for the dignity of political office, a restraint in performance, and a reasoned approach to controversial topics. There is among the Members a prevailing spirit of dedication, even of goodness, and the belief that political subjects are important and should be earnestly considered. Political debate is often vigorous, and at times it may seem to belie the above comments, but an attempt is made to keep political conflict within the bounds of moderation, and often of dignity. Some of the characteristics of Parliament are reflections of the British culture, but it is nevertheless instructive to see how the values of order and leadership and free speech and justice are applied in the parliamentary system where conflict is always present.

The pronounced opposition to delegating power to committees is related to the effect such decentralization would have on the corporate nature of parliamentary action. One of the functions which Parliament performs best is that of expressing a collective judgment on political action, and this judgment may be replete with moral undertones of justice and fair play. Indeed, the judgment may be described as a species of Calvinistic irritation with evil, expressed with episcopal decorum. There is insistence on fair play in the proceedings, and special concern is expressed for the maintenance of justice when the actions of Government seem to impinge on the rights of individuals. The standards of rectitude expected of Ministers and officials are high, and Members and Peers are quick to detect any weakness of character, indifference, or lack of vigour. Criticism is often blunt, free, and righteous. The traits which comprise the spirit of Parliament intrigue its Members, fascinate the press and the public, and perhaps help to make the parliamentary model attractive to countries now creating for the first time a centralized system of government.

POLITICAL STABILITY

The ability of the British parliamentary system to develop stable Governments over a long period of time is also one of Parliament's most satisfactory achievements. The Governments have exhibited internal strength within the United Kingdom and have had sufficient support to make external commitments which can bind their successors. During political crises arising from wars or depressions the entire membership can close ranks and form a Government whose strength is almost unassailable. It is possible for a Government to be established with the support of a variety of political combinations: Coalition Governments, National Governments, Caretaker Governments, and of course Governments supported by a party majority.

There has evolved in the British experience a distinctive concept of centralized authority which, in the political thought of the Kingdom, is intrinsic, inherent, and of fundamental importance. The question of whether or not to have a permanent, continuous authority is not a debatable point. This may sound axiomatic and obvious, yet the concept of a continuing centralized authority forming a great complex organization has not been universally held and is only now being established in the newer nations. The British system, in short, underscores the supreme necessity of government, of having a recognized legitimate authority which is able to rule.

The British culture seems to be organized in such a fashion that it requires a ruler over an ordered society. This trait of creating leaders to whom the members of the association are deferential is found in other areas of British society also; it is not limited to the creation of a Government or the relations between the Government, the Crown, and Parliament. It is manifest in the organization of the two major parties, the structure of local government, and the selection of parliamentary candidates; and one could go on.

The concept of a ruler over an ordered society, of a stable and responsible centralized authority, fits many of the requirements of a nation under modern conditions. The stable, centralized system of government can give commands within the nation, and it can make commitments and exert influence internationally. This system has considerable utility for the demands of modern times, more, certainly, than competitive systems now outmoded by events.

It is pertinent to inquire whether the organization of Parliament is such that it will continue to produce stable Governments, whether in fact the reliance for stability is not placed on the unpredictable future of the political parties. This, of course, is a speculative area, even though it is true that in the past political crises have been met successfully, without challenging the underlying requirement of stability. One may note, however, that the search for political stability is carried on constantly. The thoughts of parliamentarians and political leaders are continually aware of the problem, of the need for creating political support, and for retaining some flexibility within the system which provides support. More than that, there are accepted boundaries within Parliament and within the parties beyond which dissent does not go.

The achievement of the parliamentary system in creating political stability in Governments is only part of the story. It is also necessary to have an equilibrating force which can exercise some control over centralized authority and demand a measure of accountability.

PARLIAMENTARY CONTROLS

One may distinguish in the parliamentary system two major systems of control, that of the Ministers in the Government over their respective departments and that of Parliament over the Ministers, and it would not be too wide of the mark to say that the principal concern of those who participate in the second system is to make certain that the first system of control is continually effective. The considerable power given to the Ministers rests on the premise that they effectively control the bureaucracy. In their constant probing, Members can frequently detect some weakness in the Minister-department relationship, and perhaps it will appear that the Ministers are in some cases the agents of the department Officials and not their superior. The nature of the relationship may be revealed at Question Time, for instance, when the Minister gives short, curt answers and seems manifestly annoyed that he is being questioned at all. The failure of ministerial control may also be evident when a Minister keeps so closely to his brief that he seems powerless to accede even to the most persuasive of arguments. The rigidity of the Minister in parliamentary debate may make the proceedings formalistic and contribute to the frustration of the Members.

Having noted that Ministers do not always give the impression of

Q* 243

being on top of their jobs, we may seem perverse now to suggest that their salaries should be raised! In the constitutional sense, the Minister is superior to the Official, but this relationship has become distorted in the salary structure, and it would seem that if the systems of control are to operate effectively it should be understood that, actually and symbolically, the Minister is the boss. Note, for instance, the salary differentials in the table below:

Salary	Officials
£7,000	Permanent Under Secretary of State
£4,200	Deputy Under Secretary of State
£3,350	Assistant Under Secretary of State
	Ministers and Members
£5,000	Secretary of State
£3,750	Minister of State
£2,500	Parliamentary Under Secretary of State
£1,750	Members

In commenting on this disparity of salaries, Mr. Gresham Cooke (Cons.) once told the House of Commons that responsibility 'is one of the major factors to be taken into account in paying remuneration and that, therefore, it may be constitutionally wrong in the long run for Ministers to be paid some £2,000 a year less than permanent secretaries.'[1]

The second system of control is that exerted by Parliament over the Ministers, and there is considerable flexibility in the way in which this function is carried out. The strong ministerial system has influenced the manner in which Parliament performs its role. To a degree (but not completely) the exercise of parliamentary control over the Ministers is swept up and encompassed within the contest between the two rival groups of partisans who contend for the right to form the Government. Some control may also be exercised by the great private associations (trade unions, agriculture, industry, banking, transportation, arts) who have direct relations with the bureaucracy, and many of the compromises and agreements on policy are made in camera, without direct public participation or public controversy. Parliament, nevertheless, is often the conduit for effective influence brought on the Government: it constitutes a reservoir of talent from which Ministers are selected, and it remains the critic.

Criticism may be expressed within the party, and the Conservatives

[1] H. C. Deb., 30th April 1959, col. 1,467.

Conclusions: 'A Happy Issue out of all their Afflictions'

in particular have a bifurcated organization which gives Private Members considerable freedom of expression and considerable scope for making their criticisms known. The relationship between party and Government is an essential aspect of parliamentary control, but this phase is normally closed to and concealed from the public except for the calculated leaks which appear in the press from time to time. There is criticism also in the great public debates wherein the Government explains and defends, the Opposition attacks and questions. In modern times, however, the Opposition has little chance of bringing a Government down through public criticism and defections, although its criticism keeps the Government alert and may affect later elections.

Parliament also attempts to provide a counterbalance for the Government power, using techniques which are a throw back to an earlier day before the Government extended its power so completely over Parliament. The basic theory of this historic relationship assumes a division of power between the Executive and the Legislature with the latter having the obligation to review the acts of the former and possessing the necessary influence to make the review effective. In this area there are Select Committees especially concerned with Estimates, Accounts, Nationalized Industry, and Delegated Legislation. However, these committees are thrice handicapped—they lack professional assistance, their reports are frequently disregarded by Parliament, and there is usually an assumption that they should not deal with questions of policy.

However, one can detect a slight trend towards the increased interest of the Members in exploring policy issues for themselves and within their own organizations, and they are attracted by such topics as economic expansion, scientific development, the analysis of the Estimates, Commonwealth relations, transport, public power, education, and the like. If Parliament hopes to increase its influence in these and other areas and to sharpen its function of critic, it may wish to have access to independent sources of information. The value of parliamentary criticism, and it is valuable, would perhaps be strengthened if Parliament could look at a topic from a somewhat different angle and did not have to rely so completely on the information proffered by the Government and by interest groups.

The effectiveness of parliamentary control is also related to the calibre of the membership, to the question whether a parliamentary career is attractive to those who might eventually become Ministers or who perform their function from the back benches. Elections are hazardous, compensation is low, the political rewards uncertain, and even those especially interested in Parliament might nevertheless find it necessary to shirk parliamentary duties by supplementing their income with other work. In the changing social conditions of the times the Member who is completely independent financially is a rarity, and many Members are in effect required to work on the outside, even to take subsidies, in order to meet their obligations. Politics cannot be made safe from risk, but it might be in the interests of a happy and spirited Parliament to increase the monetary rewards of membership and of a ministerial career. This would make it easier for Members, if they wished, to apply themselves full time to Parliament and to becoming independently well informed on public issues.

It would seem that the model Member, the one able to contribute most to Parliament, is the full-time Member with enough independence, freedom, and financial resources to make the most of his unique opportunities. With the proper support he should be able to read, travel, visit, talk, think, and perhaps write as well; to get on top of his job at home, in the colonies and the Commonwealth, and in other countries; to see for himself. He would, in short, use his time in becoming a well-informed Private Member. He would not in so doing become a 'professional'. Far from it. However, with the present rate of remuneration it is not always easy for Members to take advantage of their quite exceptional opportunities.

THE TRANSFERABILITY OF PARLIAMENT

A final question concerns the adaptability of Parliament. Can the parliamentary system be transferred to other societies, or is it particularly and essentially British and unable to thrive on alien shores? In developing self-government and democracy in the colonies and former colonies, there has been a general belief in the value of transferring British political institutions: they have worked on the home front, the British people have faith in them, and all British administrators know in general how they operate. And it can be asked whether a newly independent nation could do better than to have its own Parliament, broadly representative of the people, which is able to maintain freedom and provide political stability. To bolster this position there is the proud example of India where parliamentary institutions seem to have been successfully planted in an alien land.

Yet doubts of this position are also expressed, and it has been unsettling to witness the quiet overthrow of parliaments in the Sudanese

Republic and in Pakistan, with scarcely a whisper of protest by the people against these deeds of force. In other areas parliamentary procedures have been distorted for partisan ends, and the emphasis placed on unrestrained sovereign power. These instances arouse second thoughts on the degree to which a parliament can be transplanted to alien lands without losing its essential character. It can be argued that cultures vary, that institutions are not necessarily transferable, and that every country should be allowed to develop its own variety of political institutions, adaptable to the society which they govern. It may also be said, somewhat more paternalistically, that the underdeveloped countries 'have not yet grown up to it', as a participant of the Brains Trust once expressed it. While it is true that Parliament has developed over a long, historic period, there is no assumption that with time and patience other countries would also develop a parliament through this devious process of cultural evolution. In the meantime, the attitude expressed by the Brains Trust member tends to stultify action by the implication that, for the time being, parliamentary governments are beyond the grasp of the newer nations.

There are other factors involved in determining the adaptability of parliaments, and one need not accept the thesis that the experiment is bound to succeed because of the general effectiveness of the British model or that it is bound to fail because it is not indigenous or that the participants 'have not grown up to it'. In developing broader political associations such as are found in the Commonwealth, there is much to be said from a practical point of view for encouraging the growth of similar types of political institutions. Within the Commonwealth, for instance, there are various cultures; the economies have not developed to the same extent or at the same rate; the history and background of the various states are different but at least the member states tend to share common political attitudes towards freedom and justice, towards individual rights and human dignity, and towards a benign and rational political process for resolving conflict such as is found in the parliamentary system. For the purposes of this discussion, then, we can assume without developing the point further that common political attitudes and practices and political institutions are worthwhile goals, that it would make it easier for governments to co-operate and for the several member states to exchange ideas and people.

It can also be argued that if it is desirable to develop a central government in a society where previously there was none, there is much to be said for introducing a parliamentary-type government at the centre. It

Conclusions: 'A Happy Issue out of all their Afflictions'

is true that parliaments are not indigenous to other cultures, but it is also true that no other form of central government is indigenous, effective, and adequate to meet modern demands. If such indigenous institutions did exist, the problem of creating new and nationalistic political institutions would not arise. It can be said, in short, that whatever type of institution is adopted in order to make self-government possible will by definition be non-indigenous, foreign, and essentially Western.

But even if one accepts these abstract arguments, it is nevertheless true that new parliaments seem to work better in some areas than in other areas. It is also true that there has been a certain amount of improvisation in developing colonial legislatures, and there is considerable difference in the type of assembly provided, say, in Tanganyika and in the Bahama Islands. Over a period of time, and at any one time, the transferred parliamentary design has not followed any single mould. In other words, in planting exotic legislative assemblies, some aspects of an independent parliament have been stressed and others muted. In some cases the emphasis has been placed on representation, deliberation, and law-making with the Governor retaining the power of the veto. In other cases there has been special concern with the balance of representation between various types of groups: officials, non-officials, and unofficials— whether elected or nominated; and nationalistic political parties have been encouraged to act as the Opposition until self-government is achieved, at which time there may be no Opposition. The requirement that the Government have the support of the majority of the assembly may be met by appointing Civil Servants as Ministers, although this expediency violates the distinctions between Ministers and Officials.

Although no one can say that the transfer of the parliamentary system will necessarily be successful wherever the attempt is tried, it might nevertheless be helpful to identify those aspects of the British Parliament which constitute 'the system' and which, theoretically, it would be desirable to transfer. The first factor is that of representation, and we may consider it essential that the assembly be integrated into the society which it regulates and controls. In the development of the British Parliament there has been more than a casual connection between the growth of representation and the belief that Parliament belonged to the people. Following this precedent in the newer assemblies, it would follow that the representation should be sufficiently comprehensive that the people believe that the legislature belongs to them, that they are truly represented; moreover, in order to provide some freedom of choice, the

Conclusions: 'A Happy Issue out of all their Afflictions'

electorate should constitute a base considerably broader than the membership of any single political party.

Parliamentary procedures are a puzzling topic, for procedures might lose their effectiveness if they perform no real function and are merely an empty emulation of those followed at Westminster. They might, indeed, be followed to the letter and at the same time permit effective power to be concentrated elsewhere. The legal theory of parliamentary sovereignty also creates difficulties. With the prize of unrestrained power dangling before the political party that can control the new parliament, the majority may claim the right to make all decisions, with the Opposition having no independent power and with individual rights subject to definition by a majority. The theory of parliamentary sovereignty has some inadequacies even for the British Parliament. The description may satisfy lawyers (and some lawyers in Parliament become edgy and uncomfortable when the concept is discussed), but the observable restrictions on parliamentary action must cause some wonderment that so seemingly inappropriate a concept as sovereignty is applied. The picture of an unrestrained and wilful assembly proceeding about its work in a capricious manner does not square with reality. There are effective restraints on parliamentary authority, and in practice Parliament is held down by a thousand strings, like Gulliver in the land of Lilliput.

The essence of Parliament, as it has developed over the centuries, would seem to be more correctly expressed by such concepts as representation, deliberation, and control—yes, and justice and fair play—rather than by a word implying that total power is encompassed in Parliament, to be captured by a majority, and for its use only. The procedures used in Westminster perform special functions, not necessarily described by the word 'sovereign', and the effectiveness of modern controls relies on the permissibility of an Opposition with special procedural rights; on restraints within the party system; on the broad freedom of debate; on the specific controls over Government, which have been developed over a long period of time; and on the moderation with which political power is used in Great Britain. In other words, in transplanting the parliamentary system the emphasis might well be placed on the development of full and adequate representation, on the encouragement of free and pertinent deliberation, and on the establishment of the types of accountability which seem to be particularly applicable, given the culture and historical background of the particular country and the type of society for which laws are being made. The whole process becomes a charade if total power is in effect given to a political party to be legitimized by mock parliamentary procedures. For parliamentary government not only means the power to make decisions, it also means the exercise of effective restraints on the use of power.

Index

251

Index

Index

Index

Index

Index

Index

Index